Virtue and Vice, Moral and Epistemic

♨METAPHILOSOPHY

METAPHILOSOPHY SERIES IN PHILOSOPHY

Series Editors Armen T. Marsoobian, Brian J. Huschle, and Eric Cavallero

The Philosophy of Interpretation, edited by Joseph Margolis and Tom Rockmore (2000)

Global Justice, edited by Thomas W. Pogge (2001)

Cyberphilosophy: The Intersection of Computing and Philosophy, edited by James H. Moor and Terrell Ward Bynum (2002)

Moral and Epistemic Virtues, edited by Michael Brady and Duncan Pritchard (2003)

The Range of Pragmatism and the Limits of Philosophy, edited by Richard Shusterman (2004)

The Philosophical Challenge of September 11, edited by Tom Rockmore, Joseph Margolis, and Armen T. Marsoobian (2005)

Global Institutions and Responsibilities: Achieving Global Justice, edited by Christian Barry and Thomas W. Pogge (2005)

Genocide's Aftermath: Responsibility and Repair, edited by Claudia Card and Armen T. Marsoobian (2007)

Stem Cell Research: The Ethical Issues, edited by Lori Gruen, Laura Grabel, and Peter Singer (2007)

Cognitive Disability and Its Challenge to Moral Philosophy, edited by Eva Feder Kittay and Licia Carlson (2010)

Virtue and Vice, Moral and Epistemic, edited by Heather Battaly (2010)

Global Democracy and Exclusion, edited by Ronald Tinnevelt and Helder De Schutter (2010)

Virtue and Vice, Moral and Epistemic

Edited by

Heather Battaly

A John Wiley & Sons, Ltd., Publication

This edition first published 2010
Chapters © 2010 The Authors
Book compilation © 2010 by Blackwell Publishing Ltd and Metaphilosophy LLC

Edition history: originally published as Volume 41, Nos. 1–2 (January 2010) of *Metaphilosophy*

Blackwell Publishing was acquired by John Wiley & Sons in February 2007. Blackwell's publishing program has been merged with Wiley's global Scientific, Technical, and Medical business to form Wiley-Blackwell.

Registered Office
John Wiley & Sons Ltd, The Atrium, Southern Gate, Chichester, West Sussex, PO19 8SQ, United Kingdom

Editorial Offices
350 Main Street, Malden, MA 02148-5020, USA
9600 Garsington Road, Oxford, OX4 2DQ, UK
The Atrium, Southern Gate, Chichester, West Sussex, PO19 8SQ, UK

For details of our global editorial offices, for customer services, and for information about how to apply for permission to reuse the copyright material in this book please see our website at www.wiley.com/wiley-blackwell.

The right of Heather Battaly to be identified as the author of the editorial material in this work has been asserted in accordance with the Copyright, Designs and Patents Act 1988.

Library of Congress Cataloging-in-Publication data is available for this book.

9781444335620 (paperback)

A catalogue record for this book is available from the British Library.

Set in 10/12pt SwiftEF-Regular by Macmillan India Ltd., Bangalore, India

Printed in Malaysia

01 2010

CONTENTS

NOTES ON CONTRIBUTORS

Guy Axtell is Assistant Professor of Philosophy and Religious Studies at Radford University of Virginia and critical thinking coordinator for the university's humanities and behavioral sciences core curriculum. He has written on various topics in metaphysics, epistemology, and value theory, and is administrator of *JanusBlog: The Virtue Theory Discussion Forum*, a network of close to two hundred researchers worldwide. He is currently working on book-length manuscripts on the epistemology of disagreement and the ethics of belief.

Jason Baehr is Associate Professor of Philosophy at Loyola Marymount University in Los Angeles. He works mainly in the areas of epistemology and virtue theory. Some of his recent publications include: "Evidentialism, Vice, and Virtue" (*Philosophy and Phenomenological Research*, 2009); "Is There a Value Problem?" in *Epistemic Value*, eds. Adrian Haddock, Alan Millar, and Duncan Pritchard (Oxford UP, 2009); and "Four Varieties of Character-Based Virtue Epistemology" (*Southern Journal of Philosophy*, 2008). He has recently completed a major monograph in virtue epistemology titled *The Inquiring Mind: On Intellectual Virtues and Virtue Epistemology* (forthcoming with Oxford UP).

Heather Battaly is Professor of Philosophy at California State University Fullerton. Her primary areas of research are epistemology, ethics, and virtue theory. Her publications include: "Metaethics Meets Virtue Epistemology" (*Philosophical Papers*, 2008); "Virtue Epistemology" (*Philosophy Compass*, 2008); "Teaching Intellectual Virtues" (*Teaching Philosophy*, 2006); and "Is Empathy a Virtue?" in *Empathy: Philosophical and Psychological Perspectives*, edited by Amy Coplan and Peter Goldie (Oxford University Press, forthcoming). She is currently writing a book on the virtues.

Michael S. Brady is Senior Lecturer in Philosophy at the University of Glasgow. His main research interests are in metaethics, philosophy of emotion, and epistemology. He is the editor of *New Waves in Metaethics* (Palgrave Macmillan, forthcoming) and, with Duncan Pritchard, of *Moral and Epistemic Virtues* (Blackwell, 2003), and has published articles in journals such as *Philosophical Studies, Philosophical Quarterly, and American Philosophical Quarterly.*

Amy Coplan is Associate Professor of Philosophy at California State University, Fullerton. Her research interests include moral psychology, ancient Greek philosophy, philosophy of emotion, and aesthetics, especially philosophy of film. She has published articles in these areas and is currently coediting an interdisciplinary collection on empathy and editing a collection on the film *Blade Runner.*

Roger Crisp is Uehiro Fellow and Tutor in Philosophy at St Anne's College, Oxford, and Professor of Moral Philosophy at the University of Oxford. He is the author of *Mill on Utilitarianism* (Routledge, 1997) and *Reasons and the Good* (Clarendon Press, 2006), and has translated Aristotle's *Nicomachean Ethics* for Cambridge University Press. He is an associate editor of *Ethics* and a delegate to Oxford University Press.

Thomas Hurka is Chancellor Henry N. R. Jackman Distinguished Professor of Philosophical Studies at the University of Toronto. He is the author of *Perfectionism* (1993), *Principles: Short Essays on Ethics* (1993), and *Virtue, Vice, and Value* (2001), as well as many articles on topics in normative ethics and political philosophy. He recently finished a trade book *The Good Things in Life* and is preparing to write a scholarly book, *British Moral Philosophers from Sidgwick to Ewing.*

Wayne Riggs is Associate Professor of Philosophy at the University of Oklahoma. His primary area of interest is epistemology. Recent publications include "Two Problems of Easy Credit," in *Synthese* (2009), "Luck, Knowledge and Control," in *Epistemic Value*, edited by Adrian Haddock, Alan Millar, and Duncan Pritchard (2009), and "The Value Turn in Epistemology," in *New Waves in Epistemology*, edited by Vincent Hendricks and Duncan Pritchard (2009).

Christine Swanton teaches in the Department of Philosophy at the University of Auckland, New Zealand. She is currently working on the virtue ethics of Hume and Nietzsche. Her book on virtue ethics, *Virtue Ethics: A Pluralistic View*, was published by Oxford University Press in 2003 (with a paperbound edition appearing in 2005).

Sarah Wright is Assistant Professor of Philosophy at the University of Georgia. In addition to virtue epistemology, she writes and teaches in general epistemology, cognitive science, and environmental ethics. She has published essays on virtue epistemology in the *Southern Journal of Philosophy* and *Acta Analytica* and an essay on decision theory (with David Schmidtz) in *Midwest Studies in Philosophy.*

Linda Zagzebski is George Lynn Cross Research Professor of Philosophy and Kingfisher College Chair of the Philosophy of Religion and Ethics at the University of Oklahoma. She is past President of the Society of Christian Philosophers and past President of the American Catholic Philosophical Association. In addition to many articles, she is the author of *Virtues of the Mind* (1996), *Divine Motivation Theory* (2004), *Philosophy of Religion: An Historical Introduction* (2007), and *On Epistemology* (2008).

1

INTRODUCTION: VIRTUE AND VICE

HEATHER BATTALY

The Basics

Elizabeth Anscombe's infamous 1958 paper "Modern Moral Philosophy" argued that ethical theory should jettison meaningless evaluations of *acts*, like "right act" and "wrong act," and instead evaluate the character traits of *agents*. Radically, Anscombe called for the elimination of deontological and consequentialist theories in ethics. Though few philosophers have embraced her eliminativism, Anscombe is widely credited with ushering in a revival of virtue ethics. Virtue ethics shifts the focus of ethical evaluation away from actions and onto agents. It tells us what it is to be an excellent person, and what qualities excellent people have. In short, virtue ethicists think that moral virtues matter. Many contemporary virtue ethicists employ the work of the ancients, especially Aristotle, in developing their views. Thus, in *On Virtue Ethics*, Rosalind Hursthouse (1999) argues for an account of the moral virtues that is neo-Aristotelian. In *The Morality of Happiness*, Julia Annas (1993) explores Aristotelian and Stoic views of the virtues.

Virtue epistemology developed in response to two different sets of concerns. In the 1980s Ernest Sosa introduced the notion of an intellectual virtue in an attempt to circumvent the debate between foundationalism and coherence theory, and to answer objections to reliabilism (see Sosa 1991). In 1996, Linda Zagzebski's *Virtues of the Mind* argued for a virtue theory in epistemology that is analogous to contemporary virtue theories in ethics. Both versions of virtue epistemology shift the focus of epistemic evaluation away from beliefs and onto agents. Virtue epistemology tells us what it is to be an excellent thinker, and what qualities excellent thinkers have. In short, virtue epistemologists think that epistemic virtues matter. "Virtue-responsibilists" like Zagzebski argue for accounts of the epistemic virtues that are based on Aristotle's account of the moral virtues, whereas "virtue-reliabilists" like Sosa argue that epistemic virtues are qualities that enable us to attain truths.[1]

---

[1] Guy Axtell uses the terms "virtue-reliabilism" and "virtue-responsibilism" in the introduction to Axtell 2000.

What exactly is a virtue theory in ethics and epistemology? Virtue theories can be contrasted with act-based and belief-based theories. Act-based theories in ethics, like deontology and consequentialism, take right and wrong acts—types of act-evaluation—to be more fundamental than the moral virtues and vices—types of agent-evaluation. Accordingly, act-based theories define the moral virtues and vices in terms of right and wrong acts. Virtue theories in ethics do the reverse. They take the moral virtues and vices—types of agent-evaluation—to be more fundamental than any type of act-evaluation. Accordingly, virtue theories in ethics define right and wrong acts in terms of the moral virtues and vices, rather than the other way around. For instance, Hursthouse explains right action in terms of the virtues as follows: "An action is right iff it is what a virtuous agent would characteristically . . . do in the circumstances" (1999, 28). Analogously, belief-based epistemologies, like evidentialist accounts of justification and truth-tracking accounts of knowledge, take justified beliefs and knowledge—types of belief-evaluation—to be more fundamental than the epistemic virtues and vices—types of agent-evaluation. Accordingly, belief-based theories would define the epistemic virtues and vices (if they addressed them at all) in terms of justified beliefs or knowledge. Virtue theories in epistemology do the reverse. They take the epistemic virtues and vices—types of agent-evaluation—to be more fundamental than any type of belief-evaluation. Accordingly, virtue theories in epistemology define belief-evaluations—justification and knowledge—in terms of the epistemic virtues, rather than the other way around. To illustrate, Sosa argues that knowledge requires true belief that is produced by an intellectual virtue (see Sosa 1991, 2004, 2007), while Zagzebski contends that knowledge is belief that results from acts of intellectual virtue (1996, 271). The first group of chapters in this collection addresses virtue theories in ethics and epistemology. The collection opens with "Virtue Ethics and Virtue Epistemology," in which Roger Crisp rejects the definition of virtue theory above, and offers an alternative.

What is a virtue? Roughly, virtues are qualities that make a person excellent. Which qualities make a person excellent? Arguably, there are two important but different ways to answer this question, both of which are employed in the literature. First, one might contend that virtues are qualities that attain good ends. Specifically, they are qualities that enable a thing to attain good ends or perform its function well. This concept of virtue begins with the intuition that good ends matter, and that the virtues are qualities that reliably attain good ends. Hence, to be virtuous, one *must* be effective at attaining the good—attaining the good is necessary for virtue. Attaining the good is also sufficient for virtue—any quality that reliably attains good ends counts as a virtue. This concept of virtue is employed by Plato in book I of the *Republic* and by Aristotle in book I of the *Nicomachean Ethics*. In contemporary virtue ethics, it is employed by Julia Driver (2001), who contends that the moral virtues are traits of character that systematically produce good consequences. On her view, virtuous motivations are neither necessary nor sufficient for being morally virtuous. Good consequences are all that matter. Thus, caring about others is not enough for benevolence, if one consistently fails to help others. Nor is caring about others required for benevolence, since one might consistently succeed in helping others without caring about them. In contemporary virtue epistemology, Sosa and the virtue-reliabilists employ this concept of virtue. Sosa explicitly contends that there is "a 'sense' of virtue ... in which anything with a function—natural or artificial—does have virtues" (1991, 271). He argues that since our primary epistemic function is attaining truths, the epistemic virtues are whatever qualities enable us to do that, be they natural faculties or acquired skills. He takes reliable vision, memory, induction, and deduction to be paradigmatic epistemic virtues. For him, the epistemic virtues require neither virtuous actions nor virtuous motives. Reliably getting the truth is all that matters.

Second, one might contend that virtues are qualities that involve good motives. Specifically, virtues are acquired traits of character that involve appropriate motivation, action, emotion, and perception. This concept of virtue begins with the intuition that motives matter. Attaining good ends is not enough (or not even required) for virtue, since one can attain good ends, and even perform appropriate actions, but have vicious motives. This concept of virtue is more popular among virtue ethicists than the previous concept, and is famously endorsed by Aristotle in book II of the *Nicomachean Ethics*. Aristotle there argues that moral virtue is "a state of character concerned with choice, lying in a mean, i.e. the mean relative to us, this being determined by ... that principle by which the man of practical wisdom would determine it" (1998, 1006b36–39). To illustrate, courage is a disposition to fear and yet to face the appropriate things, at the appropriate times, in the appropriate ways, and with the appropriate motivations. Courage lies in a mean between a vice of excess (foolhardiness) and a vice of deficiency (cowardice). Aristotle argues that the moral virtues are not natural faculties, because, unlike natural faculties, the moral virtues are praiseworthy. He thinks that the moral virtues are not skills (partly) because the virtuous person, but not the skilled person, must have a specific motivation in acting: the virtuous person must choose the appropriate acts for their own sakes.

In contemporary virtue ethics, this concept of virtue is employed by Rosalind Hursthouse (1999), who argues that the moral virtues are entrenched dispositions of appropriate motivation, action, emotion, and perception. For example, the honest person is motivated to do what she thinks is right, reliably tells the truth, is distressed and angry when others lie, and notices who is or is not trustworthy. Using Aristotle's notion of the *phronimos* (practically wise person), Hursthouse argues that the honest person's motivations, actions, emotions, and perceptions match those of the *phronimos*. In contemporary virtue epistemology, Zagzebski and the virtue-responsibilists employ this concept of virtue. Zagzebski (1996) argues that the epistemic virtues are acquired character traits that involve appropriate epistemic motivations, appropriate epistemic actions, and reliable success in attaining true beliefs. She thinks that attaining good ends is required, but not enough, for being virtuous. (In contrast, James Montmarquet [1993] thinks that attaining true beliefs is not even required for epistemic virtue.) Zagzebski takes open-mindedness, intellectual courage, intellectual autonomy, and intellectual humility to be paradigmatic epistemic virtues. On her view, a person with the virtue of open-mindedness is motivated to attain truths and motivated to consider alternative ideas; he also considers alternative ideas when he should, and reliably attains truths as a result. Using Aristotle's doctrine of the mean, Zagzebski argues that the virtue of open-mindedness lies in a mean between two vices.

Which of these two concepts of virtue is the "real" concept? Arguably, there is no single real concept of virtue, and arguments to that effect will be unproductive (see Battaly 2008a, 2008b). Both concepts are good: both identify qualities of an excellent person. One way to be an excellent person is to reliably get the good; for example, to reliably help others rather than harm them, or to reliably get truths rather than falsehoods. Another way to be an excellent person is to possess virtuous motivations: to care about others or about the truth.

What is a vice? If virtues are qualities that attain the good, then vices are qualities that fail to attain the good. If, on the other hand, virtues and vices are contraries rather than contradictories, then one can fall short of virtue without being fully vicious. One could instead be *akratic*—weak-willed—or *enkratic*—continent. The *enkratic* person performs, for example, benevolent acts, but must overcome competing motivations in order to do so. The *akratic* person also has competing motivations, but unlike the *enkratic* person, fails to overcome them and fails to perform benevolent acts. In contrast with the *akratic* person, the vicious person does not have competing motivations—she is not conflicted. The vicious person's motives are in fact bad. Arguably, the person who possesses the vice of cruelty is disposed to harm others, be pleased by others' failures, and notice opportunities for insulting others, and is motivated to do these things because she thinks they are good. By comparison with the literature on virtue, considerably less has been written about vice. This is especially true of intellectual vice. A noteworthy exception is Miranda Fricker's *Epistemic Injustice* (2007), which provides a detailed account of the epistemic vice of testimonial injustice. This collection contains two chapters on epistemic vices: Jason Baehr's "Epistemic Malevolence," which makes use of Robert Adams's (2006) account of moral malevolence; and my "Epistemic Self-Indulgence," which employs Aristotle's account of moral self-indulgence.

The Structure of Virtue Ethics and Virtue Epistemology

What is a virtue theory in ethics? We have seen that the standard answer is that virtue ethics differs from deontological and consequentialist ethics because it reverses "the direction of analysis" of two of the main concepts in ethical theory: the concept of right action and the concept of virtue (see Greco 2004). To explicate, it is claimed that deontological and consequentialist theories both take the concept of right action to be more fundamental than the concept of virtue, and define virtue in terms of right action. Whereas virtue ethics takes the concept of virtue to be more fundamental than the concept of right action, and defines right action in terms of virtue—as an action that a virtuous person would perform. The three chapters in the first group all address the structure of virtue theories in ethics. Linda Zagzebski and Thomas Hurka both endorse versions of the direction of analysis view, while Roger Crisp's "Virtue Ethics and Virtue Epistemology" suggests that the direction of analysis view is problematic.

Crisp explores the problems and prospects for an analogy between virtue ethics and virtue epistemology. In so doing, he defines virtue ethics, outlines a virtue epistemology that is modeled on Aristotelian virtue ethics, and enumerates several challenges for virtue epistemology. Crisp argues that all ethical theories ask and answer the following questions: How should I live? What kind of person should I be? And, how should I act? On his view, what is distinctive about virtue ethics is the *ultimate reason* it gives for its answer, rather than the answer it gives. After all, Crisp explains, virtue ethics and utilitarianism might give the same answer—live virtuously, be a virtuous person, and act virtuously. The difference is that the utilitarian gives this answer *because* she thinks that living and acting virtuously maximize utility, whereas the virtue ethicist gives this answer *because* she thinks that it is virtuous to live and act virtuously. According to Crisp, for a theory to count as an "explanatory" virtue ethics, the ultimate reason it gives for living and acting virtuously must be provided by the virtues themselves. Crisp also argues that defining virtue ethics in terms of its direction of analysis is problematic. For if we define virtue ethics in terms of its direction of analysis, then virtue ethics is committed to claiming that an act is right because it is an act that a virtuous person would perform. But that, argues Crisp, is false: "What the virtuous person would do is insufficient to explain rightness." Sometimes what makes an act right are the details of the situation, rather than the fact that a virtuous person would do it.

Crisp outlines an Aristotelian virtue epistemology that allows for two different sorts of epistemic virtues. He begins with Aristotle's notion of moral virtue and his doctrine of the mean. Aristotle famously argues that each moral virtue lies in a mean between a vice of excess and a vice of deficiency. The morally virtuous person hits the mean—he acts and feels as he should. According to Aristotle, the virtues deserve praise because we are responsible for possessing them. Likewise, argues Crisp, some epistemic virtues lie in a mean and involve actions and feelings. These virtues include: creativity, perseverance, open-mindedness, self-doubt, and joy in inquiry. Crisp suggests that these virtues deserve praise because they are traits for which we are, to some extent, responsible. But he also thinks that there are epistemic virtues for which we are not responsible, including the capacities of perception and memory. Thus, he makes space for both responsibilist and reliabilist epistemic virtues.

Crisp concludes that though it is worth developing a virtue epistemology that is modeled on virtue ethics, such a view faces several challenges. First, most virtue ethicists do not endorse virtue epistemology but instead rely on epistemological theories that virtue epistemologists reject. Second, the debates about the role of commonsense intuitions in ethics would carry over to virtue epistemology. Finally, virtue epistemology may not be able to live up to its billing: it may fail to avoid the foundationalist-coherentist debate, the internalist-externalist debate, and skepticism.

Linda Zagzebski's "Exemplarist Virtue Theory" argues for a radical kind of virtue ethics that is grounded in exemplars. Zagzebski enumerates three main desiderata of a moral theory. First, a moral theory should "simplify, systematize, and justify our moral beliefs and practices." Second, there must be some element in the theory that enables users to link the theory to the world—to recognize that a particular element of the theory refers to a particular thing in the world. Third, Zagzebski thinks that "foundational" moral theories currently have an advantage, since contemporary philosophers (unlike the ancients) assume that morality itself requires justification. A moral theory is foundational if it takes a single moral concept as its foundation, and uses that concept to define all other moral concepts. Accordingly, Zagzebski thinks, contra Crisp, that virtue ethics takes virtue concepts to be the most fundamental, and defines the concept of a right act in terms of virtue concepts.

With these desiderata in mind, Zagzebski designs an innovative moral theory that grounds moral concepts in exemplars—virtuous people. The theory is foundational, but its foundation is not conceptual. Radically, its foundation consists in virtuous people themselves. Zagzebski's moral theory begins with direct reference to exemplars. Employing the well-known Kripke-Putnam theory of reference, Zagzebski argues that direct reference to exemplars is analogous to direct reference to gold (see Kripke 1980 and Putnam 1979). Roughly, the Kripke-Putnam view argues that the referent of the natural kind term "gold" is fixed by ostention. Zagzebski highlights two features of this view. First, it argues that one can successfully refer to gold even if one does not know the essential properties of gold—those properties were in fact discovered much later via empirical research. Second, it argues that a speaker can successfully refer to gold even if she associates the wrong descriptive meaning with "gold," provided that she is connected "by a chain of communication" to other speakers who reliably pick out gold. Analogously, contends Zagzebski, we can fix the referent of the term "good person" by pointing at exemplars. Moreover, we can successfully refer to exemplars even if we do not know their essential properties. Like the nature of gold, the nature of exemplars may be discovered later via empirical research. We can also successfully refer to exemplars even if we associate the wrong descriptive meaning with the term "good person," provided that there are some speakers in our community who do succeed in picking out exemplars.

Is there anyone in our community who reliably identifies exemplars? Zagzebski thinks that we identify good people via the emotion of admiration, which she claims is "generally trustworthy when we have it after reflection and when it withstands critique by others." Hence, she thinks that people in our community who have a sufficiently developed emotion of admiration succeed in picking out exemplars. Zagzebski acknowledges that just as some of the stuff that we judged to be gold (pyrite) was not really gold, some of the people that we judge to be exemplars may not really be exemplars. We might learn later on, via empirical research and narratives, that some of our judgments were mistaken.

Zagzebski defines the concepts of a right act, a virtue, a duty, a good state of affairs, and a good life by direct reference to exemplars. Thus, a virtue is "a trait we admire in *that* person," where "that" refers directly to an exemplar. It is a trait that "makes the [admirable] person paradigmatically good in a certain respect." A right act is "an act a person like *that* would take to be favored by the balance of reasons." Zagzebski concludes that her exemplarist virtue theory satisfies the three desiderata above. It explains our practice of identifying exemplars; its direct reference to exemplars links the theory to the world; and it is foundational.

Hurka and Zagzebski agree, contra Crisp, that virtue ethics differs from deontological and consequentialist ethics because it takes the concept of virtue to be more fundamental than the concept of right action, and defines right action in terms of virtues rather than the reverse. But Hurka and Zagzebski disagree about whether we should endorse virtue ethics. Zagzebski endorses a radical version of virtue ethics, which takes exemplars—virtuous people—to be fundamental, and defines the concept of right action (and other moral concepts) in terms of exemplars. In contrast, Hurka's "Right Act, Virtuous Motive" argues against all versions of virtue ethics, and for "higher-level" accounts, which define *both* the concept of right action *and* virtue concepts in terms of a third moral concept (either the good or rightness) (see also Hurka 2001).

Hurka sets out to explain why right acts and virtuous motives often coincide. He considers four possible explanations: consequentialism, deontology, virtue ethics, and higher-level accounts. He argues that consequentialism, deontology, and virtue ethics have at least one thing in common: they all define right acts and virtuous motives directly in terms of each other. That is to say, each view treats one of the two concepts as more fundamental than the other, and then defines the other concept in its terms. Consequentialism takes the concept of right acts to be more fundamental, and argues that virtuous motives are those that tend to produce right acts. Deontology takes the concept of right acts to be more fundamental, and argues that virtuous motives are motives to perform right acts because they are right. Virtue ethics takes the concept of virtuous motives to be more fundamental, and argues that right acts are those that would be done from virtuous motives. Hurka insightfully contends that there is a fourth option. In contrast, higher-level accounts argue that rights acts and virtuous motives coincide, not because either concept is defined directly in terms of the other, but because "each involves a relation to some third [basic] moral property."

What is that basic moral property? Hurka maintains that there are two sorts of higher-level accounts. The first falls within a consequentialist framework: it takes goods and evils to be basic, and it defines both right acts and virtuous motives in terms of goods and evils. Hurka argues that virtuous motives are here defined as appropriate attitudes toward goods and evils. That is, it is virtuous to love and want goods—like another person's pleasure—and to hate and seek the absence of evils—like another person's pain. Correspondingly, it is vicious to love evils, and to hate goods. Right acts are defined as acts that produce the greatest surplus of good over evil. The second sort of higher-level account falls within a deontological framework: it takes moral rightness to be basic, and it defines right acts and virtuous motives in terms of rightness. Accordingly, it is virtuous to love and want what is right, and to hate and want to avoid what is wrong. Here, right acts are acts that instantiate the property of rightness.

Hurka defends his higher-level accounts by arguing that they have an advantage over virtue ethics. On his view, some versions of virtue ethics are committed to claiming that right acts and virtuous motives *always* coincide: all acts that issue from virtuous motives are right, and all right acts issue from virtuous motives. Other versions of virtue ethics are committed only to the former. In contrast with both versions of virtue ethics, Hurka's view contends that though right acts and virtuous motives *often* coincide, they sometimes come apart, and do so in two ways—namely, right acts are sometimes performed from nonvirtuous motives, and wrong acts are sometimes performed from virtuous ones. Hurka argues that, unlike virtue ethics, his higher-level accounts allow for these possibilities. To illustrate, take an attorney who prosecutes a defendant, and does so because of malice. Suppose the defendant is guilty. According to Hurka's higher-level consequentialist account, the attorney's act is right given that it deters crime and produces more goods than evils, even though the attorney's motive is clearly vicious. Alternatively, take an attorney who prosecutes a defendant because he cares about protecting the community and sincerely believes that the defendant is guilty. Suppose his belief is false—the defendant is innocent. As long as punishing an innocent defendant produces more evils than goods, then according to the higher-level account, the attorney's act is wrong, even though it is virtuously motivated. We can apply Hurka's objection to Zagzebski's view, by adding that the virtuously motivated attorney is an exemplar.

Virtue and Context

Guy Axtell's "Agency Ascriptions in Ethics and Epistemology: Or, Navigating Intersections, Narrow and Broad" and Sarah Wright's "Virtues, Social Roles, and Contextualism" both explore connections between the virtues and context. Axtell argues that whether we should ascribe broad traits (e.g., benevolence) or narrow traits (e.g., "dropped paper" compassion) to agents depends on the context. Wright contends that virtues are context-sensitive—they are sensitive to the social roles of agents. She uses social roles to ground a view in epistemology that she calls "virtue contextualism."

Axtell addresses two problems in ascribing character traits to people—one in epistemology, and one in ethics. The generality problem in epistemology, originally an objection to reliabilism, points out that every token belief-forming process is an instance of many different types (see Conee and Feldman 1998). For example, the token process that produces your belief that there are words on this page is an instance of multiple process-types, including: vision at a particular time t, vision of a medium-sized object in a well-lighted environment, vision, and perception. It is the process-type, not the process-token, that matters; and different process-types enjoy different degrees of reliability. The generality problem contends that there is no principled way to decide which of the process-types is relevant—there is no principled way to decide how narrow or how broad the process-type should be. Axtell points out that the generality problem applies to both reliabilist and responsibilist epistemic virtues. The second problem is the situationist challenge in ethics (see Doris 2002). Following Aristotle, contemporary virtue ethicists tend to think of the virtues as global character traits—as habits or stable dispositions of the agent that influence her motivations, actions, emotions, and perceptions in every situation. Situationists argue that there are no such character traits—there are no global dispositions like benevolence. If character traits exist at all, they are narrow and localized (e.g., "dropped paper" compassion), rather than broad and global. The situationist challenge has led to a distinction between dispositionalists (e.g., Zagzebski) and occurrentists (e.g., Hurka).

Axtell argues that these two problems are analogous. Both problems are about how narrowly or how broadly we should construe the virtues. Axtell suggests that inquiry-pragmatism can shed light on these problems. The inquiry-pragmatist argues that which traits (narrow or broad) are relevant depends on the context and on our pragmatic interests. Thus, some contexts and interests will make narrow traits relevant, others will make broad traits relevant. In short, we can and should make narrow-trait ascriptions and broad-trait ascriptions. Which ascriptions we make, and when, are determined by the context.

Using Christopher Lepock's response to the generality problem, Axtell argues that reliabilist virtues are best construed as narrow traits, whereas responsibilist virtues, like open-mindedness, are best construed as broad traits. This is because our goal in ascribing narrow traits is to evaluate particular beliefs, whereas our goal in ascribing broad traits is to evaluate people. Thus, our goals and interests in epistemology dictate when we should ascribe narrow traits and when we should ascribe broad ones. Axtell suggests that we use this same strategy to respond to the situationist problem. In ethics, our goal in ascribing narrow traits is the evaluation of particular acts, whereas our goal in ascribing broad traits is to evaluate people. In sum, Axtell argues that "narrowly and broadly typed traits [should be] . . . seen as ascribed in response to different . . . explanatory interests . . . with neither being primary over or reducible to the other." Accordingly, Axtell rejects views that reduce one sort of trait ascription to the other. Zagzebski's view takes global traits—dispositions—to be primary, whereas Hurka's takes narrow traits—occurrent virtuous motives—to be primary. Axtell argues against both of these views. He also implies that we should not define right acts in terms of virtuous agents, since act evaluation should not be reduced to agent evaluation.

In "Virtues, Social Roles, and Contextualism," Sarah Wright argues that moral and epistemic virtues are sensitive to context, specifically to the social roles of agents. The social roles of agents include being a daughter, a member of one's country and community, and a member of one's chosen profession. Wright argues that virtues are means between extremes, and that the location of the mean "depends on the social roles of the person who must act." Thus, the mean is different for agents with different social roles. To illustrate, to hit the mean associated with the moral virtue of courage, a police officer who witnesses a burglary must pursue the criminal, whereas a bystander need only call the police. To hit the mean associated with the virtue of epistemic carefulness, a doctor who reads about the effectiveness of a drug in *Time* magazine should seek further evidence, whereas a layperson can hit the mean by believing that the drug is effective. Wright argues that since we are inevitably embedded in social roles, "there is no way to be a courageous person *simpliciter*; there is no mean in a vacuum . . . there is no way to exhibit the . . . virtues except within a social role. One is only courageous *in the role of a bystander*" or *in the role of police officer*. Wright notes that some social roles are incompatible with the virtues. Virtues are excellences, but not all excellences are virtues. Excelling in the social role of thieving is not a moral virtue, nor is excelling in the social role of cult-following an epistemic virtue. But as long as a social role is compatible with living well, morally or epistemically, we can develop virtues within that social role.

Wright uses social roles to ground her "virtue contextualism." Contextualists in epistemology argue that we lack knowledge in skeptical contexts but have knowledge in ordinary contexts.[2] Different versions of contextualism disagree about which conditions fix a context and about when contexts change. Wright evaluates two versions of contextualism, which she calls "attributor contextualism" and "methodological contextualism." Suppose that person A is attributing knowledge to person B. Roughly, attributor contextualism (DeRose 1999) argues that the context of person A, the one who makes the knowledge-attribution, determines the epistemic context. So, if A assumes ordinary standards for knowledge, then "B knows that *p*" will be true. But if A mentions the possibility that B is being deceived by a demon, then "B knows that *p*" will be false. A's mere mention of a skeptical possibility is sufficient for changing the context to a skeptical one. Wright rejects attributor contextualism on the grounds that it makes the epistemic context too easy to change. In contrast, methodological contextualism (Williams 2004) argues that the context of person B determines the epistemic context. That context is fixed by B's interests—for example, in doing history—and the parameters that are specific to the methodology that B is interested in—for example, the parameters of doing history. Consequently, A's mere mention of Cartesian demons does *not* suffice to change the epistemic context to a skeptical one. To change it, A must convince B to abandon his interest in doing history and take up an interest in battling the skeptic. As a result, contexts are more stable. Wright objects to methodological contextualism on the grounds that it cannot explain what makes an epistemic context good or bad, and thus cannot explain what makes knowledge valuable. Wright contends that her virtue contextualism, which grounds methodological contexts in social roles, solves this problem. She concludes that social roles that are compatible with living well (i.e., social roles in which one can develop virtues) generate contexts "such that the knowledge had within them is valuable."

Virtue and Emotion

Aristotle argues that the virtues are, in part, dispositions to have appropriate emotions. The chapters in this group examine links between virtue and emotion. Michael Brady's "Virtue, Emotion, and Attention" addresses the role of emotion in the virtuous person's acquisition of evaluative knowledge. Amy Coplan's "Feeling Without Thinking: Lessons from the Ancients on Emotion and Virtue-Acquisition" addresses the role of emotion in the acquisition of the virtues themselves. Both chapters make use of empirical research.

[2] Some contextualists argue that knowledge-attributions are false in skeptical contexts, but true in ordinary contexts.

Brady rejects the perceptual model of emotions, which claims that the virtuous person gets evaluative knowledge from her emotional responses. The perceptual model of emotions, endorsed by Peter Goldie (2004), argues that emotional responses are like sensory perceptions. Roughly, our emotional responses provide us with evaluative knowledge in the same way that our sensory experiences provide us with perceptual knowledge. On this account, my sensory experience of a white wall gives me a prima facie reason to believe that there is a white wall. Analogously, my fear of the neighbor's dog gives me a prima facie reason to believe that the dog is dangerous. These reasons are defeasible. Like our sensory experiences, our emotional responses sometimes fail to track reality—I might be afraid of a sweet old golden retriever who is not dangerous. So, by themselves, emotional responses are insufficient for evaluative knowledge. To get that knowledge, the perceptual model claims that we must also have "virtuous habits of attention." Brady explains that these are dispositions to pay attention to, and evaluate the reliability of, our emotional systems when and only when there is good reason to do so. The person who possesses such virtues does not constantly pay attention to her emotional systems, she only does so when there is reason to. When there is no reason for her to pay attention to her emotional systems, she is right to trust her emotional responses and to regard them as "providing her with genuine information about how things are in the evaluative world." In short, the perceptual model claims that in normal circumstances, the virtuous person's emotional responses yield evaluative knowledge.

Against the perceptual model, Brady argues that it is not emotional responses but a *non-emotional* capacity that yields evaluative knowledge. Using empirical research, Brady argues that there is a key difference between sensory experiences and emotions. Unlike sensory experiences, emotional responses persist and consume us—they trigger conscious reflection and deliberation about whether or not they are tracking reality. Thus, my fear of the neighbor's dog triggers deliberation about whether I should be afraid. The fear is emotional; the deliberation is not. Brady contends that in deliberating about our emotional responses, we look for non-emotional features of their objects and conditions that confirm or disconfirm our responses. So, in deliberating, I look for features of the dog (e.g., growling) and the conditions (e.g., it is eating) that indicate that the dog is, or is not, dangerous in these conditions. Brady argues that virtuous people have learned to directly recognize the emotion-relevant features in objects and conditions; they have developed the non-emotional capacity to recognize that "these features are signs of danger, [and] those features are signs of wrongdoing." Brady thinks that emotional responses play a vital role in the *development* of this capacity—in the acquisition of this virtue. But once this non-emotional capacity is acquired, the virtuous person relies on *it* for evaluative knowledge. Consequently, in normal circumstances, it is not the virtuous person's emotional responses that generate evaluative knowledge; it is her non-emotional capacity that does so. The most important upshot of Brady's view is that virtuous people can and do gain evaluative knowledge without having emotional responses. This is their standard way of gaining evaluative knowledge. When a virtuous person has an emotional response, it is because the circumstances are "abnormal or surprising," and she cannot take it for granted that her non-emotional capacity will get the right result.

In "Feeling Without Thinking," Amy Coplan argues that the way we conceptualize emotion influences our views about how we acquire virtue. If, like Socrates and Chrysippus, we think that emotion is controlled by, or a species of, reason, then acquiring virtue will essentially be a matter of correcting our false beliefs and replacing them with knowledge. But if, like Plato and Posidonius, we think that emotion is independent from reason, then acquiring virtue will also involve the habituation of our emotions. Coplan argues against the intellectualism of Socrates, Chrysippus, and the contemporary cognitive theory of emotion, and sides with Plato, Posidonius, and the contemporary noncognitive theory of emotion.

Socrates and Chrysippus are both intellectualists. They think that knowledge is sufficient for virtue. As long as we reason well and acquire knowledge, we will acquire virtue. According to intellectualism, our emotions and actions follow directly from our knowledge or ignorance. Our emotions are not independent sources of action, since they either are themselves a species of reason (Chrysippus thinks emotions are judgments) or are completely controlled by reason. Accordingly, virtue-acquisition is essentially a matter of replacing our false beliefs with knowledge. Coplan contends that the intellectualism of Socrates and Chrysippus resurfaces in the contemporary cognitive theory of emotion, endorsed by Robert Solomon (2007) and Martha Nussbaum (2004). The cognitive theory claims that emotions are essentially cognitive judgments. Emotions need not be accompanied by physical sensations or changes in the body. Thus, fear is a judgment that something is dangerous.

Plato and Posidonius both reject intellectualism. They think that emotion and reason are independent powers of the soul, and that emotion cannot be completely controlled by reason. They argue that emotions are independent sources of action. Hence, knowledge and reason alone are insufficient for virtue. To acquire the virtues, we must also train our noncognitive emotions. Coplan contends that the views of Plato and Posidonius foreshadow the contemporary noncognitive theory of emotion, endorsed by Jenefer Robinson (2005) and Jesse Prinz (2004). The noncognitive theory claims that emotions are essentially embodied appraisals—physical sensations and changes in the body that focus one's attention and prepare one to respond. These appraisals are neither conscious nor conceptual, but they are nonetheless meaningful. Thus, according to the noncognitive theory, fear is "(1) an embodied appraisal, which represents the stimulus as dangerous through bodily changes, and (2) the perception of those changes, which is what we feel as fear."

Coplan defends the noncognitive theory of emotion, and argues against intellectualism, by using current empirical research on emotional contagion and mirror-neurons. She argues that this research supports the claim that emotions can be involuntary and automatic and do not require conscious judgment. Coplan concludes that knowledge is insufficient for virtue-acquisition. To acquire the virtues, we must also train our emotions.

Virtues and Vices

The chapters in the final group provide analyses of individual virtues and vices. Christine Swanton's "A Challenge to Intellectual Virtue from Moral Virtue: The Case of Universal Love" and Wayne Riggs's "Open-Mindedness" analyze specific virtues. Jason Baehr's "Epistemic Malevolence" and my "Epistemic Self-Indulgence" analyze specific vices.

Swanton tackles the moral virtue of universal love, and in so doing provides a much-needed secular analysis of grace. She defines universal love as "a preparedness to be, for example, beneficent, gracious, forgiving, merciful to *anyone* where appropriate, and a manifesting of that prepared-ness to assignable individuals, as appropriate" (her emphasis). This love is *universal*—it is not withdrawn on the basis of "the unattractiveness of the object, or lack of affection for the object," nor even on the basis of the object's "lack of virtue" or lack of "other merits." Accordingly, one might argue that universal love does not exhibit practical wisdom, and hence is not a moral virtue. In reply, Swanton contends that although universal love is indeed "arational" and "reasonless," it is still reason-responsive. Conse-quently, it cannot be so easily expelled from the class of moral virtues.

Is the notion of universal love incoherent? Universal love is a preparedness to manifest love toward *any individual* regardless of merit, attractiveness, and personal relations. As such, it is universal, rather than partial. But it is simultaneously a love of particular individuals in their particularity, rather than a love of humanity in general. How can these two aspects of universal love be reconciled? Swanton contends that the answer lies in the analysis of preparedness. She argues that preparedness is a *Grundstimmung*: it is a background "emotional orientation to the world at large." According to Heidegger, a Grundstimmung is a back-ground "emotional hum" that sometimes "irrupts" in intense emotion (see Heidegger 1995). Swanton thinks that this analysis of preparedness allows one to be engrossed in particular individuals, without demanding that one be engrossed in *all* individuals. For if preparedness is a Grundstimmung, then one becomes engrossed in a particular individual *only when* one's background emotional hum irrupts in an intense emotion of love. Between irruptions, preparedness is simply a readiness to become engrossed in any individual. So, it does not entail actual engrossment in all individuals.

Grace is one type of universal love. Swanton argues that grace is a form of love that is "expressed by someone in a superior position, to someone in an inferior position," as when one club member graciously accepts not being invited to another club member's birthday party. Swanton elucidates grace as a virtue by contrasting it with condescension, blind charity, failure to let be, cheap grace, excessive legalism, pride as a vice, and humility as a vice. She argues that acts of grace are "arational"; that is, that there is no intention with which the acts are done. Take Bruce*, the club member who graciously accepts not being invited to Wayne's birthday party. Though Bruce* would have loved to have been invited, he is not bitter, he does not think or speak ill of Wayne, he does not complain, and he makes kind remarks when the subject comes up. Swanton argues that these acts of grace are spontaneous; Bruce* does not perform them with a "desired upshot" in mind. Hence, they are arational. In addition, Swanton argues, they are "reasonless"—they lack contributory reasons. She borrows Jonathan Dancy's notion, according to which a contributory reason provides a justification for the agent's act. Swanton contends that there are no contributory reasons for Bruce*'s acts of grace. She concludes that though acts of grace are arational and reasonless, they are nevertheless reason-responsive.

The virtue of open-mindedness is a paradigmatic intellectual virtue; accordingly, analyses of it are much needed. In "Open-Mindedness," Wayne Riggs contends that open-mindedness requires an awareness of "one's fallibility as a believer" and dispositions that put this awareness into practice in one's behavior. He proposes three desiderata for an account of the virtue of open-mindedness. The account should ensure that open-mindedness is a thick concept rather than a thin one. It should also treat intellectual virtues (or at least one kind of them) as character traits— much as virtue-responsibilists do—rather than as cognitive faculties—as virtue-reliabilists do. That is, it should treat intellectual virtues as interesting in their own right, even if they turn out not to be necessary for knowledge. Finally, the account should solve four puzzles that arise for open-mindedness. It should explain: (a) why anyone would want to be open-minded; (b) why an otherwise intellectually virtuous person would want to be open-minded; (c) how open-mindedness is consistent with strongly held beliefs; and (d) when we should expend resources in pursuing open-mindedness. Puzzles (b) and (c) warrant brief explanation. An otherwise intellectually virtuous person appears to have little motivation to consider alternative views, since he has every reason to believe that others in his community are not as likely to get the truth as he is. But open-mindedness seems to require that he consider alternative views. Regarding (c), open-mindedness appears to be inconsistent with strongly held beliefs. It seems that if an agent is fully confident in her belief that p, then she will not seriously consider the possibility that not-p. But being open-minded about p seems to entail that she take the possibility that not-p seriously.

Following Jonathan Adler (2004), Riggs contends that open-mindedness is "an attitude toward oneself as a believer, rather than toward any particular belief." If one is open-minded, then one acknowledges the possibility that "anytime one believes something, it is possible that one is wrong." In short, the open-minded person is aware that humans are fallible—that some or other of her beliefs are false. Riggs argues that Adler's account of open-mindedness is good as far as it goes—it solves puzzles (a) and (c)—but is ultimately incomplete. To be genuinely open-minded, one must not only be aware that one is fallible, one must put that awareness into practice in one's behavior. Consequently, one must also be disposed to seek self-knowledge about one's cognitive weaknesses, to self-monitor for situations in which one is prone to such weaknesses, and to combat those weaknesses when the given situations arise. The open-minded person who knows that he is prone to wishful thinking when forming beliefs about his finances, and who realizes that he is discussing the current state of his finances, will combat that weakness by seriously considering challenges to his beliefs about his finances.

Hence, Riggs argues, the otherwise intellectually virtuous person is motivated to be open-minded because even she is subject to some cognitive weaknesses. But she need not take every challenge to her beliefs seriously—she can conserve her resources. The open-minded person can dismiss a challenge to her belief that p if: she is confident that her belief that p is well justified; and she is confident that she is not in a situation in which she is prone to cognitive weaknesses; and she is correct that she is not in a situation in which she is prone to cognitive weaknesses.

Along with Miranda Fricker's *Epistemic Injustice* (2007), Jason Baehr's "Epistemic Malevolence" and my "Epistemic Self-Indulgence" are among the first works to examine specific epistemic vices in detail. Each of these two chapters argues that there is an epistemic analogue of a moral vice.

Baehr contends that despite its failure to appear on standard lists of intellectual vices, epistemic malevolence is indeed a paradigmatic intellectual vice, the structure of which is analogous to that of moral malevolence. Accordingly, Baehr argues for five key features of moral malevolence. First, moral malevolence is an "opposition to the good as such"; an opposition that is robustly willed, active, and personally deep. The morally malevolent person is intentionally and fundamentally hostile toward the good, and attempts to diminish or destroy it. Second, the morally malevolent person regards the good as an enemy—she "enemizes" the good. Third, Baehr argues that the object of moral malevolence can be personal or impersonal. When one is opposed to an individual person's well-being, or the well-being of a specific group of people, one's malevolence is personal. In contrast, supervillains, like Milton's Satan and the Joker, are opposed to the good in general, or to goodness itself; hence their malevolence is impersonal. Fourth, a supervillain need not oppose his own good—the scope of impersonal malevolence need not be maximally broad. Fifth, Baehr advocates a subjective conception of malevolence. He argues that the morally malevolent person need not be opposed to that which is *in fact* good; she need only be opposed to that which she *regards* as good. On Baehr's view, opposition to what is *in fact* good is neither necessary nor sufficient for malevolence. Malevolence turns on whether one *intends* to undermine the good, not on whether what one opposes is *in fact* good, or on whether one reliably *succeeds* in undermining the good. Accordingly, some people who oppose what is in fact good and reliably produce harm are not malevolent, and others who oppose what is not in fact good and fail to produce harm are malevolent.

Analogously, epistemic malevolence is an opposition to the epistemic good as such. Baehr suggests that the epistemic good includes, but is not limited to, knowledge. Like moral malevolence, epistemic malevolence can be impersonal or personal. Accordingly, the epistemically malevolent person enemizes knowledge in general, or some person's or group's knowledge or epistemic well-being. Baehr provides four illustrations of the vice of epistemic malevolence: the infamous Cartesian Demon, the Foucauldian "suspicionist," the character O'Brien in George Orwell's *1984*, and the Aulds, to whom Frederick Douglass was enslaved. Finally, Baehr highlights an important asymmetry between moral malevolence and epistemic malevolence: we think that moral malevolence is a paradigmatic moral vice, but we do not think that epistemic malevolence is a paradigmatic epistemic vice. Epistemic malevolence does not appear on standard lists of intellectual vices. Baehr suggests that this asymmetry can be explained by the fact that epistemic malevolence is less common than moral malevolence.

In "Epistemic Self-Indulgence" I argue that there is an epistemic analogue of the moral vice of self-indulgence. I defend an Aristotelian account of moral self-indulgence, which I use as a model for epistemic self-indulgence. I argue that there are several distinguishing features of moral self-indulgence. First, the vice of moral self-indulgence is an "excess" of the corresponding virtue of moral temperance. The passions and actions associated with moral self-indulgence and temperance are (by and large) physical, and they famously include wanting, consuming, and enjoying food, drink, and sex. I argue that the morally temperate person desires, consumes, and enjoys only appropriate objects, only at appropriate times, and only in appropriate amounts. By way of contrast, the morally self-indulgent person exceeds with respect to objects, or occasions, or amounts. She desires, consumes, and enjoys appropriate and inappropriate objects indiscriminately (e.g., sex with her own partner, and sex with her best friend's partner); or desires, consumes, and enjoys appropriate or inappropriate objects at inappropriate times (e.g., at a job interview); or desires, consumes, and enjoys appropriate or inappropriate objects too much (e.g., hourly). Second, following Aristotle, I restrict the purview of moral temperance and its vices to desires that are "peculiar" to individuals—such as wanting chocolate cake—rather than "common" to human beings—such as a shared biological desire for food. Third, I argue that according to Aristotle, the morally temperate person desires and consumes both objects that actively contribute to his health *and* objects that do not undermine his health; in short, the temperate person eats broccoli but also eats an occasional "treat," like chocolate cake (see Young 1988). Accordingly, the morally self-indulgent person consumes objects that contribute to her health, treats, *and* objects that actively undermine her health.

Likewise, the vice of epistemic self-indulgence is an "excess" of the virtue of epistemic temperance. Accordingly, the passions and actions associated with these traits are epistemic rather than physical, and include wanting, consuming, and enjoying beliefs, knowledge, and belief-forming practices. I argue that the epistemically temperate person desires, consumes, and enjoys only appropriate epistemic objects, only at appropriate times, and only in appropriate amounts. The epistemically self-indulgent person, however, either desires, consumes, and enjoys appropriate and inappropriate epistemic objects indiscriminately (e.g., true beliefs about physics and false beliefs about physics, or reliable processes and unreliable processes); or desires, consumes, and enjoys epistemic objects at inappropriate times (e.g., while having sex with his partner); or desires, consumes, and enjoys epistemic objects too much (thus preventing him from pursuing other things of value). I contend that the purview of epistemic temperance and its vices is restricted to epistemic desires that are "peculiar" to individuals—e.g., wanting true beliefs about metaphysics—and excludes the "common" desire for perceptual information about one's surroundings. I also argue that even if trivial truths (like true beliefs about Derek Jeter's batting average and Paris Hilton's whereabouts) do not actively contribute to valuable epistemic ends, they are still "epistemic treats." Celebrity trivia may be of lesser value than truths about physics, but the occasional consumption of celebrity trivia does not undermine valuable epistemic ends. Accordingly, the epistemically temperate person will consume objects that actively contribute to valuable epistemic ends *and* epistemic treats, whereas the epistemically self-indulgent person consumes all of these *and* objects that undermine valuable epistemic ends (e.g., false beliefs or unreliable processes). Finally, I suggest that philosophers and skeptics are epistemically self-indulgent because they desire, consume, and enjoy epistemic objects too much.

Acknowledgments

I am deeply grateful to the contributors. I would also like to thank the speakers, chairs, and supporters of the California State University Fullerton International Philosophy Conference on Virtue and Vice (June 2008). Special thanks go to the Fullerton Philosophy Department, the University Missions and Goals Initiative, the Vice President of Administration and Finance, and the Vice President of Academic Affairs, all of whom demonstrated the virtue of magnificence. I am especially happy and grateful to have the support of Clifford Roth.

References

Adams, Robert Merrihew. 2006. *A Theory of Virtue*. Oxford: Clarendon Press.

Adler, Jonathan. 2004. "Reconciling Open-Mindedness and Belief." *Theory and Research in Education* 2, no. 2:127–42.

Annas, Julia. 1993. *The Morality of Happiness*. New York: Oxford University Press.

Anscombe, G. E. M. 1958. "Modern Moral Philosophy." *Philosophy* 33, no. 124:1–19.

Aristotle. 1998. *The Nicomachean Ethics*. Translated by David Ross. Oxford: Oxford University Press.

Axtell, Guy ed. 2000. *Knowledge, Belief, and Character*. Lanham, Md.: Rowman and Littlefield.

Battaly, Heather. 2008a. "Virtue Epistemology." *Philosophy Compass: Epistemology* 3, no. 4:639–63.

———. 2008b. "Metaethics Meets Virtue Epistemology: Salvaging Disagreement About the Epistemically Thick." *Philosophical Papers* 37, no. 3:435–54.

Conee, Earl, and Richard Feldman. 1998. "The Generality Problem for Reliabilism." *Philosophical Studies* 89, no. 1:1–29.

DeRose, Keith. 1999. "Contextualism: An Explanation and a Defense." In *The Blackwell Guide to Epistemology*, edited by John Greco and Ernest Sosa, 187–205. Malden, Mass.: Blackwell.

Doris, John. 2002. *Lack of Character*. New York: Cambridge University Press.

Driver, Julia. 2001. *Uneasy Virtue*. New York: Cambridge University Press.

Fricker, Miranda. 2007. *Epistemic Injustice*. Oxford: Oxford University Press.

Goldie, Peter. 2004. "Emotion, Reason and Virtue." In *Emotion, Revolution, and Rationality*, edited by Dylan Evans and Pierre Cruse, 249–69. Oxford: Oxford University Press.

Greco, John. 2004. "Virtue Epistemology." In *Stanford Encyclopedia of Philosophy*, edited by Edward Zalta. Available at http://plato.stanford.edu/entries/epistemology-virtue/ (last accessed November 12, 2009).

Heidegger, Martin. 1995. *The Fundamental Concepts of Metaphysics: World, Finitude, Solitude.* Translated by William McNeill and Nicholas Walker. Bloomington: Indiana University Press.

Hurka, Thomas. 2001. *Virtue, Vice, and Value.* New York: Oxford University Press.

Hursthouse, Rosalind. 1999. *On Virtue Ethics.* Oxford: Oxford University Press.

Kripke, Saul. 1980. *Naming and Necessity.* Oxford: Blackwell.

Montmarquet, James A. 1993. *Epistemic Virtue and Doxastic Responsibility.* Lanham, Md.: Rowman and Littlefield.

Nussbaum, Martha. 2004. "Emotions as Judgments of Value and Importance." In *Thinking About Feeling,* edited by Robert C. Solomon, 183–99. New York: Oxford University Press.

Prinz, Jesse. 2004. *Gut Reactions.* New York: Oxford University Press.

Putnam, Hilary. 1979. "The Meaning of 'Meaning'." In *Mind, Language, and Reality,* vol. 2 of *Philosophical Papers.* Cambridge: Cambridge University Press.

Robinson, Jenefer. 2005. *Deeper Than Reason.* Oxford: Clarendon Press.

Solomon, Robert C. 2007. *True to Our Feelings.* New York: Oxford University Press.

Sosa, Ernest. 1991. *Knowledge in Perspective.* New York: Cambridge University Press.

———. 2004. "Replies." In *Ernest Sosa and His Critics,* edited by John Greco, 275–325. Malden, Mass.: Blackwell.

———. 2007. *A Virtue Epistemology.* Oxford: Oxford University Press.

Williams, Michael. 2004. "Skepticism and the Context of Philosophy." *Philosophical Issues* 14:456–75.

Young, Charles M. 1988. "Aristotle on Temperance." *Philosophical Review* 97, no. 4:521–42.

Zagzebski, Linda T. 1996. *Virtues of the Mind.* Cambridge: Cambridge University Press.

2

VIRTUE ETHICS AND VIRTUE EPISTEMOLOGY

ROGER CRISP

Over the past thirty or so years, since the publication in 1980 of Ernest Sosa's seminal paper "The Raft and the Pyramid," a debate has developed over whether epistemology might benefit from reflection on that broad movement in moral philosophy which has come to be known as "virtue ethics."[1] As someone inclined to view the increasing specialization in philosophy with some concern, I find this turn in epistemology intriguing.

These are, however, somewhat murky waters. A lot of writing in virtue ethics has been either primarily critical of other views or concerned to promote a particular substantive position. There has not been a great deal of discussion of exactly what virtue ethics is. On the face of it, this might seem no bad thing. Philosophers probably spend too much time on creating and polishing pigeonholes rather than getting on with answering fundamental philosophical questions. But the question is of course unavoidable when the claim under examination itself concerns a philosophical position. In what follows, then, I begin by saying a little about how virtue ethics is best understood. Aristotle's ethics is widely thought to be the closest we have to a canonical statement of the position, and, since it strikes me as both insightful and plausible, I then sketch in broad outline Aristotelian versions of virtue ethics and, by analogy, virtue epistemology. I end by asking whether, in light of my account of virtue ethics in general and Aristotelian virtue ethics in particular, virtue ethics has anything to offer epistemology, and if so what.

Substantive and Explanatory Virtue Ethics

What, then, is virtue ethics? One helpful two-stage way to categorize philosophical theories is (a) according to which questions the theories under consideration provide answers, and then (b) according to the answers they give. To which questions, then, is virtue ethics an answer?

[1] Sosa 1991a. Informative overviews of the course of the debate are found in, e.g., Axtell 1997; Battaly 1998, 2008; Zagzebski 1998; Greco 2002, 2004. The catalyst for virtue ethics is usually said to be another seminal paper: Anscombe 1958.

A fundamental one must be that of Socrates: "How should one live?" But there are many aspects to the living of a life, and hence there are more specific questions to be asked, including: "What kind of person should I be?" and "How should I act?" Virtue ethicists unproblematically can, and do, answer all of these questions, and so we should avoid the claim that virtue ethics focuses on the questions of how one should live or what kind of person one should be *rather* than on the question of how one should act (Zagzebski 1996, xiv, 6, 15; 1998, 618; Battaly 1998, intro.; Brady and Pritchard 2003, 2; Greco 2004, sec. 1, par. 1). It may well be that those commonly thought of as virtue ethicists focus on lives and persons, and non–virtue ethicists on actions, but this would not be a result of the constraints of ethical theory itself.

So a theory might be counted as a form of virtue ethics if it answers these questions as follows: "You should live the life of virtue, as a virtuous person, acting virtuously." But here we should note an important distinction between what we might call *substantive* and *explanatory* normative theories. We want to know both *how* we should live, and *why* we should live in that way. A straightforward explanatory version of virtue ethics will state not only that we should live the life of virtue and so act virtuously (which is what the merely substantive theory says), but also that the *ultimate* (that is, *non-derivative*) normative, justifying, or grounding reason for so living and acting is provided, in some way or another, by the virtues themselves.[2] An explanatory virtue ethicist may suggest, for example, that I should act generously. But an act utilitarian may well make the same claim, since acting generously will maximize expected utility. The explanatory virtue ethicist will then go on to distinguish her position from the utilitarian explanatory view by claiming that the reason for acting generously is not that so acting maximizes utility but that it is virtuous. The view may allow that there are other ultimate reasons, but in its strict monistic version it will not. Further, monistic explanatory ethical theories imply their substantive analogues.[3]

Note that this definition of explanatory virtue ethics leaves open—as I presume it should—exactly which traits are virtuous. This suggests that the standard way of introducing virtue ethics—as a clear alternative to views such as utilitarianism or Kantian deontology—is an oversimplifica-

---

[2] Note that the claim here is not that the virtuous person herself be motivated by the virtue of her acts, or by thoughts of that virtue, or that virtue be a reason to which she herself need appeal in justifying her action. Rather, the thought is that the virtue of an act itself counts in favour of performing that act.

[3] It would be self-contradictory to be a monistic explanatory virtue ethicist but to deny that one should live virtuously. But a pluralistic explanatory virtue ethicist may claim that in certain circumstances other sources of reasons might outweigh those grounded in virtue. For example, one might think that to avoid certain catastrophic outcomes, a life of vice might be called for, though there would be *something* to be said for the life of virtue nevertheless—viz., that it was virtuous.

tion (e.g., Baron, Pettit, and Slote 1997). We have already seen how an explanatory utilitarian can be a substantive virtue ethicist, advocating the life of virtue on the ground of its promotion of well-being. And Kant himself, of course, recommends the virtues (O'Neill 1996). But an explanatory virtue ethicist, who believes that an ultimate reason for acting in some way is that so acting is virtuous, may believe also that there is only one virtue. And if that virtue is benevolence, impartially construed, on the one hand, or conscientiousness, on the other, his position will seem to most people utilitarian or Kantian, respectively. But as long as one keeps the substantive/explanatory distinction in mind, virtue ethics can be kept distinct. If it is claimed that the reason for performing a benevolent action, or for being benevolent, is that virtue itself provides ultimate reasons, and that benevolence is the only virtue, then this is explanatory virtue ethics and substantive utilitarianism. If no normative weight is attached to the virtues themselves, and what is said to favour benevolence is the maximization of well-being, then we have explanatory act utilitarianism and substantive virtue ethics.

Synchronic and Diachronic Accounts

An explanatory virtue ethicist believes that an action's being virtuous, in itself, counts as an ultimate reason—and perhaps can be the only ultimate reason—in its favour. But what is it for an action to be virtuous?

To some, an action's being virtuous requires only that the agent be in a certain state—that she be motivated in certain ways, experience certain emotions, feel certain feelings, or whatever—*at the time of action.*[4] A kind action, for example, is an action done in a kindly way, where kindness is understood as constituted by certain feelings, emotions, and so on, at some particular time.

This *synchronic* view is very close to, and may even be seen as overlapping with, what is usually described as a form of deontology. When gratitude is required, for example, a deontologist may accept that the very fact that some action is one of gratitude counts in its favour. And he will also insist on the agent's performing the grateful action in an appropriate state—with knowledge, voluntarily, for the right reasons, with appropriate feeling, and so on.

Aristotle (2000, 2.4, 1104a28–33) draws a distinction between an action's being merely virtuous, on the one hand, and being done virtuously—"in accordance with the virtues"—on the other. Acting virtuously requires that the agent (a) act with knowledge, (b) act from rational choice of the actions for their own sake, and (c) *act from a firm*

---

[4] A weaker position will allow that an action is virtuous in so far as it is what the virtuous person would do (see Aristotle 2000, 2.4, 1105b5–7). On this view, the agent's motivation is irrelevant as to whether the action is or is not virtuous.

and unshakeable character. Take a case of generosity. The situation calls for a certain action: the giving away of a certain amount of money. For that action to be "in accordance with" the virtues—fully or properly virtuous, as we might put it—the agent has to fulfil conditions (a) to (c) above.

This account throws into doubt the claim that virtue ethics is to be understood in terms of the "direction of analysis" of virtues and right action—as the view that right action should be understood in terms of what the virtuous person would do, and not the other way round (Hookway 1994, 225; Zagzebski 1996, 15; Axtell 2000, xiii; Greco 2001, 136–38; 2004, sec. 8, par. 4; Battaly 2008, 1–2).[5] Right action is of course what the virtuous person would do; but as that is not what *makes* it right, the notion of "what the virtuous person would do" is insufficient to explain rightness. In the example of generosity, it is the situation—in particular, the needs of the recipient, and the financial capacities of the potential donor—that determine which action is right. Now it is indeed true that, on condition (c), what it is to *act rightly* is indeed to be understood in terms of the virtuous person, or at least her character. But it is equally true that the notions of a virtuous person and of virtuous character have to be understood partly by reference to right action and to acting rightly.

Several modern virtue ethicists clearly hold a diachronic position. Consider Rosalind Hursthouse: "What it is that makes the agent who does what is V [virtuous] for X reasons on a particular occasion both actually and counterfactually reliable and predictable, if she is—what it is for her to be 'really committed to the value of her V act'— is that she acts 'from a fixed and permanent state', namely the virtue in question" (1999, 135–36).

An explanatory virtue ethicist must, I suggest, accept such a *diachronic* account of virtue and right action. Virtue ethics may well be a theory about right action, but a virtue itself is an enduring trait of a person, and any theory which does not make essential reference to such traits in its explanatory account of right action is best not described as a form of virtue ethics.

Why should it matter in ethics whether the agent is "really committed" to the value of his act? The answer must be that such a commitment is in itself praiseworthy. So when we praise an action performed virtuously, the object of our praise is at least in part the disposition or virtue of the agent, or rather the agent himself for his possession of such a disposition (cf. Montmarquet 1993, 97–98). Consider Hume: "If any *action* be either virtuous or vicious, 'tis only as a sign of some quality or character. It must

---

[5]   Zagzebski, for example, defines a "pure" virtue theory as one "that makes the concept of a right act derivative from the concept of a virtue or some inner state of a person that is a component of virtue" (1996, 79).

depend upon durable principles of the mind, which extend over the whole conduct, and enter into the personal character. Actions themselves, not proceeding from any constant principle, have no influence on love or hatred, pride or humility; and consequently are never consider'd in morality" (2007, bk. 3, pt. 3, sec. 1, par. 4). Despite what Hume says here, there seems no reason why a diachronic explanatory virtue ethicist has to accept that actions themselves cannot be morally praiseworthy. Nevertheless, she surely must accept that, when an action is praised for being done rightly or done virtuously, implicit in that praise of the action is praise of the agent for being the sort of person to perform such actions.

Who Is a Virtue Ethicist?

A substantive virtue ethicist will claim that we should live and act virtuously. This position, however, is likely to be of less interest to an epistemologist looking for inspiration than an explanatory view, according to which the ultimate reason for performing a virtuous action is that it is virtuous.[6]

This simple view is perhaps the purest conceivable form of virtue ethics. But I can think of no philosopher who has advocated such an austere position; and this is not surprising. For a natural way to think of at least many virtues is as dispositions to respond in the appropriate way to normative reasons that can be characterized independently of the virtue itself. And this is certainly how the virtuous agent will often see things. It may be that one reason for acting benevolently is that so acting will be benevolent. But the benevolent person's thoughts will be occupied with the suffering he can alleviate, and it is this to which he will refer if asked to justify his action.

Those I shall call *paradigmatic virtue ethicists* tend not to stop with the virtues alone when advocating the life of virtue or acts of virtue. Consider Aristotle again. The details of his position are of course a matter of some controversy, but it is clear that he has a battery of arguments in favour of the life of virtue, resting on the notions of happiness or *eudaimonia*, human nature, the noble or *to kalon*, pleasure, and so on. In fact, it is unclear even whether Aristotle is to count as an explanatory virtue ethicist at all. On one interpretation, for example, he might be seen as an egoistic eudaimonist, who thinks that ultimately our reasons rest on the promo-

---

[6] We have seen that there are different accounts of what it is for an action to be virtuous. If it consists merely in the action's being what the virtuous person would do, then the explanatory virtue ethicist is claiming that the fact that a virtuous person would φ is itself a reason to φ. This has the odd implication that, in the case of the virtuous person, the fact that he is φ-ing is itself a reason to φ. If an action's being virtuous consists in its being done from certain motives or with certain feelings, and also perhaps on the basis of a firm character, then the view is that an action's being virtuous in this way itself speaks in favour of it. Here the "direction of analysis" is indeed from virtue to right action and not vice versa.

tion of our own happiness—which turns out to consist in exercising the virtues. On another, he is a perfectionist, who believes that the good of any member of a species consists in its perfecting its own nature—and in the case of human beings that turns out to be virtuous activity. More plausibly, perhaps, his text can be seen as indeterminate on these issues of priority. If our question is how we should live, then we should take into account happiness, human nature, the virtues, and much else in our answer, and not bother to press further questions about priority relations between these different concepts unless we have to.

In more recent times, Philippa Foot, in her earlier writings (e.g., 1978), argued in favour of the virtues from the perspective of an internalist conception of practical reasons, according to which the virtues would fulfil certain basic desires of the agent, while in *Natural Goodness* (2001) she developed eudaimonist and perfectionist arguments closer to those of Aristotle. Rosalind Hursthouse (1999) has likewise advocated a form of eudaimonism, though she gives the virtues a more instrumental role than Aristotle does and denies perfectionism. And so on. None of these writers is especially clear on whether the source of normativity in their positions includes the virtues themselves, and so we cannot be sure whether any of them should be described even as pluralistic explanatory virtue ethicists.

So there has been and is no consensus among paradigmatic virtue ethicists on the role of the virtues at the level of explanatory theory. This leaves at least two options for the virtue epistemologist. One would be for her to work out her own explanatory account in ethics. That might turn out itself to be virtue ethical, or it may not, and the kind of analogies to be drawn will depend importantly on the explanatory theory in question. For example, those attracted to broadly utility-maximizing explanatory positions are perhaps more likely to accept those reliabilist accounts of knowledge that seek to explain attributions of knowledge in terms of the (epistemic) value of the states produced by the operation of certain faculties; while those who accept virtue ethical explanatory accounts are more likely to explain knowledge in terms of the virtuous exercise of those faculties itself.[7]

A second strategy for the epistemologist is of course to examine accounts offered by other philosophers. Aristotle's is beyond doubt the account most cited as authoritative by contemporary paradigmatic virtue ethicists. So let me turn to it.

Aristotelian Virtue Ethics

Aristotle (2000, 2.5–6) sees virtues as *hexeis*, or dispositions, of two broad kinds: to *act* as one should (which requires the agent to be in a certain

---

[7] See, e.g., the broadly pragmatist possibility outlined in Blackburn 2001.

state); and to *feel* as one should (where "feelings" are to be understood broadly, to include emotions, desires, and so on). Note that at this level of abstraction there is still the option of, say, a utilitarian position, if we were to state that the acts one should perform and the feelings one should experience are those that maximize utility.

Aristotle's framework for his account of the virtues is his famous doctrine of "the mean." His ethics is indeed an attempt to answer the Socratic question. But he noticed that human lives could be analysed into several significant "spheres," each of which could be characterized in terms of the feelings or actions characteristic of those spheres (see Nussbaum 1993, 243–47; Zagzebski 1996, 221–22). These spheres are significant, and all but universal, aspects of human experience. At least some of them are characterized by emotions, and the virtuous person will be the one who feels those emotions "correctly." But how should we understand correctness and incorrectness? Aristotle says: "For example, fear, confidence, appetite, anger, pity, and in general pleasure and pain can be experienced too much or too little, and in both ways not well. But to have them at the right time, about the right things, towards the right people, for the right end, and in the right way, is the mean and best; and this is the business of virtue. Similarly, there is an excess, a deficiency and a mean in actions" (2000, 2.6, 1106b18–24).

So, to take anger as an example, the even-tempered person will be the one who feels anger at the right time, about the right things, towards the right people, and so on. But how should we understand the vices between which even temper is a mean? Quite often, commentators have sought to do this in a purely quantitative way: the bad-tempered person is the one who feels too much anger, and the person with the deficient vice feels too little. But that is only part of the story, as the passage above makes clear. One can go wrong by feeling anger at the wrong time, about the wrong things, towards the wrong people; and likewise by *failing* to feel anger at the right time, and so on. And, as Aristotle frequently points out, because there are many factors that the virtuous person gets right, there are many ways to go wrong, in the direction either of excess or of deficiency.

We can now see how actions feature along with feelings in the Aristotelian account. Several virtues are characterized in terms not of an emotion but of a type of action. An example is generosity, one of its characteristic actions of course being to give away money. The virtuous person will give away money to the right people, at the right time, for the right reasons, and in the right way (which, recall, involves knowledge and rational choice of the action for its own sake, as well as a causally active disposition). The stingy person will fail to act in these various ways, while the wasteful person will give away money to the wrong people, in the wrong way, and so on. Thus, one cannot plot a person's character on a spectrum from excess to deficiency passing through the mean. For there is nothing to prevent a person's possessing both an excessive and a deficient vice in the same sphere. This happens often in the sphere of money, as Aristotle notes. The wasteful person will give money at the wrong times and to the wrong people, and this will result in his not having the money to give at the right times and to the right people, so that he will end up stingy as well.

The doctrine of the mean is often criticized. One common objection, often thought especially devastating for Aristotle's account, is that the doctrine of the mean just fails with regard to certain virtues—in particular, justice (Williams 1980). Aristotle (2000, 5.3–5) does himself seek to incorporate justice into the doctrine of the mean, but his attempts are almost universally seen as failures. In particular, he tries to attribute a specific feeling or emotion—*pleonexia*, greed—to the unjust person. This is where he went wrong. If he had reflected further upon the doctrine of the mean as he himself describes it, he would have seen that justice is like, say, generosity, in that it will have to be characterized primarily in terms of actions, understood in a certain context. There are certain things that just people will do: take their fair share; make fair distributions, according to, for example, merit; fairly rectify unfair transactions. Now it might be thought that we cannot place these actions on the kind of spectrum required by the doctrine of the mean: either you are just or you are unjust. There are no vices of excess and deficiency. But this would be too swift. Someone may make a fair distribution, for instance, but at the wrong time (too early or too late, perhaps), or for the wrong end, motivated perhaps by a desire to ingratiate herself with the beneficiaries. These are cases of *excessive injustice*. Likewise, someone may *fail* to make a fair distribution at the right time, and this would be a case of *deficient injustice*. In fact, the doctrine of the mean seems to me a major insight into the nature of virtue. Morality, Aristotle is suggesting, is not to be understood merely in terms of a set of negative prohibitions or constraints. Rather, there are certain areas of life in which all of us will be put to the test, and to live our lives morally well we must act and feel appropriately within those areas.

An Aristotelian Virtue Epistemology

Let me now consider whether the Aristotelian model of the moral virtues just outlined might serve as the basis for an account of epistemic virtues.[8] Our original and overarching question may then be specified as: "How should one live, epistemically?"—one response being: "In accordance with the epistemic virtues." And an explanatory form of virtue epistemology will claim that the epistemic virtues themselves, either on their own or more probably in conjunction with and in relation to other items, ground reasons.

---

[8] For other broadly Aristotelian conceptions of virtue epistemology, see Code 1987; Montmarquet 1993; Zagzebski 1996.

As regards the synchronic/diachronic distinction,[9] there seems no difficulty in carrying across the distinction to epistemology in cases where the actualization of a disposition makes it appropriate. So the thought would be that this particular instance of creativity, open-mindedness, or believing is admirable partly because it is caused—in an appropriate way—by a stable or reliable disposition. And (Gettier problems aside) this will surely provide one with a reasonably secure notion of justification—or at least objective justification—for any account of knowledge that employs that notion.

In the case of the virtues we have been discussing, the right response to their possession is praise, since their exercise is noble. Likewise, since the exercise of the vices is *aischron*, or disgraceful, the correct response is blame. I take it that if epistemic traits are plausibly to count as virtues, then they should at the very least be appropriate objects of some pro-attitude or other (more on this below). We should nevertheless retain a distinction between moral and epistemic virtues.[10] Moral virtues are closely related to the happiness of the agent and others in her society, or *polis*. Epistemic virtues may also be central to happiness on some conceptions of that notion, but conceptually they find their place in what we might call the *epistemic enterprise*—that is, within activities and practices that involve the acquisition of knowledge or understanding. This distinction reflects that commonly drawn between practical reasons or values, and epistemic reasons or values. There can be reasons for belief of both kinds. To take an example of Sosa's (1991a, 165), an ill person may have a practical justification for believing he will recover (the belief itself is likely to aid that recovery) and a theoretical or epistemic reason provided by the results of tests, the doctor's opinion, and so on. And of course Aristotle himself (2000, 1.13) drew a clear distinction between moral and intellectual or epistemic virtues, resting on his differentiating separate parts of the soul.

If we return to the Aristotelian account of the moral virtues, we may note first that epistemic considerations can themselves affect what is morally right. Consider courage, understood as the correct feeling of fear. Aristotle tends to limit courage to the battlefield, but there is no reason—even by Aristotle's lights—to restrict its scope in this way. Now imagine someone who is inquiring into a cover-up by her employer. She may come to a point in her inquiry at which she realizes that continuing with it will involve

---

[9] For a clear statement of the diachronic position, see, e.g., Sosa 2001, 193–94. Cf. Sosa 1991b, 225: "Whatever exactly the end may be, the virtue of a virtue derives not simply from leading us to it, perhaps accidentally, but from leading us to it reliably." See also Greco 1993b, 414. Greco brings out well how the stability of dispositions has to be understood in terms of possible worlds: see, e.g., his response to Kvanvig at Greco 2003, 470–71. For the objection that the notion of reliability can do the work here without any reference to virtues, see Dancy 2000, 77–78.

[10] Even on a Platonic conception of the moral virtues as "unified" in knowledge, we are likely to want to distinguish moral knowledge from knowledge of other kinds.

risking her job and reputation. But it may well be right for her to continue with this part of the epistemic enterprise. This is a case where knowledge is perhaps only of instrumental value. But an analogous situation might be found in pure research about some highly significant topic, when a researcher realizes that his well-founded hunches are leading him down a path likely to damage his reputation in the intellectual community in which he works. Or consider an intemperate, angry, or wasteful scholar, whose research is hindered by vice. The moral virtues, in other words, can play an executive role in the epistemic enterprise (see Hookway 2003a, 76–77).

Aristotle's moral virtues concern actions and feelings. Some actions and feelings are intrinsic to the epistemic enterprise itself, so that their role is not best understood as executive. Consider creativity. It is clear that this can be a virtue, and it has its two opposing vices: uncreativeness, and misguided creativity (there are times when one should stop creating and just get on with the epistemic job at hand). Other action-focused virtues in this area might include perseverance, listening to others (the virtue here would be something like open-mindedness), or self-doubt, while a feeling-based virtue might be joy in inquiry or discovery. This final virtue might be said to be merely a particular case of a more general virtue, involving pleasure in activity. And indeed the action-related virtues just mentioned will be found outside the epistemic enterprise as well. There may be some action- or feeling-related virtues, however, such as "proper inquiry" or curiosity, which are specifically epistemic.

The question now arises whether there might be epistemic virtues concerned with items other than actions and feelings—in particular, of course, belief. The epistemically virtuous person, we may assume, will believe in the right way, for the right reasons, and so on, while failures will consist in not believing when or in the way one should, or believing when or in a way one should not. Is believing an action? Judging plausibly is, but not the state of belief itself, which is essentially passive. Further, belief is most plausibly seen as involuntary, and so, if it is an action, not a candidate for praise and blame on the Aristotelian picture (see Audi 2001a).

In *Ethics* 3.5, Aristotle argues that people are responsible for the way they turn out. If I become unjust, it will be because I have done unjust things in the past, and if intemperate, because I have spent my time in drinking and so on. I presume that Aristotle would want to extend this account to feelings also. So if I end up bad-tempered, it will be because I have given in to feelings of anger in the past, acting on them when I should not and failing to adopt strategies to curb my feelings. Consider now what Aristotle says about vices of the body as opposed to those of the soul: "Nobody blames someone unattractive by nature, but we do if he is so through not exercising and looking after himself. The same goes for weakness and disability; nobody would criticize a person blind by nature, or as the result of a disease or an injury, but rather pity him; everyone, however, would blame a person who was blind from drinking or some other intemperance. So bodily vices in our power are blamed, while those not in our power are not. And if so, then in other cases the vices that are blamed will be those in our power" (2000, 3.5, 1114a23–31).

It is true that we do not blame someone blind by nature for her blindness. But, as Aristotle notes, we may pity her, and this is an evaluating response: blindness is something regrettable. Likewise, though we may not blame the naturally weak, we may pity them, and admire another's strength. What I suggest, then, is that we allow the scope of epistemic virtues to be fixed not entirely by praise and blame but by pro and con attitudes more broadly—including pity and admiration. Such an account is more consistent with the attitudes we do take to epistemic virtues and vices, and allows us to bypass the problem of the apparent involuntariness of belief and other cognitive states. We can admire open-mindedness, for example, *even if* we know (in the case at hand) that the possession of that trait is not the responsibility of the open-minded person.

This suggests that we might extend epistemic virtues to cover epistemic capacities, such as perception and memory.[11] There is value in seeing things in the right way (not through veridical delusion, say) and at the right time (without a delay), and corresponding deficient and excessive vices. Failure to see through blindness would be a deficiency, while blurred vision might be an excess. But what we tend to admire is the very possession of the virtuous capacity: 20/20 vision, or an excellent memory. And this does take us beyond the doctrine of the mean: either you possess that capacity or you don't.

Here, reflection on epistemic virtues enables us to see an aspect of Aristotle's *ethical* position which remains largely hidden, through his emphasis on the exercise of the virtues in particular actions and episodes of feeling (see Hookway 2003b, 189). We do praise justly performed actions and appropriately felt anger. But we also admire people for the mere possession of the virtuous dispositions towards such actions and feelings, and this is implicit in Aristotle's own condition (c) on acting or feeling virtuously—that the agent must act or feel from a stable disposition. If those dispositions do not matter, then why impose condition (c) on virtuous action? It is perhaps because he approaches the virtues through his eudaimonism, and takes the view that happiness must involve activity, that Aristotle, unlike Plato, plays down the possession of the virtues, making it a mere necessary condition of acting or feeling virtuously rather than something admirable in itself. A life in a coma, even if one possesses the virtues, cannot, he suggests, be a happy one (2000, 1.5, 1095b32–

---

[11] See Sosa 1991c, 271, and Sosa's broad definition of a "competence" as "a disposition, one with a basis resident in the competent agent, one that would in appropriately normal conditions ensure (or make highly likely) the success of any relevant performance issued by it" (2007, 29; see discussion in Battaly 2008, 5–6). See also Kvanvig 1992, 111–12. For an argument for extension in the other direction, see Baehr 2006.

1096a2). That may be right—but it could nevertheless be, to some extent, an admirable one. Further, we may be prepared to extend moral admiration to certain traits regardless of whether the agent is or is not responsible for possessing them. This, of course, will ease the passage of any analogy between epistemic and moral virtue.

Conceptual space is now available for introducing Aristotle's own epistemic virtues, analysed in the sixth book of the *Ethics*: skill, scientific knowledge, practical wisdom, wisdom, intellect, and so on. These are capacities the mere possession of which is admirable, and the lack of which is the appropriate object of a negative attitude. But of course one can also construct an analysis of these virtues in terms of the mean, so that the virtuous person is the one who exercises his skill in the right way, and so on. The only virtue for which this will not work is practical wisdom. But that is because the life of practical wisdom just is the life of virtue, and there can be no wrongful exercise of *it*.

We have then at least the beginning of an outline of a broadly Aristotelian account of the epistemic virtues, which, though consistent with the doctrine of the mean, goes beyond it, through respecting a broader range of response than praise and blame alone, to cover cognitive states and their exercise as well as actions and feelings. To return to the foundational question—How should one live, epistemically speaking?— we have an answer. One should act, feel, cognize, possess the capacities so to act and so on, as appropriate to the epistemic enterprise.

Virtue Epistemology: Challenges and Prospects

Though the above is only a sketch of an epistemology modelled on a form of virtue ethics, it does seem to support the idea that analogies between epistemology and ethics in this area could be fruitful. But let me mention some issues, both methodological and substantive, that arise for anyone developing such an analogy (see Baehr 2008, esp. final sec.).

The kind of virtue ethics that epistemological proponents of the analogy have in mind is what I have been calling "paradigmatic virtue ethics," including historical as well as contemporary theories under that heading. Since most paradigmatic virtue ethicists would not accept virtue epistemology, virtue epistemologists who are not prepared to accept without question ethical positions based on epistemologies they themselves reject will be required to develop their own version of virtue ethics based on virtue epistemology, and then draw analogies between that account of ethics and epistemology. And of course they would have to be ready to show that their procedure was not circular in any vicious way.[12]

---

[12] They would also have to explain the epistemology they use in epistemology, and ward off concerns here about a regress. But this is a problem for any epistemologist. For a virtue epistemological account of virtue epistemology, see Lehrer 2001.

In his own dialectical epistemology of ethics, Aristotle puts a lot of weight on common sense (see esp. 2000, 7.1, 1145b2–7), and this explains why his ethics can plausibly be seen as a systematization and development of common-sense morality. Modern paradigmatic virtue ethicists say less about epistemology, but the fact that they tend to advocate common-sensical positions suggests that they also are inclined to attach weight to common-sense morality. This inclination could be questioned.[13] (i) Serious ethical disagreements have arisen and continue to arise between those who accept common-sense morality, both within and across cultures and sub-cultures. (ii) There are powerful evolutionary explanations available of central components of common-sense morality, and while these are not automatically debunking they do demand more epistemological support for common-sense morality than is usually provided. (iii) As Sidgwick pointed out more clearly than anyone else, our own common-sense morality contains various contradictions and peculiarities that require more systematization of the position than is commonly found in paradigmatic virtue ethics.

These three problems are likely to carry over to virtue epistemology. Indeed, recent epistemology as a whole contains many examples of appeals to common-sense intuitions which seem functionally quite similar to the same sort of appeals in ethics in arguments against ethical theories which go against common sense (so the brain lesion or demon arguments against reliabilism remind one of, say, the sheriff case against utilitarianism, or the hospital visit case against Kantianism).

Even more worrying, perhaps, is the possibility that there is no analogue to common-sense morality in epistemology. We do not, it might be suggested, set out explicitly to teach our children epistemological principles in the way that we teach them moral principles. Nor does there appear to be anything analogous to rights or other deontological restrictions that might put obstacles in the way of a "truth-maximizing" position such as reliabilism, in the way that these notions pose problems in ethics for welfare-maximizing views such as act utilitarianism. This leaves it open for a reliabilist to claim that she is in fact defending a more secure area of common sense against less respectable intuitions about particular cases, such as the demon. Quite how those involved in such disagreements should proceed is itself a substantial and difficult question.

The advantages claimed for an epistemology that mirrors virtue ethics in certain key respects are many (Greco 1993a, 521; Zagzebski 1998, 618; Baehr 2008, 3–4). They include an expansion of the scope of epistemology beyond individual beliefs to epistemic traits more generally and the intellectual virtues in particular, especially understanding and wisdom. The hope of a unified axiology, which collapses any distinction between moral and epistemic values, has been raised. It has been suggested also

---

[13] For a defence of common sense in this context, see Lemos 2001.

that various philosophical difficulties—in addition to the obvious one of re-inventing the wheel—can be avoided, including scepticism, Gettier problems, and the apparent stand-offs between epistemic internalism and externalism, on the one hand, and between coherentism and foundationalism, on the other (Greco 2004, intro.; Battaly 2008, 1).

The way forward, however, is not entirely clear. One general lesson of the discussions of virtue ethics and virtue epistemology above is that any plausible virtue epistemology is going to have to say quite a lot about individual beliefs and their grounding and justification. So any attempt to avoid philosophical puzzles about beliefs by focusing instead on epistemic traits is unlikely to succeed.

There are more specific potential difficulties. Consider first the foundationalist-coherentist debate (or indeed stand-off) (see esp. Sosa 1991a). Here, the essence of the Sosa-influenced position that has emerged is that, since the justification (that is, the justifiedness) of some belief will depend on its being the result of the exercise of a virtuous trait, the question does not arise of whether justification must end with some foundational or self-evident belief or proposition or consists rather in relations of coherence between beliefs. Unfortunately, however, the move to virtue epistemology avoids the foundationalist-coherentist stand-off not through a mere change of focus from beliefs alone to traits but through the importation of a particular conception of the virtues. Reliabilism, as a form of externalism, can indeed claim to sidestep the stand-off. But because of their externalism, reliabilist traits will appear to many to be too distant from what we understand by "virtues" to deserve that name. The reliabilist can probably anyway do without attributing reliability to virtues in particular. Further, because epistemic traits include the disposition to believe, there is nothing to prevent a foundationalist and a coherentist rephrasing their debate in terms of the virtues, with each describing as virtuous the dispositions towards the beliefs he holds to be justified.

Similar problems arise in the attempt to avoid the internalism-externalism debate. That debate concerns which beliefs are justified. And since according to virtue epistemology one central epistemic virtue will be a disposition to believe with justification, there will be both internalist and external accounts of virtue epistemology available.[14] It is true that a virtue epistemologist may claim that aspects of each position are correct, with internalists having latched onto certain properties of certain virtues, and externalists certain properties of certain others (see

[14] Virtue epistemologists have been resistant to the claim that virtues are dispositions to have justified beliefs (where justification can be explained in terms of foundationalism, coherentism, internalism, externalism, or whatever), on the ground that this is to get the "direction of analysis" backwards. But just as virtue ethics requires a notion of right action independent of virtue, so virtue epistemology requires a notion of belief which can be justified on grounds independent of epistemic virtue.

Zagzebski 1998, 621; Bloomfield 2000, 35–40). But again this hybrid view does not require expression in terms of the virtues.

What about scepticism? It is clear how a reliabilist virtue epistemologist can allow a person to have knowledge without her having an answer to the sceptical question, and how the reliability of the trait that results in knowledge is intended to provide justification. But note again how this position relies on a particular conception of a virtue, one of which many virtue ethicists would be unhappy to accept an ethical analogue. Virtue ethicists are likely to require that the virtuous agent have some kind of access to her justification for action, and not wish to permit luck to play such a role in the determination of moral value. For them, a virtuous believer deceived by an evil demon will be no less virtuous for that, just as the virtuous actor whose entirely justifiable and reasonable action leads to unforeseeable disaster is not to be criticized.[15] We cannot, then, assume that the virtues have to be "successful" in any sense that requires them to achieve some external goal.[16]

Finally, it is not clear that virtue epistemology provides any special opportunities for a unified axiology.[17] Aristotle's notion of the noble could perhaps be carried over to epistemology. But it is hard to see how virtue epistemology could provide the resources to collapse the distinction between practical value, on the one hand, and epistemic value, on the other. Consider again Sosa's ill patient. Her reasons to believe that she will recover appear to come from two entirely different sources: her own well-being, and the evidence (see Driver 2003, 110).

What, then, of the prospects for an analogy between virtue ethics and virtue epistemology, given all these issues awaiting resolution? I suspect the difficulties here will turn out to be no harder to surmount than those in many other areas of philosophy, and much progress has already been made by several thinkers in outlining strategies for dealing with them. Further, just as in philosophical ethics modern virtue ethics raised especially clearly questions that were largely being ignored—What is a virtue? Which traits are virtues? and so on—the same is true in epistemology of virtue epistemology. Developing various different answers to these questions, along common-sense "responsibilist" or more radical reliabilist lines, seems to me a very promising strategy for epistemology. But what is urgently required in both ethics and epistemology is further reflection on the methodology, and especially the epistemology, of those disciplines themselves. It would unwise to expect convergence within these disciplines in advance of consensus on how they are to be pursued. Epistemology, in this sense, is prior to both virtue ethics and virtue epistemology.

[15] For helpful discussion, see Audi 2001b, 88.
[16] *Pace* Zagzebski (1996, 137, 176–84, 248, passim). See Annas 2003, 23–31.
[17] Cf. Zagzebski 1999, 94. The success of the programme here is related to that promoting the idea of the unity of the virtues.

Acknowledgments

For comments on previous drafts and helpful discussion, I am grateful to Robert Audi, Tim Beaumont, Leonard Kahn, Matthew Liao, Tim Williamson, Chris Woodard, Nick Zangwill, and audiences at the Universities of Nottingham, York, Birmingham, and Cambridge; Queen's University Belfast; the Peter Strawson Society, Oxford; and the *Virtues and Vices: Moral and Intellectual* Conference at Cal. State Fullerton, June 2008. I owe a special debt of gratitude to Heather Battaly, whose penetrating comments improved the chapter at many points.

References

Annas, Julia. 2003. "The Structure of Virtue." In *Intellectual Virtue*, edited by Michael DePaul and Linda Zagzebski, 15–33. Oxford: Clarendon Press.

Anscombe, G. E. M. 1958. "Modern Moral Philosophy." *Philosophy* 33:1–19.

Aristotle. 2000. *Nicomachean Ethics*. Edited and translated by Roger Crisp. Cambridge: Cambridge University Press.

Audi, Robert. 2001a. "Doxastic Voluntarism and the Ethics of Belief." In *Knowledge, Truth, and Duty*, edited by Matthias Steup, 93–111. New York: Oxford University Press.

———. 2001b. "Epistemic Virtue and Justified Belief." In *Virtue Epistemology*, edited by Abrol Fairweather and Linda Zagzebski, 82–97. New York: Oxford University Press.

Axtell, Guy. 1997. "Recent Work on Virtue Epistemology." *American Philosophical Quarterly* 34:1–40.

———. 2000. "Introduction." In *Knowledge, Belief, and Character*, edited by Guy Axtell, xi–xxix. Lanham, Md.: Rowman and Littlefield.

Baehr, Jason. 2006. "Character, Reliability and Virtue Epistemology." *Philosophical Quarterly* 56:193–212.

———. 2008. "Four Varieties of Character-Based Virtue Epistemology." Unpublished manuscript.

Baron, Marcia, Philip Pettit, and Michael Slote. 1997. *Three Methods of Ethics*. Oxford: Blackwell.

Battaly, Heather. 1998. "What Is Virtue Epistemology?" 20th World Congress of Philosophy, available at http://www.bu.edu/wcp/Papers/Valu/ValuBatt.htm (last accessed 3 September 2009).

———. 2008. "Virtue Epistemology." *Philosophy Compass: Epistemology* 3, no. 4:639–63.

Blackburn, Simon. 2001. "Reason, Virtue, and Knowledge." In *Virtue Epistemology*, edited by Abrol Fairweather and Linda Zagzebski, 15–29. New York: Oxford University Press.

Bloomfield, Paul. 2000. "Virtue Epistemology and the Epistemology of Virtue." *Philosophy and Phenomenological Research* 60:23–43.

Brady, Michael, and Duncan Pritchard. 2003. "Introduction." In *Moral and Epistemic Virtues*, edited by Michael Brady and Duncan Pritchard, 1–12. Malden, Mass.: Blackwell.

Code, Lorraine. 1987. *Epistemic Responsibility*. Hanover, N.H.: University Press of New England.

Dancy, Jonathan. 2000. "Supervenience, Virtues, and Consequences." In *Knowledge, Belief, and Character*, edited by Guy Axtell, 73–85. Lanham, Md.: Rowman and Littlefield.

Driver, Julia. 2003. "The Conflation of Moral and Epistemic Virtue." In *Moral and Epistemic Virtues*, edited by Michael Brady and Duncan Pritchard, 101–16. Malden, Mass.: Blackwell.

Foot, Philippa. 1978. "Moral Beliefs." In *Virtues and Vices*, 110–31. Oxford: Blackwell.

———. 2001. *Natural Goodness*. Oxford: Clarendon Press.

Greco, John. 1993a. "Virtue Epistemology." In *A Companion to Epistemology*, edited by Jonathan Dancy and Ernest Sosa, 520–22. Malden, Mass.: Blackwell.

———. 1993b. "Virtues and Vices of Virtue Epistemology." *Canadian Journal of Philosophy* 23:413–32.

———. 2001. "Virtues and Rules in Epistemology." In *Virtue Epistemology*, edited by Abrol Fairweather and Linda Zagzebski, 117–41. New York: Oxford University Press.

———. 2002. "Virtues in Epistemology." In *Oxford Handbook of Epistemology*, edited by Paul Moser, 287–315. New York: Oxford University Press.

———. 2003. "Further Thoughts on Agent Reliabilism: Replies to Cohen, Geivett, Kvanvig, and Schmitt and Lahroodi." *Philosophy and Phenomenological Research* 66:466–80.

———. 2004. "Virtue Epistemology." In *Stanford Encyclopedia of Philosophy*, edited by Edward. Zalta. Available at http://plato.stanford.edu/entries/epistemology-virtue/ (last accessed 3 September 2009).

Hookway, Christopher. 1994. "Cognitive Virtues and Epistemic Evaluations." *International Journal of Philosophical Studies* 2:211–27.

———. 2003a. "Affective States and Epistemic Immediacy." In *Moral and Epistemic Virtues*, edited by Michael Brady and Duncan Pritchard, 75–92. Malden, Mass.: Blackwell.

———. 2003b. "How to Be a Virtue Epistemologist." In *Intellectual Virtue*, edited by Michael DePaul and Linda Zagzebski, 183–202. Oxford: Clarendon Press.

Hume, David. 2007. *A Treatise of Human Nature*, vol. 1. Edited by D. F. and M. J. Norton. Oxford: Clarendon Press.

Hursthouse, Rosalind. 1999. *On Virtue Ethics*. Oxford: Oxford University Press.

Kvanvig, Jonathan. 1992. *The Intellectual Virtues and the Life of the Mind*. Savage, Md.: Rowman and Littlefield.

Lehrer, Keith. 2001. "The Virtue of Knowledge." In *Virtue Epistemology*, edited by Abrol Fairweather and Linda Zagzebski, 200–213. New York: Oxford University Press.

Lemos, Noah. 2001. "Commonsensism in Ethics and Epistemology." In *Knowledge, Truth, and Duty*, edited by Matthias Steup, 204–18. New York: Oxford University Press.

Montmarquet, James. 1993. *Epistemic Virtue and Doxastic Responsibility*. Lanham, Md.: Rowman and Littlefield.

Nussbaum, Martha. 1993. "Non-relative Virtues: An Aristotelian Approach." In *The Quality of Life*, edited by Martha Nussbaum and Amartya Sen, 242–69. Oxford: Clarendon Press.

O'Neill, Onora. 1996. "Kant's Virtues." In *How Should One Live?*, edited by Roger Crisp, 77–99. Oxford: Clarendon Press.

Sosa, Ernest. 1991a. "The Raft and the Pyramid: Coherence versus Foundationalism in the Theory of Knowledge." In his *Knowledge in Perspective*, 165–91. Cambridge: Cambridge University Press.

———. 1991b. "Knowledge and Intellectual Virtue." In his *Knowledge in Perspective*, 225–44. Cambridge: Cambridge University Press.

———. 1991c. "Intellectual Virtues in Perspective." In his *Knowledge in Perspective*, 270–93. Cambridge: Cambridge University Press.

———. 2001. "Reflective Knowledge in the Best Circles." In *Knowledge, Truth, and Duty*, edited by Matthias Steup, 187–203. New York: Oxford University Press.

———. 2007. *A Virtue Epistemology*. Oxford: Clarendon Press.

Williams, Bernard. 1980. "Justice as a Virtue." In *Essays on Aristotle's Ethics*, edited by Amelie O. Rorty, 189–99. Berkeley: University of California Press.

Zagzebski, Linda. 1996. *Virtues of the Mind*. Cambridge: Cambridge University Press.

———. 1998. "Virtue Epistemology." In *Routledge Encyclopedia of Philosophy*, edited by Edward Craig, 9: 617–22. London: Routledge.

———. 1999. "What Is Knowledge?" In *Blackwell Guide to Epistemology*, edited by John Greco and Ernest Sosa, 92–116. Malden, Mass.: Blackwell.

3

EXEMPLARIST VIRTUE THEORY

LINDA ZAGZEBSKI

1. Introduction

In this chapter I outline a radical kind of virtue theory I call "exemplarism," which is foundational in structure but which is grounded in exemplars of moral goodness, direct reference to which anchors all the moral concepts in the theory. I compare several different kinds of moral theory by the way they relate the concepts of the good, a right act, and a virtue. In the theory I propose, these concepts, as well as the concepts of a duty and a good life, are defined by reference to exemplars, which are identified directly through the emotion of admiration. It is an advantage of the theory that what makes a good person good is not given *a priori* but is determined empirically. The same point applies to what good persons do and the states of affairs at which they aim. The theory gives an important place to empirical investigation and narratives about exemplars, analogous to the scientific investigation of natural kinds in the theory of direct reference.

2. My Theory of Moral Theory

I think of a moral theory as an abstract structure that aims to simplify, systematize, and justify our moral beliefs and practices. Constructing a moral theory is part of moral practice. Moral practice includes the construction of theories about the practice.

Since one of the aims of a moral theory is to simplify, it will leave out many subtleties and complexities in the practice of morality. There is nothing wrong with that as long as we do not think that the features of moral practice left out of the theory disappear. We are simply not attending to them when we are engaged in theory building and discussion. They will reappear when we engage in some other part of the practice. But we wouldn't construct theories unless we thought that there is something to be gained by attending to certain features of our moral practices and their relations at the expense of others. Given the limitations of the human mind, we are not able to understand a domain taken as a whole unless we ignore part of the domain we want to understand. The bigger and more complex the domain, the more we have to leave out if we want to understand it. Morality is an enormous domain that involves almost every aspect of human life and, to some extent, nonhuman life. It is not surprising that we cannot get our minds around it without mentally stripping away much of interest in the practice of morality.

I think this is a general point about understanding that applies even to the understanding of something as simple as the layout of a city. If every feature of the city was on the city map, the map would be as complex as the city is, and the map would not help us understand the city's layout. So the map leaves out many things, and it may also distort some things. Think of the shape of a country like Canada or Russia on a two-dimensional map. The map can be misleading, but a two-dimensional map is often more useful than a globe, even with the distortion. The distortion does no harm as long as we are aware of it.

Similarly, it is more useful to conceptualize moral reality without certain things in it, but it is helpful to keep in mind that we made a choice to leave those things out and the result might be a distortion. Most moral theorists believe that a good moral theory leaves out the identity of the persons in the practice and there is no first person pronoun in the theory. Others believe it would be better if we identified certain persons, or at least put thicker descriptions of persons into a theory. It seems to me that just as a two-dimensional map of the world distorts the shape and relative size of countries, a moral theory without personal identity distorts the moral relations among persons. However, it does not follow that we should put identities into our theories. Leaving out identity gives us an understanding of general moral relations between persons that would be very hard to grasp with the identities specified. If you want to highlight the fact that a person is a member of the community of moral agents, you don't want to add that the person is the same one your grandfather despised until his death because of an injury to your grandmother. But that information would be relevant to other parts of moral practice, such as those involving loyalty. Since I am going to make the unusual move of proposing a kind of moral theory that identifies certain individuals, I think it is worth thinking about the fact that we make a choice to leave out personal identity in a moral theory, and the choice is made for a reason. As long as we are aware of the reason for the choice, we might decide that it is not always an advantage to make that choice.

You might think that a theory should include reference to oneself and the identity of some other persons because you think a good theory should include all the conditions relevant to moral decisions. The identity of some persons is relevant to many decisions, particularly those arising from loyalty, friendship, and familial relations. But even though I think that we hope to get moral guidance from a good theory, a moral theory is not primarily a manual for decision making, and it is not constructed to be a manual. Again, a moral theory can be compared to a map. A detailed street map will help us get around a city, but a map of the world is not detailed enough to do that and it is not intended to do so. I think of a moral theory as more like a map of the world than a street map. Theories of parts of morality may be closer to street maps, and it is good that we have them, but even a street map is not constructed with the sole purpose of guiding a person from place to place. If your primary purpose was to get from one place to another, you might not use a map at all. A Global Positioning System would be a more efficient tool for getting around. But a navigation system cannot give you the understanding of the layout of the city that you get from a map. Similarly, if our main purpose was to get guidance in moral decision making, we would want a manual, not a theory. But the manual would not give us understanding of the domain of morality as a whole.

I think, then, that moral theory aims primarily at explaining and justifying moral beliefs and practices, and correlatively, showing us which beliefs and practices are unjustified. The aim of telling us what to do in any given situation is secondary. The different elements to be explained include reactive emotions such as admiration, blame, praise, and remorse, practices of punishing some but not all acts of wrongdoing, rules such as the Golden Rule or the Ten Commandments, and values such as freedom, fulfillment, and social cohesiveness, which are often revealed in narratives that are cherished by a particular community. These are only some of the elements of our moral practices that preexist our theory. My point is that there is already something there that we seek to understand through a moral theory.

What we seek to understand can be altered by the process of seeking to understand it. In this respect a moral theory is unlike a street map. I suppose we can imagine a map that we liked so much that when the map and the layout of the streets did not coincide, we changed the streets, not the map. But assuming that we do not want to move the streets around, the point of a map is to give us understanding of the physical layout of a city that is already there and that will change for reasons that have nothing to do with the map. Moral theory is different because even though there are moral practices that are already there in advance of the creation of theory, since one of the purposes of the theory is to justify the practices, we might find out that some element of the practice is not easily justified if it is related to other elements of the practice in certain ways.

That could lead us to change the practice in response to the theory. In contrast, a city map does not seek to justify the layout of a city, it seeks only to depict it.

If a moral theory is intended to explain our moral beliefs and practices in a way that can lead us to revise those practices, it is natural to wonder how a theory can do that. For whom is a theory intended? Would we want to promulgate it for the whole society? Is it instead for moral leaders? Or is there a class of people whose business it is to produce moral theories—the moral philosophers? I assume it is the latter. We produce moral theories first for other philosophers, and secondarily for students in philosophy classes. But we think that theoretical discussions can ultimately influence practice. In this chapter I compare a variety of moral theories at the most abstract level of theoretical structure. It is pretty obvious that theory at that level does not influence practice, but one of the issues I am interested in is the path from abstract theory to revisions of practice. I suspect that the path goes through disciplines other than philosophy, publications aimed at the general educated public, the arts and the media, and sometimes the law, and most of the time the path withers before ordinary people are affected, but theory can influence practice. I think that it is an advantage if a theory can link up with moral practice in a plausible way, particularly if it can link up with narratives that capture the imaginations of ordinary people.

Since we are going to compare moral theories, an obvious question to ask is whether the theories are in competition with one another. Presumably, some theories are better than others, but it is not obvious that there cannot be two equally good theories that are dramatically different. Most of us would strongly hesitate to allow the possibility of two equally good moral manuals that give conflicting moral directions. If we also think a manual is generated from a theory, that can explain our resistance to the idea that there can be two equally good moral theories. We don't want to be committed to allowing two equally good but incompatible manuals. But as I've said, the connection between a theory and a manual is not straightforward. Most moral theories generate most of the same moral directions, so the theories differ more than the manuals they generate. In fact, the manuals would be mostly the same, assuming the moral practices the theories explain and justify preexist the theories. But a comparison of theories often becomes most interesting in precisely those places in which they lead to conflicting directions—differences in the manuals they produce. I am going to propose a theory that does not produce a manual by itself but produces it in conjunction with other components of our moral practices, particularly narratives. The manual we get from such a theory is no doubt vague, but I prefer a vague manual to the wrong manual. In any case, I am not going to say much about moral manuals and how we get them.

3. The Structure of Some Moral Theories

If we want a comprehensive yet simple moral theory, I think we should start by looking at three very general concepts of positive moral evaluation. (Theories are almost always built around positive rather than negative evaluation). Deep differences between theories can be revealed by comparing the ways they relate these three concepts: *the good* (G), *a virtue* (V), and *a right act* (R). The good applies to different kinds of things in different theories, and it might seem misguided to compare the good in hedonistic utilitarianism, Aristotle's idea of *eudaimonia*, Kant's notion of a good will, and Plato's Form of the Good. Clearly, there is a sense in which Plato, Aristotle, Kant, and Mill are not talking about the same thing, but there is a sense in which they *are* because each has selected a form of the good that is allegedly pivotal in understanding moral practice, and that has important relations to the evaluation of acts and persons.

There is another complication that I want to mention before we compare the theories. There are more concepts of act evaluation than of anything else. In addition to the concept of a right act, there is the concept of a virtuous act and the concept of a duty. Furthermore, the concept of a right act is ambiguous because sometimes it is treated as the complement of a wrong act—an act that is not wrong, in which case it includes the evaluatively neutral as well as the evaluatively positive. Sometimes, instead, it is treated as the equivalent of what one *should* do— the act that is favored by the balance of moral reasons. And sometimes it is treated as the equivalent of the even stronger notion of duty—what one *must* do. If something is a duty, it is wrong not to do it. So a right act can be understood as (a) an act it is not wrong to do, or (b) an act it is wrong not to do, or (c) an act that one has most moral reason to do. A virtuous act is typically treated as an act that expresses a virtue and is hence good, but it is not a duty, nor is it conceptually equivalent to what one should do in the sense of an act that is favored by the balance of moral reasons.

The purpose of the diagrams below is to help us in comparing theory structure and to reveal what a theory leaves out, as well as the different ways the theories organize these three moral concepts. In each diagram the foundational concept is at the bottom, and the concepts above are defined in terms of their relations to the concepts below. For instance, in utilitarianism, a right act is defined in terms of a good state of affairs, and the relation is one of promotion. A right act is one that promotes a good state of affairs. In some cases the relation in question is one of constituency. (I use "<" to mean "is a constituent of".) In some theories the real foundation is something outside ethics, such as reason or human nature or what everyone desires, and I indicate this below the line separating the moral concepts from the nonmoral foundational concept.

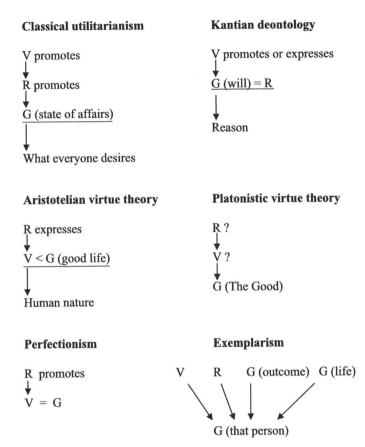

The diagrams reveal some differences among the theories. Whatever is at the bottom of the diagram is most fundamental in the theory, and I think also most important. What is derivative is less important and typically gets less attention. In fact, virtue gets no attention in Mill and only a small amount of attention in contemporary forms of consequentialism. Plato and Aristotle talk about virtuous acts but give little attention to a right act and arguably none at all to duty. So I am trying to illustrate both a difference in patterns of understanding these three fundamental moral concepts, and the difference in the importance these concepts have in the respective theories. There are things that one theory considers important that another theory leaves out entirely or mentions only in passing. This might seem obvious, yet it is common for a philosopher to critique the account of his favorite moral concept by another philosopher who really is not interested in the concept. That sometimes happens in critiques of the way virtue theorists use the concept of a right act.

A comparison of the diagrams also shows us some features that these theories have in common. Perhaps the most obvious one is that they are all foundational in structure. Making one concept foundational has the advantage of theoretical elegance, but I think it should be acknowledged that if the aim of moral theory was just to simplify and systematize our moral practices, there would be no special advantage in a foundational structure. Any clever person could make up structures using the concepts of good, right act, and virtue that are just as simple as the theories in the diagrams, but that do not have a hierarchical form with a single foundational concept. The attraction to foundationalism, I believe, is due to the fact that in the modern era a moral theory is not only expected to justify our individual moral practices, it is assumed that the entire practice of morality itself is in need of justification, and it is assumed further that a secure foundation is the best way to justify the practice of morality. Neither of these assumptions is obvious. I have already said that I accept the fact that justification is a purpose of moral theory, but I do so as a concession to modern moral philosophy. This aim would not have been recognized in the premodern era, and I imagine that that is the reason it is so difficult for modern philosophers to recognize anything in the premodern period that constitutes moral theory at all. It is only at the risk of severe artificiality that the moral philosophies of Plato and Aristotle can be squeezed into the structures I have labeled "Platonistic" and "Aristotelian," nor can they be easily aligned with any alternative foundationalist structure. Readers may have their own view on whether any moral philosopher before the modern period advocated a theory with a foundationalist structure. I suspect there is none, and that is because nobody before the modern era thought that moral theory needed to justify moral practice. Moral philosophers would have thought that moral theory is a part of philosophy that simplifies and systematizes a complex practice, but there would have been no thought that the practice itself had to be justified. Granted, they sometimes used moral theory to adjudicate disputes about issues such as justice in war, but they surely did not think that morality itself is in need of justification. That assumption is probably due to the naturalistic tenor of our times. The thought now is that we can be confident of the existence of nature in the sense of nature investigated by empirical science, but morality is not part of that, and we cannot be confident of its credentials. Morality needs something outside it to justify it, something of which those who question the credentials of morality can be confident.[1]

---

[1] It is interesting that the motive for Divine Command Theory is different. The Divine Command theorist rejects the independence of moral authority from divine authority, not because our moral practices are in need of justification, but because divine authority is threatened if moral authority has a source independent of God.

This is why it is desirable that moral theory be foundational in structure. It doesn't actually have to be, but it is much easier if it is. Presumably it is hard enough to tie even one of the fundamental concepts of moral evaluation to something outside morality; to tie more than one would be more challenging than philosophers can tolerate. But we could declare victory if there is a single concept foundational to morality that is justified by reference to something outside morality on which everyone can agree, and which in turn can support all other moral concepts. And that is the aspiration of at least three of the theories in the diagram. The foundational concept is tied to something else that is not moral and that is accepted by anybody who might be inclined to question the justifiability of moral practice.

The three I have in mind are Kantian moral theory, neo-Aristotelian moral theory, and utilitarianism. Kant grounds the concept of a right act in reason understood formally or, at least, in some uncontroversial way. Neo-Aristotelian virtue theory grounds the good for human beings in human nature, understood in a way that makes minimal claims about the substance of human nature. Hedonistic utilitarianism grounds the good of human beings in something every human, indeed, every animal, naturally desires: to get pleasure and to avoid pain. In each case, morality derives from something that is allegedly less in need of justification, and it does so in a simple and elegant way. I think this is also the reason that Platonistic theories seem nonexplanatory to most modern philosophers.

Now I would like to propose another feature that a good theory should have, whether or not it is foundationalist in structure. Since a theory is a theory *of* something, there has to be some way that a user of the theory can connect the theory to what the theory is about. If a theory can be compared to a map of some domain, the user of the theory should be able to superimpose the map on the domain. She should be able to say, "*This* element in the theory refers to *that* element in the domain." Sometimes the elements of the theory are objects of the user's background experience, and this feature is easy to satisfy. When the economist refers to prices and interest rates, he assumes the users of the theory can identify those elements in the world of economic exchange. Sometimes the theorist gives directions for finding the elements of the theory, as when the botanist draws pictures of the plants she is classifying. The same point applies to a city map. It is useful only if the user can find something in the city that hooks it to the map—that intersection over there is this one on the map. A stationary map will sometimes say "You are here" in order to orient the user. It seems to me that a moral theory needs something that serves that purpose—something that tells him that *this* element of moral belief or practice is *that* element in the theory. Unlike a map of an imaginary city, a moral theory is like a map of an actual city, and a user needs to connect the map with moral practice in order to negotiate the practice.

Let me now review the desiderata of a moral theory as I understand it.

1. A moral theory should simplify and systematize our pretheoretical moral beliefs and practices, aiming at giving us understanding of the practices of morality, and sometimes resulting in a revision of those practices. It is possible that simplifying and systematizing results in some distortion, but that can be tolerated if something is gained from the distortion and the distortion is not forgotten.

2. A moral theory is not a manual and its main purpose is not to give directions in decision making, but it is an advantage if a theory can help us in our practical lives. Many directions for making moral decisions already exist in our pretheoretical practices, including narratives, parables, and practical rules.

3. A moral theory should also justify our moral beliefs and practices. I am not convinced that the entire domain of moral practice needs to be justified by something outside the practice, but I am willing to accept both the aim of producing a foundationalist structure, and the need to make the foundation something relatively uncontroversial.

4. A moral theory needs a hook to connect it to the domain of moral practices of which it is a theory. Just as a map is useless unless we can identify something on the map by reference to something in our experience, a moral theory is useless unless we can find a place where the theory connects to a part of the moral domain we can identify independent of the theory.

4. Exemplarism

The theory I want to propose is foundational in structure, but the foundation is not conceptual. Instead, the construction of the theory begins with direct reference to exemplars of moral goodness. My model for the foundational move in constructing a theory of this kind is the Putnam-Kripke theory of direct reference, particularly in the form in which it was used to define natural kind terms.[2] Leaving aside differences in the versions of the theory, the basic idea is that a natural kind term such as "water" or "gold" or "human" refers to whatever is the same kind of thing or stuff as some indexically identified instance. For example, gold is, roughly, whatever is the same element as *that*, water is whatever is the same liquid as *that*, a human is whatever is a member of the same species as *that*, and so on, where in each case the demonstrative term "that" refers directly—in the simplest case, by pointing. One of the main

---

[2] This theory originated with Saul Kripke's *Naming and Necessity* (Kripke 1980) and Hilary Putnam's "The Meaning of 'Meaning'" (Putnam 1979, first published in Gunderson 1975).

reasons for proposing this account of reference was that Kripke and Putnam believed that often we do not know the nature of the referent, and yet we know how to construct a definition that links up with its nature. We may not know the nature of gold—its deep structure, and for millennia nobody did, but that did not prevent people from defining "gold" in a way that fixed the reference of the term and continued to do so after it was discovered what distinguishes gold from other elements. In fact, we would not say that modern humans "discovered" the nature of gold unless we thought that modern speakers know the nature of the same stuff of which people used to be ignorant. The theory of direct reference has the advantage of explaining how "gold" referred to the same thing before and after the discovery of the atomic structure of gold.

This proposal began a revolution in semantics because it meant that competent speakers of the language can use terms to successfully refer to the right things without going through a descriptive meaning.[3] Unlike a term such as "hammer," the referent of natural kind terms like "water" and "gold" is not whatever satisfies a description given in advance. Because speakers need not associate descriptions with natural kind terms in order to successfully refer to the right kinds, an important consequence of this theory is that it is possible that speakers succeed in referring to water and gold even when they associate the wrong descriptions with terms like "water" and "gold."[4] What is required instead is that they be related by a chain of communication to the actual stuff water and gold.[5] It is not even necessary that every speaker be able to identify water and gold reliably herself as long as some speakers in the community can do so and the other speakers rely upon the judgment of the experts.

An interesting feature of this theory is that a definition through direct reference is only a contingent truth. It is not a necessary truth that what I am pointing to right now is gold. Of course, *if* I am pointing to something gold and if it is essential to anything gold that it is gold, then it is essential to the thing I am in fact pointing to that it is gold. However, it is not a necessary truth that I am pointing to *this* thing, and so it is not necessary that I am pointing to gold. Hence, we must accept either that some definitions are not necessary truths or that the way we connect words with

---

[3] Initial discussion focused on natural kind terms and proper names, but later the theory was applied to a broader class of terms. The extent of the class of terms which can refer directly is not important for my point in this chapter.

[4] On one version of the theory, natural kind terms have no meaning; they are purely denotative (like Mill's theory of proper names). On another version of the theory, natural kind terms have a meaning, but meanings are not in the head. That is, they are not something a speaker grasps and through which he finds the referent. See Putnam 1979.

[5] In some later versions of the theory the chain is thought to be causal, hence the term "causal theory of reference," but the idea that the use of a term by many speakers is causally connected is not a necessary part of the theory.

objects in the type of "definition" we have been considering is not actually a definition. For my purposes, it does not matter which option we take. One other interesting consequence of the theory of direct reference is that there are necessary *a posteriori* truths. Kripke thought that once the reference of a natural kind term like "water" is fixed by ostension, scientists can then discover the nature of water empirically. Under the assumption that the nature of water is essential to it, it follows that certain necessary truths such as "Water is H_2O" are discovered *a posteriori*.

This idea can be used in the construction of a moral theory. I suggest that basic moral concepts are anchored in exemplars of moral goodness, direct reference to which are foundational in the theory. Good persons are persons *like that*, just as gold is stuff *like that*. Picking out exemplars can fix the reference of the term "good person" without the use of descriptive concepts. It is not necessary that ordinary people engaged in moral practice know the nature of good persons—what makes them good. In fact, it is not necessary that anybody know what makes a good person good in order to successfully refer to good persons, any more than it was necessary that anybody knew what makes water water to success-fully refer to water before the advent of molecular theory. We need not associate any descriptive meaning with "good persons," and users of our language can successfully refer to good persons even when they associate the wrong descriptions with the term "good person." As with natural kinds like gold and water, people can succeed in referring to good persons as long as they, or at least some people in their community, can pick out exemplars.[6]

Practices of picking out such persons are already embedded in our moral practices. We learn through narratives of both fictional and nonfictional persons that some people are admirable and worth imitating, and the identification of these persons is one of the pretheoretical aspects of our moral practices that theory must explain. Moral learning, like most other forms of learning, is principally done by imitation. Exemplars are those persons who are *most imitable*, and they are most imitable because they are most admirable. We identify admirable persons by the emotion of admiration, and that emotion is itself subject to education through the example of the emotional reactions of other persons. I am proposing, then, that the process of creating a highly abstract structure to simplify

---

[6] It is an important part of the theory of direct reference that a person can successfully refer when she is not good at identifying the referent herself, and even when she has never had any experience of the referent. So we all can refer to uranium, and Putnam says he can refer to elm trees even though he is not good at recognizing them. Nonetheless, those of us who are only distantly related to uranium or elm trees are epistemically disadvantaged relative to the experts who are good at identifying them. We lack the understanding that the experts have. But given the importance of moral understanding by as many people as possible in a moral community, it is important that the ability to identify exemplars is spread as widely as possible. This is one of the functions of narrative, mentioned below.

and justify our moral practices is rooted in one of the most important features of the pretheoretical practices we want to explain, the practice of identifying exemplars, and in a kind of experience that most of us trust very much—the experience of admiration, shaped by narratives that are part of a common tradition.

I am assuming that the emotion of admiration is generally trustworthy when we have it after reflection and when it withstands critique by others. We have no guarantee that what we admire upon reflection is admirable, but then we do not have any guarantee that our vision or memory is trustworthy if it withstands reflection either. All we can do is the best we can do by using our faculties as conscientiously as we can, and our disposition to admiration is one of those faculties.

This theory is compatible with the possibility that paradigmatically good individuals are only contingently good,[7] and it is also compatible with the theory that our identification of exemplars is revisable. Just as we can be mistaken in our judgment that some portion of a substance we identify as water is really water, we can also be mistaken in our judgment that some person we identify as paradigmatically good is really good. However, given that there is a conceptual connection between water and stuff "like that," we cannot be mistaken in thinking that most of what we take to be water is water. Similarly, there is a conceptual connection between good persons and persons "like that," but unlike the case of natural kinds, this conceptual connection guarantees that we are usually right only if we can generally trust our disposition to admiration. It is possible that a community of persons is so radically wrong in its identification of exemplars that even its concept of the good is mistaken. I don't think we need worry about anything analogous in the case of natural kinds, since there is nothing to get right when we point to a material substance or element.

One of the most interesting features of the Kripkean account of natural kinds is the way empirical investigation can reveal natures, and I think this also is a feature of exemplarist virtue theory. If the concepts in a formal ethical theory are rooted in a person, then narratives and descriptions of that person are morally revealing. It is an open question what it is about the person that makes him good. For the same reason, when we say that a good person is a person like that, and we directly refer to Saint Francis of Assisi, or to Confucius, or to Jesus Christ, we are implicitly leaving open the question of what properties of Francis, Confucius, or Christ are essential to their goodness. Perhaps there are nonevaluative descriptions of these persons that are sufficient to determine their moral goodness; perhaps not. Perhaps their goodness is not determined by any descriptive properties we know how to apply. The exemplarist approach has the advantage that neither these metaphysical matters nor substantive matters about what makes a person

---

[7] Unlike water, which is probably water essentially.

good need be settled at the outset. I am assuming that Kripke is right that deep and important, perhaps even necessary properties of the object class can be determined by empirical observation, although the determination of what counts as deep and important is not itself empirical.[8] Since narratives are a form of detailed observations of persons, exemplarism gives narrative an important place within the theory analogous to scientific investigation in the theory of natural kinds. Narratives might even reveal necessary features of value by uncovering the deep properties of a good person. If so, there would be necessary *a posteriori* truths in ethics that can be discovered in a way that parallels the discovery of the nature of water.[9] Furthermore, new empirical research on virtuous exemplars may reveal interesting features of their attitudes and behavior.[10] The theory therefore has a place for both stories and empirical research within its abstract structure.

Are there any historical examples of exemplarist virtue theory? I have suggested that Aristotle's definition of *phronesis* involves an essential demonstrative reference, but there is no indication that persons with *phronesis* play a foundational role in his theory. However, Amy Olberding (2008) argues that Confucius's *Analects* can be read as rooting moral concepts in the experience of paradigmatically good individuals like the Duke of Zhou, heroes of Chinese history, and Confucius himself.[11] If she is right, the conceptual schemata of the *Analects,* including its account of specific virtues, human flourishing, and the path of self cultivation, originate in the experiences of admiration for the figures the text vividly describes. As I said above, there is reason to think that the search for a foundationalist moral theory is a feature of modern Western philosophy, so it would be very surprising if Confucius aspired to such a theory, but I find it interesting that Confucius and his followers may have used an

---

[8] The parallel point applies to the discovery of the necessary truth, "Water is H_2O." Empirical observation yields the conclusion that water is H_2O, but the judgment that the molecular structure of water is essential to it is *a priori.*

[9] I have not said anything about the difference between fictional narratives and biography. The place of fiction in philosophy is an interesting one, but I am leaving it aside for this chapter.

[10] For example, research by Lawrence Walker and Karl Hennig (2004) suggest that there are three distinct types of moral exemplarity: just, brave, and caring. Exemplars have been the subject of other psychological studies, for instance, Kevin Reimer and David Wade-Stein's (2004) work on adolescent exemplars, and research on the participants in the L'Arche communities. Currently, a research group headed by Michael Spezio at Cal Tech is studying the way exemplars play economics games with neuroimaging during the playing of the games.

[11] Olberding is not suggesting that Confucius treated himself as an exemplar. *The Analects* is a compilation of teachings of Confucius, conversations with his students, observations of his behavior by his students, and teachings of his students. The work has several strata in its composition, and Olberding argues that the function of exemplars operates both in Confucius's own teachings and in the way Confucius is treated by his followers.

exemplarist approach to explain how the abstract concepts of most significance in Confucian moral practice arise.

5. A Comprehensive Exemplarist Virtue Theory

An exemplarist moral theory does not have to be a virtue theory. There can be exemplary acts and exemplary lives, and possibly exemplary states of affairs, as well as exemplary persons, and any of these could be defined by direct reference. Whether all of these concepts have the potential to be the foundation of a plausible moral theory is another question. If the exemplary is the most imitable, I doubt that there are exemplary states of affairs. There can be exemplary acts, but reference to a few exemplary acts will not be helpful in constructing a comprehensive theory. The idea of beginning the construction of a theory with direct reference to exemplary lives is more promising, but a difficulty with that approach is that only some of the features of a life good as a whole can be imitated. In contrast, admirable persons can be imitated insofar as they are admirable, and if all important moral concepts could be defined by reference to these persons, that would not only give us a comprehensive moral theory, it would allow a smooth connection between moral theory and moral training.

Let me review. What I mean by an exemplar is a paradigmatically good person. An exemplar is a person who is most admirable. We identify the admirable by the emotion of admiration. I assume that our emotion of admiration is generally trustworthy, but I do not assume that we always trust it. When we do, we take the object of admiration to be admirable. A person who is admirable in some respect is imitable in that respect. This is rough because there are many reasons why we do not or cannot imitate the admirable. But the feeling of admiration is a kind of attraction that carries with it the impetus to imitate. The ways in which the exemplar are admirable, and hence imitable, can be used to give us both a way of understanding significant moral concepts and a way of using those concepts as a way of making ourselves and our lives conform to the admirable.

Here is a suggestion for defining a series of basic moral concepts in terms of a paradigmatically good or admirable person.

A *virtue* is a trait we admire in an admirable person. It is a trait that makes the person paradigmatically good in a certain respect.
A *right act* (an act that a person would have most moral reason to do) in some set of circumstances C is what the admirable person would take to be most favored by the balance of reasons in circumstances C.
A *duty* (an act it would be wrong not to do) in some set of circumstances C is what the admirable person would feel compelled to do in C in the sense that if he did not do it, he would feel guilty for not doing it.

A *good state of affairs* (more precisely, that subset of states of affairs that can be the outcome of human acts) is a state of affairs at which admirable persons aim.

A *good life* (a desirable life, a life of well-being) is a life desired by admirable persons.[12]

In each case, the concept to be defined (virtue, good state of affairs, right act, and so on) is defined via indexical reference to a paradigmatically good person. So a virtue is a trait we admire in *that* person and in persons like that. A good state of affairs is a state of affairs at which persons like that aim. A good life is a life desired by persons like that. A right act is an act a person like that would take to be favored by the balance of reasons. A duty is an act a person like that would feel compelled to do, and so on.

Is the theory I have described a type of virtue theory? That depends, of course, upon what it takes to be a virtue theory. Exemplarism does not make the virtues primary, although it does make virtuous persons primary. Perhaps a comparison of the theory with other theories in the diagrams near the beginning of the chapter suggest that it is a distinct class of theory, neither act-based nor virtue-based. I don't want to insist that it is closer to traditional virtue theories than it is to act-based theories, but it seems to me that it is more easily combined with work in virtue ethics than with work in consequentialist and deontological theories. However, it probably does not much matter how it is ultimately classified.

In talking about my theory of theory, I mentioned that sometimes a theory distorts what it explains, and moral theory distorts moral practice by not putting the first person pronoun and other descriptive features into the theory. What is right or a duty or a good life *simpliciter* is determined by an act or attitude of a certain kind of person, the paradigmatically admirable person. But it is possible that the exemplar differs from me in ways that affect the way the evaluative concepts we have considered apply to me. Maybe the most desirable life for me is a life no exemplar has ever desired, nor would desire it if she thought about it because its desirability for me is due in part to my idiosyncrasies. Maybe acts that for me are right, even duties, are not acts that any exemplar would do or feel compelled to do because no exemplar is exactly like me and perhaps no exemplar has ever been in my circumstances. And if an exemplar were in my circumstances, then perhaps the exemplar would not have most reason to do what I have most reason to do precisely because being an exemplar gives a person reasons for acting that do not apply to the ordinary person, and conversely, the ordinary person may have reasons for acting that do

---

[12] I propose variations of these definitions of virtue, right act (permissible act), and a duty in Zagzebski 2004, and the above definition of a good life in Zagzebski 2006.

not apply to the exemplar. This is one of the ways that features of persons and situations left out of theory can sometimes be relevant to practice. A theory should give us moral guidance, but it is not primarily a manual. Nonetheless, even when a theory does not generate guidance, it should help us construct a manual that guides us in particular situations.

Let me end by summarizing some advantages of exemplarism. Exemplarist virtue theory has the theoretical simplicity and power of foundationalism without the problems of a conceptual foundation. Perhaps grounding moral theory in the concept of human nature or reason or uncontroversial objects of human desire can succeed, but I doubt it. In any case, the success of those approaches is not so convincing as to make it unnecessary to look for an alternative approach. Exemplarism puts at the foundation of the theory a crucial element of moral practice and, indeed, of moral experience: the identification of persons we admire and whose admirability is something of which we are confident.

Direct reference to exemplars serves another desideratum for an adequate theory mentioned in section 3. It gives the theory a hook that links it to the real world of moral practice—something comparable to a map that says "You are here."

Exemplarism provides a theoretical structure within which the empirical side of ethics can be linked with the traditional *a priori* side of ethics. Lately, the issue of how moral philosophers ought to use empirical research has attracted a lot of attention (see, e.g., Appiah 2008). This theory is one way to do that. Similarly, exemplarism gives an important place to narrative ethics within the structure of the theory. In my opinion this is critically important. Only a tiny percentage of people in the world care about moral theory in the sense I have been discussing, whereas 100 percent of the people in the world like stories. Most moral insights come from stories, but it is the special virtue of the philosopher to organize those insights. As I said at the beginning of the chapter, I do not see any reason why there cannot be more than one equally good moral theory, but I think that exemplarist virtue theory has some notable advantages over other types of theory.

References

Appiah, Kwame Anthony. 2008. *Experiments in Ethics*. Cambridge, Mass.: Harvard University Press.

Gunderson, Keith, ed. 1975. *Language, Mind, and Knowledge*. Minneapolis: University of Minnesota Press.

Kripke, Saul. 1980. *Naming and Necessity*. Oxford: Blackwell.

Olberding, Amy. 2008. "Dreaming of the Duke of Zhou: Exemplarism and the *Analects*." *Journal of Chinese Philosophy* 35:625–39.

Putnam, Hilary. 1979. "The Meaning of 'Meaning'." In *Mind, Language, and Reality*, volume 2 of *Philosophical Papers*. Cambridge: Cambridge University Press.

Reimer, Kevin, and David Wade-Stein. 2004. "Moral Identity in Adolescence: Self and Other in Semantic Space." *Identity* 4:229–49.

Walker, Lawrence, and Karl Hennig. 2004. "Differing Conceptions of Moral Exemplarity: Just, Brave, and Caring." *Journal of Personality and Social Psychology* 93:845–60.

Zagzebski, Linda. 2004. *Divine Motivation Theory*. Cambridge: Cambridge University Press.

———. 2006. "The Admirable Life and the Desirable Life." In *Values and Virtues*, edited by Timothy Chappell, 53–66. Oxford: Oxford University Press.

4

RIGHT ACT, VIRTUOUS MOTIVE

THOMAS HURKA

In this chapter I explore the relation between right acts and virtuous motives. The two are, I take it, closely connected, since we expect people with virtuous motives to at least often act rightly. But what exactly is the connection, and what is its basis? Why do right acts and virtuous motives so often coincide?

The answer I give arises out of the account of virtue defended in my book *Virtue, Vice, and Value* (2001). This "higher-level" account, as I now call it, was widely accepted in the late nineteenth and early twentieth centuries, for example by Hastings Rashdall, Franz Brentano, G. E. Moore, and W. D. Ross, and in my view it is far more illuminating than the better-known one derived from Aristotle. I will not say a great deal that is new about the account, but will highlight a feature of it that was underemphasized in my book and that contrasts interestingly with the dominant views in present-day writing about virtue.

In exploring the relation between rightness and virtue, I will abstract from an issue that arises on one side of it. This concerns the relation between occurrent virtuous motives, such as my compassionate desire now to relieve your pain now, and longer-lasting virtuous traits of character, such as standing compassion. Theorists influenced by Aristotle take traits of character to be the primary subjects of virtue, and call occurrent motives virtuous only if they issue from virtuous traits; a rival view treats occurrent states of mind as primarily virtuous, with virtuous traits just dispositions to have or be in those states. I believe the second view, which emphasizes occurrent virtuous states, is both philosophically more persuasive and truer to everyday thinking about virtue than is the first (Hurka 2006); here as elsewhere Aristotle is a poor guide. But I will ignore this issue and consider the relation between right acts and virtuous occurrent motives however the latter come to count as such.

The two best-known views about this relation each take one side to be primary and identify the other in its terms. The first view is instrumentalist about virtue. It takes the rightness of acts to be determined independently of virtue, and identifies virtuous motives as those that tend to result in right acts, so they are reliable means to right acts. Since there are different kinds of right act, there are different kinds of virtuous motive. Thus a benevolent motive tends to result in acts that promote others' happiness when that is right, a courageous motive to result in acts that accept the risk of harm when that is right, and so on. This instrumentalist view has been defended by Henry Sidgwick (1907, 392), G. E. Moore (1903, 172), and others, and it grounds the coincidence between right acts and virtuous motives in its understanding of the latter, since it takes them to be simply those motives that tend to cause right acts.

The second and opposite view is virtue-ethical. It takes the virtuousness of motives to be determined independently of rightness and identifies right acts by some relation to virtuous motives. One version of this view is Michael Slote's agent-based virtue ethics, which says acts are right when they are in fact done from virtuous motives. While allowing that there can be virtuous motives that do not issue in right acts, this approach has the radical implication that all right acts are virtuously motivated (Slote 2001). A weaker version of the virtue-ethical view identifies right acts counterfactually, as those that would be done by a person with virtuous motives, or those a fully virtuous person would perform. Defended by Rosalind Hursthouse, it differs from Slote's view in allowing that there can be right acts done from non-virtuous motives, but it joins him in implying that if a person has and acts from a virtuous motive, his act is necessarily right (Hursthouse 1999).

Despite their differences, both these views explain the connection between right action and virtue by treating one of the two concepts as primary and understanding the other in its terms. But this is not the only possible explanation, as the parallel case of causal explanation shows. If event types A and B are statistically correlated, the explanation can be that A causes B or, conversely, that B causes A. But it can also be that A and B are joint effects of a common cause C and so occur together even though neither causally influences the other. For example, it may be that smokers drink more than non-smokers, and drinkers smoke more than non-drinkers. But the explanation of this correlation need not be that smoking causes drinking or that drinking causes smoking; some third factor such as sociability or a fondness for parties may cause people both to smoke and to drink without any causal connection between the two. The association will then rest on a shared link to a common cause rather than any causal influence between its effects.

The same possibility exists for right action and virtue. They may be connected not because either is identified in terms of the other but because each involves a relation to some third moral property whose shared role explains their frequent coincidence. Their relations to this third property cannot be the same if they are different concepts, but if each is somehow linked to the same property, their parallel links can explain their association.

This is precisely the type of explanation given by the higher-level account of virtue. My book presented this account primarily within a consequentialist framework, which is also how its first clear-headed proponents, Rashdall, Brentano, and Moore, presented it, and where its distinctive features are most evident. But the account can also be extended to fit within a deontological theory and was so extended by Ross. I will again first present it within a consequentialist setting and then add deontological elements later.

1. The Higher-Level Account: Consequentialist Virtues

Described most generally, the higher-level account understands virtue and vice as higher-level moral concepts, identified by an intentional relation to other, more basic moral concepts. More specifically, it takes virtue and vice to be intrinsic values consisting in, respectively, morally appropriate and inappropriate attitudes to other moral concepts or to items falling under them. In consequentialist moral theories the basic moral concepts are those of intrinsic good and evil, so virtue and vice consist in appropriate or inappropriate attitudes to other, previously given goods and evils. It does not matter so much what these other goods and evils are, but let us follow Rashdall and assume that they are pleasure and knowledge as goods and their contraries pain and false belief as evils.

Now, the morally appropriate attitude to an intrinsic good is positive, so on the higher-level view it is virtuous and good to love for itself, or to desire, seek, and take pleasure in for itself, anything else that is good. This means that if another person's pleasure is good, it is virtuous and more specifically benevolent to desire, seek, and take pleasure in her pleasure for itself—certainly an intuitive implication. And the appropriate attitude to an intrinsic evil is negative, so it is virtuous and intrinsically good to hate—to desire and seek the absence of and be pained by the presence of—that evil for itself. So if another's pain is evil, it is virtuous and more specifically compassionate to want his pain to end, and to be pained when it does not. But the contrary attitudes to goods and evils, namely, loving the evils and hating the goods for themselves, are inappropriate and therefore vicious. It is vicious and evil to maliciously want and take pleasure in another person's pain, and similarly evil to enviously want to destroy or to be pained by her pleasure. Just as loving goods and hating evils are intrinsically good, so loving evils and hating goods are intrinsically evil.

These various claims embody a simple pattern. What are appropriate are attitudes whose orientation matches the value of their objects, so positive attitudes to positive values and negative attitudes to negative ones are virtuous and good. But unmatching attitudes—positive to negative and negative to positive—are vicious and evil. The virtues match orientation to value; the vices clash. And for each virtue the relevant attitude can have either of two forms. I can desire a good like knowledge because I think it is good, therefore desiring it as something good. But I can also, without any thoughts about goodness, simply desire knowledge as knowledge, say, from simple curiosity. In the one case my attitude is based on an evaluative thought, about the goodness of knowledge; in the other it is not. But in both cases I desire a good either for its goodness or for the property that makes it good, and my doing so is a further intrinsic good.

A virtue ethicist may object that the higher-level account is wrong to treat pleasure and knowledge as goods independent of virtue. Pleasure, for example, is not always good; it is only good when it is such as a virtuous person would feel and not when it is, say, malicious pleasure in another's pain. The higher-level account partly agrees and partly disagrees with the premise of this objection. It holds that malicious pleasure is good as pleasure and evil as malicious, with the evil in most cases outweighing the good, so the pleasure is in most cases on balance evil.[1] In making malicious pleasure usually on balance evil the account agrees with the virtue-ethical premise, but in making such pleasure good as pleasure it does not. And in doing the latter it continues to treat pleasure always as such good and therefore as good independently of virtue. The argument that this is the right treatment of pleasure and other goods such as achievement is too complex to give here, but interested readers can consult the relevant sections of my book (Hurka 2001, 144–52).

The account as so far described is consequentialist because it relates virtue and vice to the central consequentialist concepts of intrinsic good and evil, though the relation is, more specifically, intentional. But consequentialism also identifies right acts by relation to good and evil, though the relation is now causal, with those acts counting as right that produce the most good or, more precisely, result in the greatest surplus of good over evil possible in the circumstances. So we have exactly the possibility described above: neither virtue nor right action is identified in terms of the other, but each involves a relation, either intentional or causal, to a more basic third concept of intrinsic goodness or evil.

Nor is this general structure possible only with these three concepts. Shelly Kagan has made a similar suggestion for the relation within consequentialist moral theories between the rightness of acts and the rightness of moral rules. Again two main views have been defended on this topic, each identifying one of the two rightnesses in terms of the other. Act-consequentialism identifies right acts directly by relation to the good, as those that in themselves maximize the good, and then takes right rules to be those whose acceptance is most likely to lead to

---

[1] Intense pleasure in another's mild distress, as when one laughs at a David Letterman joke—and every Letterman joke is at least mildly malicious—can be on balance good. But that seems to me the right result.

right acts. Rule-consequentialism, by contrast, identifies right rules directly, as those whose acceptance will maximize the good, and right acts as those that are, say, prescribed by the right rules. But Kagan defends a third possibility, which he calls "direct consequentialism," and in which neither kind of rightness is understood in terms of the other. Right acts are related directly to the good, as those that maximize the good; right rules are also related directly to the good, as those whose acceptance will maximize the good. But there is no conceptual tie between the two: each is independently connected to the same basic concept of intrinsic value, just as in the higher-level account of virtue both virtue and right action are independently connected to that concept (Kagan 2000).

We can illustrate these connections by adapting some diagrams of Kagan's. Assuming a general consequentialist structure, the instrumentalist view of virtue is represented in figure 1, where the arrows show identification relations: the basic concept of intrinsic value is used to identify right acts, which are then used to identify virtuous motives, so right acts are related directly to the good and virtuous motives only indirectly.

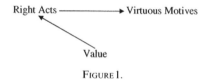

Right Acts ⟶ Virtuous Motives

Value

FIGURE 1.

The competing virtue-ethical view—given the consequentialist framework, it will be unlike the best-known such views—uses the concept of intrinsic value to identify virtuous motives, namely, those involving an appropriate attitude to good or evil, and then uses those motives to identify right acts, say, as those that do or would spring from virtuous motives so understood. The resulting view, represented in figure 2, relates virtue directly to the good and right acts only indirectly.

But the higher-level account I have sketched relates both right acts and virtuous motives directly to the good, though by different relations. It is represented in figure 3, which mirrors Kagan's diagram for direct consequentialism by having separate arrows running from the basic consequentialist concept to these other two.

What are this account's implications for the connection between right acts and virtuous motives? The first is that the connection is not exceptionless. On the contrary, the higher-level account allows that there can be both right acts performed from non-virtuous motives and wrong acts performed from virtuous ones. To illustrate the first possibility, consider Sidgwick's famous example of a prosecutor who prosecutes a

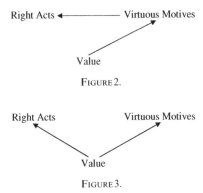

Right Acts ◄─────────── Virtuous Motives

Value

FIGURE 2.

Right Acts   Virtuous Motives

Value

FIGURE 3.

defendant from personal malice (Sidgwick 1907, 202). His act of prosecuting may by consequentialist standards be right, because it incapaci-
tates the defendant from further crimes and also deters others from crime,
but if it is done from malice it has a vicious motive. For the converse
possibility, imagine an act done from virtuous motives but with false
empirical beliefs. For example, imagine that the prosecutor prosecutes
believing sincerely and on the basis of good evidence that the defendant is
guilty, and from a benevolent desire to protect society and its members.
But in fact the defendant is innocent, and punishing him will cause more
harm than good. Here the prosecutor acts from a virtuous motive, but
given his act's actual effects it is wrong.

  This implication should not be surprising, since Ross, one of the main
defenders of the higher-level account, insisted precisely on the logical
separateness of rightness and virtue or moral goodness, arguing that
whether an act is right is independent of its motive while whether it is
virtuous depends only on its motive (Ross 1930, chap. 2). The implication
is surely also intuitively attractive. Slote's virtue-ethical view implies that
an act is right if and only if it is virtuously motivated, while Hursthouse's
implies, more weakly, that it is right if it is virtuously motivated. But
surely commonsense moral thought recognizes that one can not only do
the right thing for the wrong reason (contra Slote) but also do the wrong
thing for a right reason (contra both Hursthouse and Slote). If the
prosecutor in the second example above in fact convicts an innocent man,
he has, despite his admirable motives, done something objectively wrong,
and it is a merit of the higher-level account to allow that possibility.

  At the same time, however, the account implies that there is the
following significant tie between rightness and virtue: if a person has
ideally virtuous motives *and* all relevant true empirical beliefs, she will of
necessity act rightly. While there can be wrong acts done from virtuous
motives, they require false empirical beliefs or at least the absence of true

ones; given all relevant true beliefs, virtue and right action coincide. To see why, however, we must elaborate the higher-level account somewhat.

As described so far, the account says only that morally appropriate attitudes like loving the good are good and inappropriate ones, such as loving evil, are evil. But as fully developed, the account also says that ideally virtuous attitudes are proportioned to their objects' degrees of value, so one loves greater goods more and lesser ones less, and by as much more or less as their relative values make appropriate. If you can produce either a small pleasure for one person or a ten times greater pleasure for another, you should ideally desire the latter ten times as much. If one person is feeling a mild pain and another a five times more intense pain, you should be five times more pained by the latter. This perfect proportioning of attitude to value is only an ideal: if you care only four times as much about a five times worse pain, that is just a slight shortfall in virtue rather than any vice. But significant disproportions in one's divisions of concern do constitute vices, and some familiar vices have just this basis. If you care much more about your own mild pleasure than about the vastly greater pleasure of other people, you are viciously selfish; if you care more about avoiding some slight harm to yourself now than about preserving a significant good such as your nation's independence long into the future, you are cowardly; and so on. So an ideally virtuous agent will not only love goods and hate evils, but do so with intensities proportioned to their degrees of goodness and evil (Hurka 2001, chap. 3).

This explains why, given all relevant true empirical beliefs, an ideally virtuous agent will always act rightly. Imagine that he can and knows that he can produce either some greater good A or some lesser good B. Given the ideal of proportional division, he will want to produce A more than he wants to produce B and, acting on his stronger desire, will therefore produce A. But the very fact that makes this his ideal combination of desires—that A is a greater good than B—also makes it by consequentialist standards right for him to produce A, because then he is producing more good. So if he acts on his ideally virtuous desires, he will of necessity act rightly. Because both virtue and right action are identified by relation to the good, and in a way that prefers relations to greater goods to relations to lesser ones, they necessarily coincide in this way: given all relevant true empirical beliefs, a person with ideally virtuous motives will always produce greater rather than lesser goods and so always act rightly.[2]

This initial connection is very tight but of limited application, since few if any agents are ideally virtuous. But we can make a more broadly applicable claim if we weaken the connection somewhat. Imagine some-

---

[2] This may not be so if some of the relevant beliefs are probabilistic; then, given bad luck, the person can fail to produce the most good. The beliefs must therefore all be non-probabilistic, so they concern what the consequences of different choices actually will be.

one who is slightly selfish, caring, say, 30 percent more about her own good than about other people's. Even with true empirical beliefs she will not always act rightly: given a choice between nine units of good for herself and ten for another person, she will prefer the nine for herself. But because she is reasonably virtuous—I am assuming her degree of self-ishness is not enough to constitute a vice—she will act rightly a reasonable amount of the time. More specifically, she will act rightly whenever she has a choice between seven or fewer units of good for herself and ten for another person. And the explanation of this looser connection is the same as for the initial tighter one: since the very same fact that tends to make a combination of desires virtuous—that the thing one wants more is a greater good—also tends to make the action those desires would issue in right, we should expect agents who are reasonably virtuous and have all relevant true beliefs to act rightly a reasonable amount of the time. That is another connection, though a looser one, implied by the higher-level account's commitment to proportionality.

These connections run from virtuous motivation to right action, but what about the converse connection? Can we say that if an act was wrong, the agent had to have less than ideally virtuous motives? We cannot say this, because of the possibility of innocent empirical error. But there are also culpable errors, where a person acts from a false empirical belief that he should not have had and is to blame for having. In one case of this type, a prosecutor should know that the defendant she is prosecuting is innocent, because there is readily available evidence proving that, but she did not do the simple work needed to discover it. When there is culpable error of this kind the person will of necessity have had less than ideally virtuous motives, but showing why again requires elaborating the higher-level account.

The simplest forms of virtue involve attitudes to goods and evils one knows about or has noticed. For example, one's hatred of the evil of pain will show itself in wanting and trying to prevent pains that one knows threaten another person or in being pained by pains one knows he is feeling. But another form of virtue involves wanting to know about goods and evils and making sure you do. If you really care about another person's pain you'll be attentive to signs that he's feeling it, even if he's trying to hide the fact; you'll also be alert for threats of pain to him, so you can ward them off. Your virtue will make you look for opportunities to benefit others, so you can exploit those opportunities, and threats of harm, to ward them off. And if you don't look when you could—if you blithely prosecute a defendant you should know is innocent—that shows that you didn't really care about avoiding those harms. Your act was thoughtless, and since thoughtlessness involves a lack of virtuous con-cern, it involves at least a lack of full virtue.

More strongly, in many cases it involves a vice. My initial formulation of the higher-level account made all loves of evils vicious, and all hatreds of evils virtuous. This implies that the intermediate state of being indifferent to an evil, where you have neither a positive nor a negative attitude to it but are neutral, is itself of intermediate or neutral value. But while that is a possible view, it is not intuitively most plausible. Complete indifference to another's intense suffering is callous, and callousness is not just the lack of a virtue; it is a vice and therefore evil. Similarly, a complete lack of interest in goods you could achieve if you tried is sloth or apathy, which are also vices. So the most attractive versions of the account treat indifference to goods and evils as not just neutral in value but evil, which requires some very mild hatreds of evil and loves of good also to be evil. If a soldier liberating a concentration camp at the end of World War II feels only mild distress at what he has discovered, say, as much as he would at a friend's hangnail, then his attitude is surely still callous. Though appropriately oriented, it is so inadequate to the evil he has stumbled upon that it is positively vicious. The same can be true of thoughtless action: someone who performs a wrong act because he couldn't be bothered to find out that it would cause immense harm can act from motives that are not just less than fully good but positively evil. What makes him culpably ignorant is a lack of concern serious enough to constitute a moral vice.

So the higher-level account underwrites a number of connections between virtuous motivation and right action. Going in one direction, agents with virtuous motives and all relevant true empirical beliefs tend to act rightly; going in the other direction, when wrong acts are due to culpably false beliefs, the agent's motives are less than ideally virtuous and often vicious. But the basis of these connections is not that one of the two concepts is understood in terms of the other; rather, each is identified by a relation to the same concepts of intrinsic good and evil. And though the relevant relations are different, one intentional and the other causal, they both favour relations to greater goods over relations to lesser ones, so desiring a greater good is other things equal more virtuous and producing a greater good is other things equal right. And that overlap between the relations grounds the connections between virtue and right action.

The overlap has another implication, for the role of virtue in our first-person deliberations about what it is right for us to do. If consequentialism identifies right acts as those that produce the most good, and among the relevant goods is virtue, then in evaluating an act we should include the value of any virtue it may express or lead to. But in an important range of cases doing so can make no substantive difference to the outcome of our deliberation: counting the value of virtue can change by how much a right act is preferable to its alternatives, but not which act that is.

These are cases where the virtue in question will be expressed in an act we can perform now, given the motives from which it will spring. Imagine that I can now produce either greater good A or lesser good B, so it is on that basis right for me to produce A. The most virtuous motive I can act from now is the desire for A; just because B is less good, the desire for it is also, given the ideal of proportionality, less good than the desire for A. But if I produce A, it will have to be from the desire for A: the desire for B could not have that effect. So if in my deliberation I consider the values of the motives I will act on, the act of producing A will have an overall outcome that is better than the act of producing B by a larger margin than if I did not consider my motives. It will have not only the non-moral superiority of A over B but also the moral or virtue superiority of acting from the desire for A over the desire for B. But considering the value of my motives now cannot change which act my deliberation finds right, for the very fact that made the choice of A initially right—that A is better than B—also makes my desire for A more virtuous. So counting the value of my motive only amplifies the superiority of a choice that was already on other grounds best.[3]

It may be objected that this is true only if I can in fact be most virtuously motivated. Imagine that I can produce either a slightly greater good A, but only from malice, or a slightly lesser good B from benevolence. Can it not be on balance preferable, counting both outcome and motive, for me to produce B? And does my present motive's value not then make a substantive difference? It does, and this can be recognized from a third-person perspective; thus, another person can see that it would be on balance better, given my present motives, to produce B rather than A. But the limitation discussed above applies only to first-person deliberation, and it is harder to see how my present motive's value can make a substantive difference there. If it does, I will choose to produce B from benevolence rather than A from malice because I believe the former is better. And it is puzzling how a desire for what is better could motivate me only at this higher level, where I consider my motives as well as A and B, and not also at the lower level, where I consider just A and B. If I can desire and then choose the greater good when considering outcomes-plus-motives, why can I not do the same when considering just outcomes? Why can the knowledge that A is better than B not by itself motivate me to produce A, independently of my malice? At the very least, cases where considering the value of my present motives changes which act my first-person deliberation identifies as right will be very rare.

This limitation on the role of virtue in deliberation holds only for the virtue that will be expressed in my own act now, and not to other people's virtue or even my own virtue at other times. It may be that if I raise my child to be compassionate that will make her less happy, because in an evil or unjust world she will be saddened by suffering around her that she would not be troubled by if she were callous. Counting the value of virtue can then favour developing compassion in her, whereas counting only the value of happiness would not. And the same can hold if I contemplate my

---

[3] For an early statement of this point, see Rashdall 1907, 2:42–43.

own future. If one course of self-development will make me more compassionate but less happy in later years, then counting virtue among the relevant goods may make me prefer that development where not doing so would not.

The fact remains, however, that the higher-level account implies that considering the value of my own virtue now cannot usually change my first-person judgment about which act is right for me now. And this claim may seem to support a further conclusion. One of its implications is that it can almost never be right for me to decide to act in a way that involves less than my own greatest possible virtue now: whatever the right act is, it can almost always be done from the best possible motives. But the idea that it can never be right to sacrifice my own virtue now may seem to suggest that virtue is more valuable than other goods, and even infinitely more so, as several philosophers have held (Ross 1930, 150–54). I have elsewhere argued against this view, holding to the contrary that virtue is always a lesser good, in the sense that an attitude to an object always has less intrinsic value than that object; so, for example, my compassion for your intense pain, though good, is always less good than your pain is evil (Hurka 2001, chap. 5). And it does not count against this lesser-good view that it can never be right to decide to sacrifice my own virtue now: the latter is not a point that bears on virtue's comparative value but simply follows, for the specific context of first-person deliberation, from the way virtue and right action relate to the same concepts of intrinsic good and evil.

2. The Higher-Level Account: Deontological Virtues

So far I have presented the higher-level account and its explanation of the link between virtue and right action within a consequentialist framework. To some this may seem of limited interest: since consequentialist theories are utterly implausible, they may say, so is any account of virtue couched in their terms. But the higher-level account can also fit into deontological theories, where it gives a similar explanation of the tie between virtue and right action.

Showing how is a little difficult, however, for there are different kinds of deontological theory. The simplest, typified by Ross, holds that alongside any duty to promote the good are underivative duties forbidding, other things being equal, such acts as lying, harming the innocent, and breaking promises. These deontological duties have no deeper explanation, and in particular none in terms of intrinsic good and evil (Ross 1930, chap. 2). But two other kinds of deontology do ground these duties in claims about good and evil. The neo-Thomist theory championed by John Finnis agrees with consequentialism that goodness always inheres in states of affairs, but holds that alongside the consequentialist duty to promote the intrinsic goods is a separate and stronger requirement not to destroy or choose directly against them, with Ross's deontological duties just specific instantiations of this single more basic one (Finnis 1980, chap. 5). And some Kantian theories ground deontological duties in a requirement to respect value, not in states of affairs, but in entities such as persons; here the prohibitions on lying and harming are specific expressions of the more general duty to respect valuable persons (see Audi 2004, chap. 3).

Neo-Thomist and Kantian deontologies make distinctive claims about virtue, finding important forms in appropriate attitudes of respect for values in states of affairs or in persons. But I will concentrate on Ross's simpler theory, because the duties it treats as underivative at least appear in all deontologies, and there are deontological virtues that involve attitudes to acts having the properties they pick out.

The higher-level account defines virtue as involving appropriate attitudes to other, more basic moral concepts, and so far, working within consequentialism, those concepts have been limited to intrinsic good and evil. But moral rightness is also a basic moral concept, and there can be virtues defined by relation to it. This is already possible in consequentialism if, as most consequentialists believe, an act's being right is analytically distinct from its producing the best outcome. Then it will be appropriate even within a consequentialist framework to desire and perform acts because they are right—since rightness is a positive property of acts, doing so will involve a positive attitude to something positive. And this attitude will express a virtue, namely, conscientiousness, that is distinct from any virtue of loving good or hating evil.

Deontological theories will also recognize the virtue of conscientiousness, as in the desire to perform an act that is all things considered right because it is right. But they can go further. If there are deontological duties making it other things equal wrong to lie, harm the innocent, and break promises, then a person can have desires, other things equal, not to do those things, because they are other things equal wrong. These desires will involve an appropriately negative attitude to acts with a morally negative property, making the desires in question virtuous and good. But the virtues they express will be distinctively deontological, since they will concern a property of other-things-equal wrongness not found in consequentialism.

It may be said that these claims are not very novel: deontologists have always taken virtue to involve a desire to perform right acts because they are right. This is true, but it only shows that deontologists have always understood virtue in a higher-order way, as involving attitudes to an independently given property of rightness. And the deontological virtues they have emphasized share other features with the consequentialist ones described above. For example, they are guided, like the consequentialist virtues, by an ideal of proportionality. If being a lie tends to make an act slightly wrong while seriously harming an innocent makes it very wrong, an ideally virtuous person will be more averse to acts of harming the innocent than to acts of lying. More generally, if a given act has various right- and wrong-making properties, he will desire it for each right-making property and shun it for each wrong-making one in proportion to that property's right- or wrong-making weight. Thus, if a given act will involve a white lie but save many lives, he will be mildly averse to it given that it will involve a lie, strongly inclined to it given that it will save lives, and inclined to it on balance or given both properties. And his virtuous attitudes will again have two forms: he can be averse to lying either because he thinks lying is other things equal wrong or because, without any thoughts about wrongness, he simply does not like lying or prefers to avoid it. Just as he can desire knowledge without thinking it good, so he can prefer not to lie without thinking that lying is wrong but just because he dislikes untruthfulness. Finally, it is again not just not virtuous but positively vicious to be completely indifferent to these properties. Someone who is not at all averse to lying, feeling no hesitation whatever about intentionally telling untruths, displays the deontological analogue of callousness about lying, which is again a moral vice.

The account of deontological virtue therefore parallels that of consequentialist virtue in defining virtue by an intentional relation to a more basic moral property, though that is now rightness, either all-things-considered or other-things-equal, rather than goodness. But there is also a deontological account of right action. This too identifies right acts by a relation to the property of rightness, but instead of being causal this relation is now one of instantiation. An act is all things considered right if it instantiates the property of all-things-considered rightness, and it is other things equal right if it instantiates the property of other-things-equal rightness, because it instantiates some other property that makes acts other things equal right. So a deontological theory that includes the higher-level account has the same basic structure, and can be represented in the same kind of diagram, as a consequentialist theory. It too defines deontological virtue and right action by different relations to a single central property, either an intentional relation or that of instantiation. And neither virtue nor right action is understood by relation to the other; instead, each relates in a different way to a common core concept of rightness (figure 4).

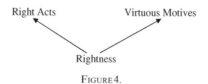

FIGURE 4.

Because of this, the deontological theory has similar implications for the connection between right action and virtuous motives. Again the connection is not exceptionless. A person can fulfill a deontological duty such as that of keeping a promise from a vicious motive, as when she repays a debt to a heroin addict because she wants him to buy the drugs that she believes will kill him. And she can act wrongly from a virtuous motive, as when she fulfils what she innocently but falsely believes is a binding promise rather than promote some significant good.

But the theory also implies that there are significant connections between the concepts. A person who is ideally deontologically virtuous and has all relevant true beliefs will always act rightly, again because of proportionality. Imagine that some act has several properties that tend to make it right and several that tend to make it wrong, but where the right-making properties outweigh the wrong-making ones and the act is on balance right. If a person's desires to do and not do the act given these various properties are proportioned to the properties' deontological weights, as proportionality requires, his desires to do the act will be stronger than his desires not to, and he will do it. And if he is not ideally but only reasonably virtuous, his coming reasonably close to proportionality implies that he will act rightly a reasonable amount of the time.

A similar point holds in the reverse direction. An ideally virtuous person may act wrongly if she has innocently false beliefs, but if her error is culpable then she is in some way not ideally virtuous. She has not cared enough about avoiding harming others or about keeping her promises to check what effects her act will have or to remember what promises she made, and her doing so again involves, if not a vice of indifference, then at least a shortfall in virtue.

So the higher-level account of virtue can easily be extended to incorporate deontological ideas and fit within a deontological moral theory, and the same holds for the account's explanation of the connection between virtue and right action. In both theoretical frameworks this connection rests not on identifying one of the two concepts in terms of the other, as in the instrumentalist and virtue-ethical views, but on relating both to another, more basic concept: in consequentialist theories that of the good, which virtue is intentionally directed toward and right acts promote, and in deontological theories that of rightness, which virtue is intentionally directed toward and right acts instantiate. And in both cases the overlap between the relations is sufficient to make virtue and right action go together as often as they do.

Of course this explanation will only be compelling if the higher-level account is acceptable in its own right, and I cannot address that issue here. My aim has only been to show that this account gives an explanation of the connection between virtue and right action different from either of the two more familiar views in the literature, an explanation that treats the two concepts as on a par rather than giving one primacy over the other.

References

Audi, Robert. 2004. *The Good in the Right*. Princeton: Princeton University Press.

Finnis, John. 1980. *Natural Law and Natural Rights*. Oxford: Clarendon Press.

Hurka, Thomas. 2001. *Virtue, Vice, and Value*. New York: Oxford University Press.

———. 2006. "Virtuous Acts, Virtuous Dispositions." *Analysis* 66:69–76.

Hursthouse, Rosalind. 1999. *On Virtue Ethics*. Oxford: Clarendon Press.

Kagan, Shelly. 2000. "Evaluative Focal Points." In *Morality, Rules, and Consequences*, edited by Brad Hooker, Elinor Mason, and Dale E. Miller, 134–55. Lanham, Md.: Rowman and Littlefield.

Moore, G. E. 1903. *Principia Ethica*. Cambridge: Cambridge University Press.

Rashdall, Hastings. 1907. *The Theory of Good and Evil*, 2 vols. London: Oxford University Press.

Ross, W. D. 1930. *The Right and the Good*. Oxford: Clarendon Press.

Sidgwick, Henry. 1907. *The Methods of Ethics*. 7th ed. London: Macmillan.

Slote, Michael. 2001. *From Morals to Motives*. New York: Oxford University Press.

5

AGENCY ASCRIPTIONS IN ETHICS AND EPISTEMOLOGY: OR, NAVIGATING INTERSECTIONS, NARROW AND BROAD

GUY AXTELL

The sea is still the aporetic place par excellence, and it is still the best metaphor for the aporia of discourse.
—Sarah Kofman, "Beyond Aporia?" (1988, 78)

1. Introduction: Major Problems with Trait Ascriptions

Character-trait ascriptions serve a variety of purposes, philosophical and non-philosophical. The appeal to human character and personality traits in folk psychology is arguably something of a mishmash of explanatory and evaluative intentions. Philosophers often try to render commonsense character psychology self-consistent and informative. There are, however, major problems they encounter on this journey, and for virtue theorists in particular these are often presented as a Scylla and Charybdis that cannot both be evaded.[1]

A major problem concerning the ascription of intellectual or epistemic character traits to an agent is the Generality Problem. Is there a non–ad hoc way to select the proper level of generality at which to describe a belief-forming process in order to evaluate its reliability?[2] If every token of a belief-forming process belongs to many different types of such processes, there may be no principled way to select the proper level of generality to describe the process token that produced the belief. The Generality Problem has sometimes been presented as an objection to reliabilist theories of justification (Conee and Feldman 2004, chap. 6), but it is more accurately a problem that must be a concern for any theory that

---

[1] For other recent and related treatments of character-trait ascriptions see Fricker 2007 and 2008 and Upton 2005.

[2] "For example, suppose I form a true belief based on a coin toss. One would normally think that this process is unreliable. But one could always cite a more fine-grained individuation of the type to undermine that verdict, say, for example, forming beliefs about who will win the 2007 NCAA basketball tournament based on flipping this coin on the Monday afternoon before the championship game. If the belief is true, this 'process' is correct 100% of the time, hence adequately truth-conducive, hence reliable" (Becker 2008, 354).

has even a reliability component. This is in part why Linda Zagzebski, in *Virtues of the Mind* (1996), acknowledges that there is relatedly a problem for virtue epistemologies in setting the level of generality at which epistemic virtues are described, and this will be true whether the virtue epistemology is one that acknowledges "faculty" virtues, as agent reliabilist theories do, or restricts the virtues to acquired habits in the way that Zagzebski and other neo-Aristotelian accounts do.

A major problem concerning the ascription of moral character traits is what can here be called the Global Trait Problem, the problem often alternatively described (in a large and growing literature) as the "situationist challenge" to character theory. When we ascribe a global character trait like honesty or kindness to someone, we typically think of this trait as robustly held such that it resists undermining, and as one so settled or habitual that the agent will manifest it not just in a few situations that invite it, but in many. Situationists say that character-trait ascriptions are poor explainers and that "minor and seemingly irrelevant differences in the perceived situation appear more readily to explain behavior and behavioral differences than character traits" (Harman 2000, 223).[3]

Gilbert Harman (1999, 2000) claims that ascriptions of character traits to individuals in folk psychology and philosophical ethics is subject to a "fundamental attribution error"—we far too often jump to conclusions about underlying personality and character traits from the behavior we observe in people. Ultimately, Harman holds that there is in fact "no character or personality" (2000). John Doris (2002) holds that there are moral character traits, but that the only kinds of moral character traits that can be rightly attributed to persons are local or narrowly construed dispositions. Both Harman and Doris make philosophic hay from empirical psychology, arguing that "Aristotelian-style virtue ethics" can have little empirical content—little value for predictive and explanatory purposes—since they "share with folk psychology a commitment to broad-based character traits of a sort that people simply do not have" (Harman 2000, 7).

The Global Trait Problem, I want to argue, *is largely a kind* of generality problem, a problem about the right level of generality at which moral trait ascriptions best serve the explanatory and normative interests involved in moral evaluation.[4] But my aim here is comparative and methodological; it is not an attempt to *solve* these problems in the abstract but an attempt to address them as *problems of practice* faced in a variety of fields cutting across philosophy and the social and

---

[3] The thesis of the explanatory salience of robust and cross-situationally manifested moral dispositions is claimed to come open to empirical refutation by studies, many of them well known and even infamous, like the Milgram and the Stanford Prison experiments. See Doris 2002 for extended discussion and interpretation.

[4] I thank John Greco for discussion of this point.

behavioral sciences. By relating these two problems directly and revealing their shared logic, we might hope to reap the benefits of an improved understanding of the explanatory and evaluative practices that make use of character-trait ascriptions. One further aim of this chapter is to show that whereas the Global Trait Problem is often held captive to stale debates in metaethics over which elements in a theory should be taken as conceptually primary or foundational, it could more profitably be treated in the way that an inquiry-focused or "inquiry-pragmatist" epistemology would suggest we treat the Generality Problem. On a pragmatist account, facts alone do not determine relevant types (Kappel 2006). Rather, in any particular case, the relevant reliability is determined by the agent's epistemic competence and performance, and the ways to settle on what field (or domain) and conditions a character trait is efficacious in turns upon pragmatic concerns related to our evaluative epistemic practices (Kappel 2006, 539–40). There is no question of identifying the total cause of an agent's action or belief, and the partial causes we select and deem salient and usefully generalized upon, whether triggering or configuring causes, situational or agential, are contextual and have much to do with the *interests-in-explanation* of the persons providing the disposition-citing explanation.

First I will explore what common structure or logic our two problems share, insofar as they each necessitate distinguishing the functions of narrowly and broadly typed trait ascriptions, and the explanatory purposes that each of these is good for. In my view the narrow and broad kinds of trait ascription are strongly interconnected in our practices of agent evaluation, whether moral or epistemic, and can only be separated in theory. Philosophers have noted these interconnections, but when they have tried to explain them, they haven't done a very good job. To do a better job, we need to think seriously about how to apply a sliding scale, allowing some cases to be best addressed by trait ascription of a narrow sort, with other cases best addressed by more global or broadly typed trait ascriptions.

More study of this scale—of the *narrow-broad spectrum* of trait ascription—is needed if we are to meet the burdens of the two problems. The present account recognizes that both narrowly and broadly typed traits serve indispensable functions and that narrowly and broadly typed traits often are interconnected in agent and act evaluation. But I also view this, if correct, as leading away from or having a "deflating" effect on some of the debate surrounding whether we should be "internalists" or "externalists" (Feldman, Goldman) in epistemology and "localists" or "globalists" (Doris, Annas) or "occurrentists" or "dispositionalists" (Hurka, Zagzebski) in our accounts of moral character. Thus I will treat especially the debate between equally reductionistic occurrentist accounts like Thomas Hurka's and dispositionalist accounts like Linda Zagzebski's (both in this collection) as subordinate to our shared need for a more comprehensive and flexible account of trait attributions. Setting aside such unmotivated "priority" debates is needed today if we are to get a clearer view of what really lies in the "intersections" between ethics and epistemology.

2. The Logic of Intellectual Trait Ascription and the Generality Problem

The Generality Problem is, as we briefly described it, the problem that any process token is an instance of several process types, and it is not clear which process type is relevant for evaluating reliability. Most responses to the problem came from reliabilists, and followed the lead of Alvin Goldman, who holds that the best way to navigate through the dual potential pitfalls of defining the belief-forming process too narrowly or too broadly, is to try to locate the narrowest (content-neutral) process that is causally operative in belief production (Becker 2008, 363).[5]

But according to Christopher Lepock in "How to Make the Generality Problem Work for You" (forthcoming a), different types of appraisals pick out processes at different levels of generality, even when appraising the same belief. While many epistemologies and even some virtue epistemologies are reductionist in this way, granting conceptual or explanatory primacy to narrowly or broadly typed trait ascriptions, Lepock develops the logic of a matter of gradations or levels from narrowest to broadest, as an interpretation of the distinction between the faculty virtues that are the especial focus of the causal/explanatory interests of externalist epistemology, and the virtues and vices that bear upon the conduct of inquiry. An antireductionist account able to properly acknowledge the distinction between and relationships among trait ascriptions at various levels of generality emerges from "mixed" accounts such as Christopher Hookway's, which the present work on the narrow-broad spectrum helps motivate. The philosophic importance of virtue-theoretic concepts goes beyond what contribution they may make to an analysis of knowing; at the broad end of the spectrum reside, according to inquiry-pragmatist forms of epistemology like Hookway's (2006) Peircean form, thickly describable inquiry and deliberation-regulating cognitive character traits, that is, the *reflective* virtues (cf. Putnam 2002; Axtell and Carter 2008).

The problem we are addressing is fundamentally a problem of *practice*, since we can and likely should continue to use both narrow- and broad-type ascriptions but lack, in current theories, the resources to properly

---

[5] Conee and Feldman relate the Single Case, No Distinction, and Generality Problems by saying that "the problem for defenders of the reliability theory, then, is to provide an account of relevant types that is broad enough to avoid The Single Case Problem but not so broad as to encounter The No-Distinction Problem. Let us call the problem of finding such an account 'The Problem of Generality'" (2004, 144). See also Beebe 2004 for a sound overview.

relate them. Recognition that trait ascriptions necessarily run along a spectrum from narrow to broad, together with acknowledgment that our explanatory interests shape the determination of what situational and agential factors we deem explanatorily salient, provides us a fresh start.

We can discern at least two distinct ways of attributing abilities or other efficacious character traits to agents, each underlying a different sort of appraisal of beliefs and believers: "One is based on the reliability of the process narrowly construed, and appraises the status of the particular belief. Another makes use of reliability of a more broadly construed process, and describes the creditworthiness of the agent in having formed the belief" (Lepock forthcoming a).

So when we look at how we actually ascribe or attribute epistemic traits to agents, we find indications that there isn't a single level of generality at which the ascriptions are directed. "When a [belief-forming] process is reliable at the narrow end of the scale, it is NTR [narrow-type reliable]; when it is reliable at the broad end, it is BTR [broad-type reliable]" (Lepock forthcoming a). A narrow or local trait is one that yields its evaluatively relevant behavioral outputs in a relatively narrow or local set of circumstances (compare Sosa 2008). Broad or global traits also support desirable behaviors, but their applications go beyond even behaviors, to the agent's internal life. But while it might seem that distinguishing between two distinct uses of reliability only complicates the problem of generality, Lepock argues that we should exploit this situation, and try to "put the generality problem to work" for us.

To this end Lepock asks what sorts of appraisals make use, respectively, of narrowly typed and broadly typed reliability (NTR and BTR for short). Trait ascriptions range from "low-level" to "high-level" virtues, from those dispositions most directly involved in perceptual knowledge to the acquired virtues as capacities for metacognitive control. "There are *prima facie* important differences between these two categories and the sort of evaluations they are involved in.... It appears that the value of low-level virtues is transmitted directly to their products and only indirectly to the agents who have them, while the value of high-level virtues attaches directly to their possessor but only tenuously to their products" (Lepock forthcoming b).

To compare them more closely, narrowly typed epistemic trait ascriptions primarily serve to appraise the status of a particular belief, and it was primarily in this context that the generality problem was framed. Says Lepock,

NTR tells us a great deal about the etiology of a particular belief or narrow range thereof.... It tells us whether we can trust the particular belief in question, or whether that particular belief is appropriately grounded. However, the epistemic status identified by NTR does not necessarily accrue to the agent. NTR tells us little about the agent's overall capacities or cognitive practices, because it reflects only the etiology of such a narrow range of beliefs on such a narrow range of occasions. Thus while NTR seems central to assessing the status of a single belief, it is less important for assigning credit or blame to believers. (Forthcoming a)

Broadly typed reliability, by comparison, does not convey very specific information about the particular belief at hand, yet it can convey a great deal about the believer's abilities and practices in the general area. Whereas the main function of narrow trait ascriptions may be belief evaluation, the main function and natural home of broad trait ascriptions is in the evaluation of agents themselves and the quality of their motives and efforts at inquiry. Also, when we are not in a position to evaluate whether someone's belief is knowledge but we do have some experience of his or her belief-forming practices, we typically fall back on BTR evaluations. "We are thus more willing to praise or blame believers for BTR, since it says more about their status as cognitive agents" (Lepock forthcoming a). We can see then that the two kinds of epistemic reliability serve different basic explanatory functions. But it is also highly useful to see that they are often intimately connected in epistemic evaluation of agents and their beliefs. Broadly typed reliability may exculpate agents from blame for beliefs formed in non-NTR ways. It can work the opposite way as well: "Using non-BTR processes prevents agents from receiving credit for their NTR beliefs" (Lepock forthcoming a).

NTR and BTR evaluations can come apart, as they do in several cases Lepock discusses, with the effect of undermining an initial intuition we may have had about the creditability to the agent for a particular true belief. There is an important role of credit in knowledge ascriptions, and creditability for true belief is most straightforward when an NTR success is backed by a BTR.

This way of framing the narrow-broad spectrum of trait ascription is necessary if we are to make sense of the challenges of the two problems to virtue theory. The flexibility of the spectrum or range account also helps us to recognize and to cut across certain unmotivated debates, and to recast the distinctions between propositional, doxastic, and personal justification. Some writers treat virtue epistemology as little more than an innovation within generic reliabilism. But "the trouble with treating virtues as belief-forming processes is that it seems to rule out any possibility of uniting the high-level and low-level virtues" (Lepock forthcoming a). The focus on processes neglects the importance in the upper range of cases with problem-solving strategies, and with the social and communal nature of the norms of inquiry. The notion of a process's "excellence" involves BTR; "achievement" and "reliability" are both diachronic concepts, terms denoting agential success across time, and as diachronic concepts they too involve BTR. Epistemic credit as credit for "getting it right" carries the externalist's acknowledgment of the diachronic and of personal justification through sound motivation and efforts at inquiry, as an important source of epistemic value. This recognition of the contribution to epistemic value made by stable intellectual character traits is part of the insight of reliabilism, and provides mixed theories with a substantial advantage over internalist epistemologies like Conee and Feldman's (see 2004). These accounts vainly attempt to cash out epistemic justification exclusively in terms of *synchronic* considerations of the agent and his or her present evidence, ignoring altogether the quality of the inquiry leading the agent to have just that total evidence to work with (for extended defense of the epistemic value of diachronic epistemic rationality see Axtell forthcoming, and Axtell and Olson forthcoming). These theories retain the importance of personal justification but are committed to viewing diachronic traits, including the intellectual virtues, *as* regulators of inquiry, as strictly nonepistemic. This, as I argue elsewhere, denatures the centrality of these virtues in explanations attributing epistemic credit to the agent for the truth of his or her belief.[6]

Lepock thinks it is better to conceive of intellectual virtues as capacities for metacognitive control of our actions of inquiry and methods and strategies of problem solving. "Open-mindedness, intellectual courage, and the like are not dispositions to form beliefs, though they are (speaking loosely) dispositions ... [to] engage in inquiry in certain ways" (2008a, 17). Most intellectual virtues have essential connections to capacities to search in some particular manner, and capacities to know when that kind of search is a good idea (Morton 2006). This way allows for the centrality in epistemology of the analysis of doxastic justification and what Feldman calls synchronic epistemic rationality but also for what Hookway (2006) says contrasts with the doxastic paradigm, an *inquiry-focused* epistemology. Even if, as Lepock holds, BTR isn't as directly involved in knowledge as it is in other important epistemic standings, such as theoretical understanding, intellectual virtues like intellectual humility and open-mindedness guard against certain biases and promote the agent's epistemic reliability in a variety of ways. They are praiseworthy traits that can be seen as configuring causes of belief or of action. The manner in which they are valued reflects diachronic goals of maintaining a stable set of beliefs over time. But the argument is not that there is any neat mapping of narrow-type ascription onto belief evaluation, or of broad-type ascription onto agent evaluation. Nor is it the need to prioritize one over the other for the assuaging of reductionist aspirations. The proper way to distinguish and relate the different levels of generality is in terms of the driving *interests-in-explanation* that philosophers have in a particular case; and of course, the nature of the case itself partly

---

[6] See Axtell 2009; see also Crisp 2010 on the centrality of diachronic traits in virtue epistemology as well as virtue ethics.

TABLE 1. Lepock's *narrow-broad spectrum* of intellectual-character-trait attributions

---

NTR: Narrowly typed reliability

—Low-level virtues (faculty virtues). Dispositions construed as genetically endowed cognitive capacities.

—Best suited to evaluating the etiology of a single belief or narrow range of beliefs; tells us nothing about an agent's other beliefs.

—The value of low-level virtues is transmitted directly to their products and only indirectly to the agents who have them.

BTR: Broadly typed reliability

—High-level virtues (reflective virtues). Best suited to explaining the agent's intellectual abilities and methods/strategies in a certain domain/area of inquiry.

—Best suited to holistic evaluation of agents, including the quality of their activities of inquiry.

—The value of high-level virtues attaches directly to their possessor but only tenuously to their products.

---

determines this although our own special purposes matter as well. Thus the present account both draws from and supports virtue-based contextualism (see Sarah Wright 2010, Greco 2009, Thomas 2008, and Upton 2005).

Recognition of the different, even if overlapping functions of NTR and BTR ascriptions (see table 1), together with the view that reflective intellectual virtues should properly be conceived as capacities for meta-cognitive control of inquiry, offers other potential benefits. Lepock argues that his view is needed to make good sense of the commonsense ascription of intellectual virtue to figures like Newton and Aristotle. For we do so without presupposing that many of their particular scientific beliefs are in fact true. But this ascription is rendered senseless if virtues are identified strictly with reliably truth-conducive *processes*, as austere forms of reliabilism appear committed to. Such persons are commonly regarded as exemplars of scientific reasoning, despite the fact that the reliability, power, and portability of their faculties are unexceptional compared to those of educated people today.[7]

So by way of review of our distinction between levels, intellectual-character-trait attributions vary across a narrow-broad spectrum. The approach recommended here, as we have seen, begins by asking why we have such different ways of ascribing intellectual traits to persons, and what distinctive functions are served by ascriptions made at different levels of generality. Knowledge is a collective good, and this kind of "genealogical" question prevents us from divorcing epistemological

---

[7] Lepock 2007, 167; Riggs 2003, 210–13. Lepock argues that "what makes it possible to explain our appraisals here is the fact that a virtuous trait can be valuable in part because of its own power and portability, even though it does not typically have enough effect on belief-formation to make one's beliefs into knowledge" (2007, 167).

concerns from the realities of social interaction. Inquiry-focused virtue epistemologists argue that the uses of trait concepts at different levels of generality have quite distinctive functions, yet are also clearly connected in many instances of epistemic evaluation. NTR and BTR can both be seen as playing a justificatory role, or perhaps even as supplying different important *kinds* of justification, doxastic and personal. We will later return to develop more fully the suggestion that we might put such a solution to the Generality Problem "to work" in epistemology by taking it as an opportunity to utilize the resources of the narrow-broad spectrum of attributions. But let's now turn to another problem where narrow and broad construal of character traits is central, the situationist challenge to virtue ethics.

3. The Logic of Moral Trait Ascription and the Global Trait Problem

When we look at our commonsense ascriptions of *moral* traits to agents, we find again that there is no single level of generality at which they are directed. Doris describes the most important differences as those between "local" and "global" trait ascription, and he rejects "theory of character" insofar as it aims to be a theory with substantial empirical content (a theory that is "realist" in contrast to antirealist, or fictionalist) about the efficacy of global traits like moral virtues and vices. We will briefly look at the local/global distinction as Doris employs it, and then at Hurka's (2001, 2009) equally suspect treatment of that same distinction.

Resurgent interest in ethical virtue is often dated to a half-century ago, 1958, when influential papers in ethics by G. E. M. Anscombe and Philippa Foot were published. Anscombe's "Modern Moral Philosophy" criticized a thin-focused "law conception of ethics" in British moral philosophy, for its neglect of individual and social psychology. Anscombe suggested that ethical theory would not advance unless and until philosophers attended to the neglected psychology of character and emotion. But the rallying cries of many self-described virtue ethicists, "moral psychology," "practical wisdom," and "the resources of thick concepts," all find them caught up in various ways with the globalist assumptions that Doris, Harman, and other situationists find so problematic in light of empirical psychology (see Goldie 2000). However disconnected virtue ethics may have been from empirical psychology in previous decades, a general climate of trading armchair philosophy for empirically informed theory, as well as Doris's spirited polemic against globalist virtue ethics, has today brought the global trait problem to center stage.

Commonsense morality posits persons of good character who are not easily swayed by circumstance. Aristotelian good character is supposed to be an integrated association of robust traits and evaluatively consistent personality structures. But, wrote one situationist author recently, "Experiments show that efficacious traits are not global, and allegedly global traits are not efficacious ... character traits are either narrow and efficacious or broad and inert. Either way, the conception of traits favored by Aristotelian virtue ethics finds little empirical confirmation in these studies" (Prinz 2009, 118).

Doris thinks we must restrict ethical trait ascriptions to the local, or situational, like "dime-finding," or "dropped-paper" compassionate (Doris 1998; see Webber 2006, 2007, 2008 for criticism). We should altogether eliminate or at least treat as very error prone "highly general trait ascriptions like 'honest' or 'compassionate'" (Doris 2002, 112). Doris holds that one of the key upshots of the social psychological research is a "'fragmented' conception of character, which countenances a plethora of situation-specific 'narrow' or 'local' traits" that aren't unified with other traits (2005, 665). Doris's use of the local/global trait distinction reflects his contrast of his "fragmentary" account of personality with the Aristotelians' "evaluative consistency thesis," and his localism with their globalism. Doris's fragmentary account holds "that systematically observed behavior, rather than suggesting evaluatively consistent structures, suggests instead *fragmented* personality structures—evaluatively inconsistent associations of large numbers of local traits" (1998, 508). So the opposition as Doris constructs it is between globalists, who posit character as "an integrated association of robust traits and evaluatively consistent personality structures," and localists or situationists, who posit character only as "evaluatively inconsistent associations of large numbers of local traits" (1998, 508).

Now there have been many responses made to Doris's book, evoking a variety of stances. Many philosophers do think the situationist studies should be a wake-up call, to virtue theorists in particular. Ernest Sosa thus concedes that "it seems incumbent on virtue theory to grant that the experiments do raise legitimate doubt as to how global and robust is human practical wisdom, and how global and robust are its more specific component virtues, such as kindness ... honesty, [and] courage" (2008, 281). But Sosa and Webber both argue that holding Doris's "fragmentary account" isn't mandatory. Some philosophic defenders of broadly based moral trait ascriptions think that a theory of virtue can get by without as much empirical content as others expect it to have. The most obvious move in this regard is what Doris calls the "rarity argument" many virtue ethicists give: it matters little to virtue ethics how rare full virtue is, so long as it is not an impossible goal; even if full virtue or integrated character *is* rare, we all have *some* capacity and opportunity to inculcate virtue in ourselves. We still have reason to take character education as important, too, and to resist the prescriptive implication situationists draw, that we ditch it in favor of (presumably) enlightened "situation management."

Other defenders of broadly typed moral traits note that Doris takes latitudinal or cross-situational studies to supply all the data needed to reject a unitary account of character in favor of a fragmentary one, whereas our best defense of our characterological intuitions is our *longitudinal* acquaintance with the individuals around us—our knowing them over an extended period of time. What allows us to attribute global traits like honesty to an agent may be our long-term or longitudinal acquaintance with that person, but for practical reasons there is very little useful experimental study of this available. We can acknowledge that, as one defender of global traits put it, there are "contingent difficulties that often beset the ascription of traits, particularly their attribution to strangers and loose acquaintances, but also that "there is no fundamental attribution error that impugns [global] attribution itself, [though there is] . . . a range of attribution difficulties that account for the ways in which [global] attribution can go wrong" (Webber 2007, 90–91, 102–3). There need be nothing wrong with ascribing stable and robust traits to people of whom we have long acquaintance, though the empirical studies should impact folk practices so as to improve them. The kind of character traits of interest as one moves toward the global end of the local/global spectrum include fundamental motives, desires, and goals, much as I earlier said that the broad end of intellectual trait ascription brings in diachronic as opposed to merely synchronic considerations.

Thomas Hurka's (2001, 2006, 2009) treatment of the local and global trait distinction also dichotomizes, turning it into fodder for debate between philosophical analyses of virtue deemed mutually exclusive and exhaustive. In "Virtuous Act, Virtuous Disposition," Hurka's initial thesis is actually strongly analogous to Lepock's: "Everyday moral thought uses the concepts of virtue and vice at two different levels" (Hurka 2006, 69). At the *global* level, says Hurka, it applies these concepts to persons or to stable character traits or dispositions. In contrast to these standing traits, the *local* applications of concepts of virtue and vice are applications to specific acts or mental states, such as occurrent desires or feelings. Hurka writes that "the global and local uses of the virtue-concepts are clearly connected, in that we expect virtuous persons to perform and have, and virtuous traits to issue in, particular virtuous acts, desires, and feelings. A philosophical account of virtue should explain this connection, but there are two different ways of doing so. Each takes one of the two uses to be primary and treats the other as derivative, but they disagree about which is the primary use" (2006, 69).

The Dispositional View, says Hurka, "takes the global use to be primary and identifies virtuous acts, desires, and feelings in part as ones that issue from virtuous dispositions. Aristotle famously took this view. In the NE he said that for an act to be virtuous it must meet some initial conditions, including about its occurrent motivation, but must also 'proceed from a firm and unchangeable character'; if it does not, it may be such as a brave or generous person *would* perform, but is not *itself* brave or generous. . . . The dispositional view . . . treats virtuous dispositions as primary and defines virtuous occurrent states derivatively, as ones that proceed from such dispositions" (2006, 70). The Occurrent-State View, says Hurka, "takes the local use to be primary and identifies virtuous dispositions as ones to perform virtuous acts and to have virtuous desires and feelings.... It applies the virtue concepts first to such states and then defines virtuous dispositions derivatively" (2006, 70).

Hurka identifies the local and global uses of virtue concepts with two competing accounts of virtue, each supporting a different, albeit equally reductive, systematic account of the nature and value of the virtues (see also Hurka and Epstein 2009). He thus polarizes the debate strongly in at least two ways: first, by accepting an occurrentist *definition* of virtue against Slote's and Zagzebski's incompatible but equally contentious dispositionalist definitions; and second, by prioritizing aims over rules and virtues among the basic elements of moral theory. He describes the dispositional view as "overwhelmingly dominant," but argues against it on a number of scores, including by claiming that the contemporary commonsense understanding of virtue is actually the occurrent-state one: "When everyday moral thought applies the virtue-concepts, it is primarily to occurrent states considered on their own" (2006, 70).

One example Hurka gives is of the soldier who is awarded a Medal of Honor for throwing himself on a hand grenade to save others. The members of a military committee are considering whether or not to give the soldier a medal for bravery: "Would they say, 'We know he threw himself on a grenade despite knowing it would cost him his life and in order to save the lives of his comrades. But we cannot give him a medal for bravery because we do not know whether his act issued from a stable disposition or was, on the contrary, out of character'?" "They would say no such thing," Hurka judges, "and they would be obnoxious if they did" (2006, 72).

The folk certainly make global judgments about virtue, but they treat those judgments "as derivative from local judgments about the virtuous-ness of particular acts, desires, and feelings, and takes those states' virtuousness to be independent of any tie to dispositions." "Moreover," Hurka goes on to contend against dispositionalists, "it is right to do so: an act of helping another from a desire for his welfare is no less admirable when out of character than when dispositionally based" (2006, 74).

In summary, this section has described two of the main uses of narrowly and broadly typed moral trait ascriptions in the literature today: Doris's contrast between the local and the global construal of traits, and the localist/globalist debate it engenders; and Hurka's own treatment of local and global uses of virtue concepts, and the occurrentist/dispositionalist debate it engenders. I compared briefly the importance of latitudinal studies and longitudinal acquaintance in defense of the legitimate functions of broadly typed moral trait ascriptions. Hurka constructs his either/or choice (between dispositionalism and occurentism) much as Doris constructs those between globalists and localists, and between traits and situations. While I said little in direct criticism of either author, directing attention to the rhetorical strategy of dichotomizing between the two kinds of trait ascription sets off our own nonreductionist approach by contrast. This sets us up, then, for a closer comparison between our two problems regarding trait ascription, and for arguing that such dichotomization is uncalled for and that our handling of the Global Trait Problem would benefit from following the same sort of approach we found Lepock bringing to the Generality Problem.

4. The Common Structure of the Two Problems

We have taken our two problems about trait ascription as serious problems in ethics and epistemology. But an approach by way of putting the narrow-broad spectrum to work rejects the primacy-granting reductive "higher-level accounts" offered by Hurka and by Zagzebski, in favor of allowing our actual evaluative practices to be our focus and our guide. As Nicholas Rescher notes, "The understanding/explanation orientation is much less atomistic and more social than the certainty/justification orientation" (2001, 237). An epistemology that does not make inquiry central will likely also be unable to satisfactorily integrate the findings and perspectives of social and collective epistemology. Why try to reduce one kind of attribution to the other, when it is possible through a more flexible model to accommodate both? The main reason why I have been attracted by Lepock's development of the narrow-broad spectrum, as his own interpretation of Hookway's distinction between faculty and reflective virtues, is that it facilitates such a nonreductive account and undercuts unmotivated debates such as those between localists and globalists, occurrentists and dispositionalists. Narrowly and broadly typed traits are thus seen as ascribed in response to different, even if overlapping, explanatory interests, with neither being primary over or reducible to the other. Our actual epistemic appraisals may not just be measures of NTR or BTR; often added to these are other considerations, from anti-Gettier conditions to internalist conditions, which additions make the quest for reducibility that much more difficult. Mostly, the approach entreats us to carefully distinguish different sorts of appraisal, and to use this information to help determine the relevant process type or relevant level of generality that responds to the explanatory interests we have in any particular case. As a problem of practice, it is easier to be clear about the different types of appraisal or evaluation we employ—for instance, even reliabilist and internalist appraisal—when we treat them as concerned with things addressed at different levels of generality.

The forms of virtue epistemology that are distinguished both from virtue reliabilist and neo-Aristotelian forms by a strongly antireductionist stance are those most closely associated with inquiry pragmatists, or those that Hookway, citing Peirce, describes as supporting "epistemology-as-inquiry" (Hookway 2006, 95). It is here also that I locate my own approach.[8]

If we consider what virtue theories the global trait problem is most serious for, they are globalist virtue ethical theories, including Stoic and neo-Aristotelian versions of virtue theories, since these make the strongest claims about the causal efficacy and philosophical importance of broadly typed traits of character. The focus on habits of responsible and successful inquiry among the pragmatist virtue theories helps them resist the flaws of globalism, while addressing empirical challenges to folk epistemological practices as well. If there is no single level of generality at which trait ascriptions in either area aim, and especially if, as I've suggested but not set out to prove here, narrowly and broadly typed traits are interconnected in evaluation of agents and their actions, then we need a nonreductionistic approach, which is what we are denied by engagement in undermotivated debates like those between the situationist localist and neo-Aristotelian globalist or again between the occurrentist and dispositionalist analyses of moral virtue. If we want to facilitate more constructive work at the intersections of ethics and epistemology, we need to see that our ability to do so is improved by our adopting a more deflationary attitude toward a number of contentious debates over the conceptual primacy of the narrow or the broad, the local or the global, the occurrent or the dispositional, the "thin" or the "thick" (on the latter, see Hurka and Elstein forthcoming, Axtell and Carter 2008, Battaly 2008, and Elgin 2008). With this deflationary attitude in place, I suggest we place ourselves on a more constructive footing to put salience contextualist approaches to the Global Trait Problem and the Generality Problem to work for us.[9] We might draw the further upshot that Zagzebski's virtue theory, sometimes called neo-Aristotelian or "pure" virtue theory on account of some of its other commitments, comes out looking especially problematic (see also 2003, 2006). This is not because it attempts a unified account of virtue across ethics and epistemology, for that is something that opposing inquiry-focused accounts can also endorse. It is acutely problematic because it is structured in ways that leave it especially

---

[8] This approach is akin to that suggested in Dewey's account of reflective morality, in which at whichever end we begin we find ourselves intellectually compelled to consider the other end. Prioritizing or reductionistic definitions of virtue such as those we find the occurrentist and dispositionalist employing are immediately suspect if in fact "we are not dealing with two different things but with two poles of the same thing" (Dewey 1989, 7:173).

[9] This reply to Hurka, then, is not so much different from Robert Adams's reply when he writes of dispositional and occurrent uses of virtue concepts that "both types of conception have their uses," and that there is little harm with being pluralist about the sources of virtue, and with operating with both, "provided we are clear about what we are doing" (Adams 2009, 124).

challenged by each of the two specific problems we've examined. Zagzebski's view is:

1. especially challenged by the Generality Problem, because of the robust (or "motive reliabilist" [Levin]) use of the "because of virtue" idea to entail truth and preclude Gettier and environmental forms of epistemic luck; and
2. especially challenged by the Global Trait Problem (and directly targeted by Doris) because of her neo-Aristotelian demand that the sources of virtuous actions be "entrenched" moral virtues, and that moral agents be *motivationally self-sufficient*.[10]

Of course, these are not faults of Zagzebski's approach alone. Extant theories of virtue do not do a very good job of unifying low- and high-level virtues. Here as in science, unification and reductionism are not the same thing, though a zealous reductive spirit wants to treat them that way and limits itself by creating but another "great divide" in ethics, this time between concern with what we ought to "do" and concern with who we want to "be."

The case for a unified virtue-theoretic account of normativity need not and should not be cast, as Roger Crisp rightly warns, as "the question of how one should live or what kind of person one should be *rather* than the question of how one should act" (2010). What we can say is that the broad end of the spectrum of trait ascriptions in both ethics and epistemology is concerned with diachronically described traits, and with more holistic evaluations of agency than with narrower concerns about the rightness of a particular act or the justification of a particular belief.[11]

---

[10] While Doris has to date restricted the situationist challenge to ethical theory, he at one point in the book gives reason to think that it could be generalized to target at least some versions of virtue epistemology. He writes: "[T]he contextual variability of cognitive functioning may problematize globalist, highly general, accounts of intelligence. A wealth of empirical work indicates that people experience remarkable difficulty 'transferring' cognitive skills across even closely related domains; they may perform well in one context and poorly in other, seemingly very similar situations, rather like the case of moral behavior. If the 'contextualism' about cognitive ability this empirical work inspires is right (see Ceci 1996), it would be a nuisance, not only for conceptions of practical reasoning emphasizing reliable flexibility but also for recent 'virtue epistemologies,' that import globalist psychological theories from the ethics literature in an attempt to elucidate central epistemic notions (e.g., Zagzebski 1996, esp. 178)" (Doris 2005, 670).

[11] Gregory Pappas's book *John Dewey's Ethics* gives us another and still more challenging response, in terms of which Dewey's thought should not be assimilated to that of self-described virtue ethicists, despite the criticisms they share of deontology and consequentialism: "It has been assumed that the great divide in ethics is between act-centered views, ethics of doing, and character-centered views, ethics of being; in other words, morality should be conceived as a matter of doing good or being good. ... John Dewey anticipated it and evaluated its legitimacy. Dewey undermines the grounds for the divide issue, and he proposes a way to move beyond the debates between character-centered and act-centered ethics" (Pappas 2008, 129).

So a final implication I want to draw from our comparison of the two problems is that the dichotomizing and reductive spirit of Doris's and Hurka's approaches to moral trait ascription obscures the need to recognize the interrelatedness of the narrowly and broadly-typed traits in moral evaluation. Both authors, as we've seen (section 3), turn the differences between narrowly and broadly typed trait ascriptions into fodder for philosophical debates motivated only by prioritizing the one or the other. Doris's use of the local/global distinction threatens to turn it into a false dichotomy wherever and whenever he uses it to insinuate an inexorable choice between (realistic) fragmentary and (utopian) global conceptions of personality; Hurka's use of the distinction follows a similar dichotomizing strategy, but in the service of a consequentialist "higher-level" reduction of dispositionalist to occurrentist moral theory. The choice he presents as inexorable is between virtues treated and defined atomistically and virtues treated and defined holistically—that is, between a view that privileges "specific acts or mental states such as occurrent desires of feelings," and one that privileges "persons, stable character traits or dispositions" (2006, 70). But from the present perspective I think we can see that the intended forced choice is wholly factitious.

Hurka's account, which acknowledges that systems of ethics proceed from emphasizing one pole or the other, is refreshingly blunt. Most philosophers try much more actively to "sink" the fact of such privileging or selective emphasis. For instance, should internalists and externalists about epistemic justification acknowledge that what motivates their debate is merely their respective selecting of one meaning of justification from among several, they would most plausibly be construed as *giving up* the claim that their account constitutes a "complete" account of epistemic justification. If the situationist and the neo-Aristotelian virtue ethicist acknowledge that they mean quite different things by behavior, or the occurrentist and the dispositionalist that the facts pertaining to occurrent states and to diachronic traits are potentially *independent* sources of value, then the contrary systems of thought they generate could still be resources for the active agent engaged in moral deliberation and reflection, but the conflict *between* such systems couldn't really be expressed. But would that be a bad or a good thing?

To be sure, the systems or theoretical perspectives in question do fit particular cases better or worse, and the Global Trait Problem isn't skirted merely by pointing out that appeal to dispositions serves an indispensable role in ethics. Preserving the philosophical importance of explanations involving the broadly typed character virtues may well require distancing ourselves from certain aspects of what Doris targets in his critique of globalism, especially the conception of the morally virtuous agent as motivationally self-sufficient.

To move toward conclusion, it is useful to point out that up to a point there are some quite strong analogies between Hurka's and Lepock's understandings of the narrow-broad spectrum of trait ascriptions. What is both shared and highly useful in Hurka's and Lepock's approaches may be summarized in the following series of steps:

    (a) there is no single level of generality at which trait ascriptions in their respective subfields of philosophy are aimed;
    (b) ascription varies across a narrow-broad spectrum;
    (c) the uses of trait concepts at different levels are clearly connected;
    (d) a philosophical account of virtue should explain this connection;
    (e) there are different ways of doing this; and
    (f) this often fuels debate between competing accounts of virtue based on the primacy of the concepts at one end of the spectrum or the other.

I find these points to be an excellent start for a logic of trait ascription that can help us navigate the intersections of ethics and epistemology. There, however, the approaches of Lepock and Hurka begin to diverge dramatically, as Lepock goes on to argue that:

    (g) both levels of trait ascription are often involved in epistemic appraisal of agents and their beliefs;
    (h) there is no *general* answer to the question of which end of the spectrum is logically or conceptually prior to the other;
    (i) we should therefore take nonreductionism as our default position and avoid contentious debates motivated only by the privileging of one end of the narrow-broad spectrum; and
    (j) this allows us to put the narrow-broad distinction (whether in the Generality Problem *or* in the Global Trait Problems) *to work* for us in concrete and constructive ways.

It is these latter steps, missing in Hurka's treatment of these same issues, that I think aid us in navigating clear of the Scylla and Charybdis so often claimed to shipwreck philosophical attempts to render characterological attributions both informative and philosophically consistent. The epistemological contextualism that ensues from putting the narrow-broad spectrum to work is just a demand for better awareness of the different roles played by our own explanatory interests as we try to say what method, field, and conditions should be employed when assessing the epistemically relevant reliability of any particular belief. Salience contextualism argues for the need to nonreductively balance and utilize the resources of trait concepts that function at different levels of generality.[12] Can we, by following Lepock's rather than Hurka's example here, apply this same approach to the Global Trait Problem? At this stage I hope that readers will share the conviction that we can and should, but also see that both Doris's and Hurka's approaches militate against it. Although Hurka, in his manner of treating the Global Trait Problem, appears to confer with our present approach in (a) to (f) he takes a quite contrary stance with respect to (g) to (j). The dispositionalist (Zagzebski, Slote) argues from the idea that it can never be right to sacrifice virtue to the view that virtue is more valuable than other goods, even infinitely more valuable. Hurka has "argued against this view, holding to the contrary that virtue is always a lesser good" (2010). So Hurka's stance implicitly holds (g*) to (j*):

(g*) the levels of trait ascription cannot be independent sources of value, but one or the other must be deemed primary;
(h*) this primacy of the local or occurrent end of the spectrum explains the value of the other end;
(i*) we should therefore view this and similarly structured primacy debates and the choices they entail as inevitable in systematic theories in ethics; and
(j*) we should reject the pluralism inherent in the spectrum approach in favor of one or another reductivism—either that of the occurrentist or that of the dispositionalist.

From what has been said, it should be clear that Hurka and Zagzebski, if not epitomizing the occurrentist/dispositionalist debate, are at least the most sharply opposed of the contributors over this issue in the present collection, opposed over what elements of a moral theory—goods, virtues, and duties—are conceptually primary or foundational. While I have benefited from the richness of thought in both authors, I do want to suggest that one upshot of our study is to cast doubt on the usefulness of their respective ways of turning the distinction between dispositional and occurrent uses of virtue terms into a clash of competing philosophical *systems*.

This comes with some qualification. Hurka's "higher-level account" (2010) provides a consequentialist model that is in an important sense less reductionistic than other and better known consequentialist models. To be sure, Hurka makes an insightful critique of virtue ethics. He says that a moral philosophy should not make global dispositions a condition for the value of occurrent attitudes, and I agree. He also says that we should not let the importance accorded by virtue ethicists to thick concepts in recent

---

[12] Indeed, without studying the shifts in explanatory frames that occur as we move from trait ascriptions of one level to those of another, it would arguably be impossible to determine when two explanations as occurrentists and dispositionalists typically present them are consistent or inconsistent with or irrelevant to one another.

years be used to deride the importance of thin normativity and act evaluation, and I agree as well. But these are not best accomplished by taking sides on opposed Occurrentist and Dispositionalist systems of ethics.[13] They are instead best accomplished by respecting the quite different functions that local and global trait ascriptions serve, and acknowledging their interconnectedness in the explanatory and normative interests that we have in the moral evaluation.

Acknowledgments

I thank John Greco, David Kaspar, Christopher Lepock, and Ken Lucey for discussion of earlier versions of this chapter, and Heather Battaly, Amy Coplan, Roger Crisp, Thomas Hurka, and other "Virtue and Vice: Moral and Epistemic" conference participants, June 26–27, 2008, for helpful discussion. Heather, Christopher, and the editors of *Metaphilosophy* helped immensely with editing suggestions.

References

Adams, Robert M. 2009. *A Theory of Virtue: Excellence in Being for the Good*. Oxford: Oxford University Press.

Anscombe, G. E. M. 1958. "Modern Moral Philosophy." *Philosophy* 33, no. 124:1–19.

Appiah, Kwame Anthony. 2008. *Experiments in Ethics*. Cambridge, Mass.: Harvard University Press.

Axtell, Guy. 2009. "Diachronic Rationality and Epistemic Value." Unpublished manuscript under review.

Axtell, Guy. Forthcoming. From Internalist Evidentialism to Virtue Responsibilism." In *Evidentialism and Its Discontents*, edited by Trent Dougherty. Oxford: Oxford University Press.

Axtell, Guy, and J. Adam Carter. 2008. "Just the Right Thickness: A Defense of Second-Wave Virtue Epistemologies." *Philosophical Papers* issue entitled "Epistemology Through Thick and Thin," 37, no. 3:413–34.

Axtell, Guy, and Phillip Olson. Forthcoming. "Three Independent Factors in Epistemology." *Contemporary Pragmatism*.

---

[13] Compare Appiah's discussion of how virtue ethics became distorted when during the 1960s and 1970s it repurposed itself to that narrower conception of morality that is the subject of mainstream moral philosophy. This is the shortcoming of virtue ethicists themselves, of course, but also of Kantians and consequentialists who would reduce an account of excellence to a cluster of duties or consequences, and procedures for fulfilling them. Once this is the case, the eudaemonist approach is lost: "Virtue ethics rather loses its point. And its way" (Appiah 2008, 63).

Battaly, Heather. 2008. "Metaethics Meets Virtue Epistemology: Salvaging Disagreement About the Epistemically Thick." *Philosophical Papers* 37, 3:435–54.

Becker, Kelly. 2008. "Epistemic Luck and the Generality Problem." *Philosophical Papers* 139:353–66.

Beebe, James. 2004. "The *Generality Problem*, Statistical Relevance and the Tri-Level Hypothesis." *Nous* 38, 1:177–95.

Conee, Earl, and Richard Feldman. 2004. *Evidentialism: Essays in Epistemology*. Oxford: Oxford University Press.

Crisp, Roger. 2010. "Virtue Ethics and Virtue Epistemology." Included in this collection.

Dewey, John. 1989. *The Later Works*. Carbondale: Southern Illinois University Press.

Doris, John. 1998. "Persons, Situations, and Virtue Ethics." *Nous* 32, no. 4:504–30.

———. 2002. *Lack of Character: Personality and Moral Behavior*. Cambridge: Cambridge University Press.

———. 2005. "Replies: Evidence and Sensibility." *Philosophy and Phenomenological Research* 71, no. 3:656–77.

Elgin, Catherine. 2008. "Trustworthiness." *Philosophical Papers* 37, no. 3:371–87.

Foot, Philippa. 1958. "Moral Arguments." *Mind* 67:502–13.

Fricker, Miranda. 2007. *Epistemic Injustice: Power and the Ethics of Knowing*. Oxford: Oxford University Press.

———. 2008. "Scepticism and the Genealogy of Knowledge: Situating Epistemology in Time." *Philosophical Papers* 37, no. 1:27–50.

Greco, John, ed. 2004. *Sosa and His Critics*. Oxford: Blackwell.

———. 2009. *Achieving Knowledge*. Cambridge: Cambridge University Press.

Goldie, Peter. 2000. *The Emotions*. Oxford: Clarendon Press.

Harman, Gilbert. 1999. "Moral Philosophy Meets Social Psychology: Virtue Ethics and the Fundamental Attribution Error." *Proceedings of the Aristotelian Society* 99:315–31.

———. 2000. "The Nonexistence of Character Traits." *Proceedings of the Aristotelian Society* 100:223–26.

Hetherington, Stephen (ed.). 2006. *Epistemology Futures*. Oxford: Oxford University Press.

Hookway, Christopher. 2006. "Epistemology and Inquiry: The Primacy of Practice." In Heatherington 2006, 95–110.

Hurka, Thomas. 2001. *Virtue, Vice, and Value*. Oxford: Oxford University Press.

———. 2006. "Virtuous Act, Virtuous Dispositions." *Analysis* 66, 1:69–76.

———. 2010. "Right Act, Virtuous Motive." Included in this collection.

Hurka, Thomas, and Daniel Elstein. Forthcoming. "From Thick to Thin: Two Easy Reduction Plans." *Canadian Journal of Philosophy*.

Kappel, Klemens. 2006. "A Diagnosis and Resolution to the Generality Problem." *Philosophical Studies* 127:525–60.

Kofman, Sarah. 1988. "Beyond Aporia?" In *Post-Structuralist Classics*, edited by Andrew Benjamin, 77–88. London: Routledge.

Lepock, Christopher. 2006. "Adaptability and Perspective." *Philosophical Studies* 129, no. 2:377–91.

———. 2007. "Metacognition and Intellectual Virtue." Ph.D. dissertation, University of Alberta.

———. 2008. "Metacognition and Epistemic Virtue," available at http://www.ualberta.ca/ ~ clepock/lepock%20-%20metacognition%20& %20epistemic%20virtue.doc (last accessed 22 September 2009).

———. Forthcoming a. "How to Make the Generality Problem Work for You." *Acta Analytica*.

———. Forthcoming b. "Unifying the Intellectual Virtues." *Philosophy and Phenomenological Research*.

Levin, Michael. 2004. "Virtue Epistemology: No New Cures." *Philosophy and Phenomenological Research* 69, no. 2:397–410.

Lockie, Robert. 2008. "Problems for Virtue Theories in Epistemology." *Philosophical Studies* 138, no. 2:169–91.

Morton, Adam. "Knowing What to Think About: When Epistemology Meets the Theory of Choice." In Heatherington 2006, 111–28.

Pappas, Gregory. 2008. *John Dewey's Ethics.* 2008. Bloomington: Indiana University Press.

Prinz, Jesse. 2009. "The Normativity Challenge: Why Empirically Real Traits Won't Save Virtue Ethics." In *Virtue Ethics, Character, and Moral Psychology*, edited by Candace L. Upton, 117–44. Oxford: Oxford University Press.

Putnam, Hilary. 2002. *The Collapse of the Fact/Value Dichotomy.* Cambridge, Mass.: Harvard University Press.

Rescher, Nicholas. 2001. *Epistemology.* Oxford: Oxford University Press.

Sosa, Ernest. 2008. "Situations Against Virtues: The Situationist Attack on Virtue Theory." In *Philosophy of the Social Sciences: Philosophical Theory and Scientific Practice*, edited by C. Mantzavinos, 274–91. Cambridge: Cambridge University Press.

Thomas, Alan. 2008. "The Genealogy of Epistemic Virtue Concepts." *Philosophical Papers* 37, no. 3:345–69.

Upton, Candace. 2005. "A Contextual Account of Character Traits." *Philosophical Studies* 122:133–51.

Webber, Jonathan. 2006a. "Character, Consistency, and Classification." *Mind* 115, no. 459:651–58.

———. 2006b. "Virtue, Character and Situation." *Journal of Moral Philosophy* 3, no. 2:193–213.

———. 2007. "Character, Global and Local." *Utilitas* 19, no. 4:430–34.

Wright, Sarah. 2010. "Virtues, Social Roles, and Contextualism." *Metaphilosophy* 41, nos. 1–2:95–114.

Zagzebski, Linda. 1996. *Virtues of the Mind.* Cambridge: Cambridge University Press.

———. 2003. "Epistemic Value and the Primacy of What We Care About." *Philosophical Studies* 33, no. 3:353–77.

———. 2006. "Ideal Agents and Ideal Observers in Epistemology." In Heatherington 2006, 131–48.

6

VIRTUES, SOCIAL ROLES, AND CONTEXTUALISM

SARAH WRIGHT

When considering the correct way to allow context to effect our epistemic responsibilities, it is instructive to look to the example of the sensitivity of the moral and epistemic virtues to the social roles of those who possess, or are developing, the virtues. With this type of sensitivity in mind, we can then turn to examine current theories of epistemic contextualism, select the strongest of those theories, and see how it might be helpfully supplemented by a sensitivity to social roles. The resultant view, which I call virtue contextualism, combines insights of virtue theory and of epistemology.

Virtues and Our Social Roles: Moral and Epistemic

Any account of knowledge which leads to the conclusion that there is little or no knowledge in the world may rightly be challenged as being too demanding. Within the realm of ethics, a similar challenge is often leveled at virtue theories. Rather than setting a standard for action and asking agents to live up to that standard, virtue theory requires not only that actions are correct but also that the motivations behind those actions are correct, and that those same motivations are embedded in deep character traits of the agent. In addition, one may worry that living a virtuous life is a standard that few can achieve because most of us do not have the time or freedom to develop and perfect our virtues or to engage in solitary contemplation. Rather, we are embedded in lives with already existing obligations, and as a result there is a concern that living a life of virtue is not an option for most people.

This is a serious worry addressed by many ancient philosophers, including the Stoics. In reasoning about how to live a life of virtue, the Stoics were concerned that virtue not be a standard that is in principle out of reach for most people. And they realized that most people, particularly by the time they were considering how to live a life of virtue, are already embedded in a life with its own demands and obligations.[1] One starts out

---

[1] As Annas explains, "[B]ecoming a Stoic is aspiring to live according to the Stoic ideal in your life: it is not a process of abstractly working out a way of life from Stoic principles and then trying to live it by ignoring or discarding your particular contexts of action and deliberation, replacing them by a more abstract one" (2002, 115).

to live a virtuous life as the daughter of particular parents, and perhaps also as a mother to particular children. One has particular abilities and particular limitations. One is a member of one's country, state, and community. And one is a member of the community in particular ways. In choosing a profession, one has chosen a particular way to contribute to the community at large as well as to one's own professional community.[2] We might summarize these commitments and obligations, both chosen and unchosen, as an agent's social role. This social role influences what the virtuous life will look like for a particular agent.[3] If one has living parents, one needs to live the life of a virtuous daughter. If one has children, then the virtuous life for that person will include being a virtuous parent. Thus there are many different types of virtuous lives that different agents might live, and these types of virtuous lives might vary widely from each other.

The variety of virtuous lives will be particularly obvious when we look at the individual actions of the virtuous agents with different social roles. When different agents are faced with the same circumstance, it might be virtuous for them to perform very different actions. If a police officer witnesses a burglary, the courageous thing for her to do is to pursue the criminal. If a bystander witnesses a burglary, the courageous thing for him to do is just to call the police. Calling the police is not a cowardly action for him; it may take courage for him to speak out and perhaps eventually be called in a trial. For him to chase the burglar, unarmed and unsupported as he is, would not be courageous, it would be foolhardy— even though that same action is not foolhardy for the police officer. The virtuous action to take in a particular circumstance thus depends on the social role of the agent in question.

Virtue can be sensitive to social roles when virtuous action is seen as the mean between two extremes.[4] This is to be contrasted with an alternate conception on which the virtues aim at producing some good,

---

[2] These are three of the four roles that Cicero assigns to us in *On Duties* 1.100–121 (Cicero 1991). The fourth is that of a human being generally. It is this, most general, role that we often focus on in epistemology, to the exclusion of the other roles.

[3] See for example Epictetus, *Discourses* 2.10.10–11 (Epictetus 1995): "If furthermore, you are on the council of any city, you should remember that you are a councilor, if a youth, a youth; if an old man an old man. For each of these names, if rightly considered, always point to the acts appropriate to you."

[4] As with Aristotle's account of the virtues in *Nicomachean Ethics* 1107ª 2–7 (Aristotle 1984), "[e]xcellence, then, is a state concerned with choice, lying in a mean relative to us. . . . Now it is a mean between two vices, that which depends on excess and that which depends on defect: and again it is a mean because the vices respectively fall short of or exceed what is right in both passions and actions, while excellence finds and chooses that which is intermediate." Long (2002, 240) notes that Epictetus makes reference to the Aristotelian model by considering the example of Milo in the context of encouraging us to develop ourselves even though we may not be able to achieve all the things that others are able to achieve (*Discourses* 1.22.35–7).

and more of that good is always better. Seeing virtues as an extreme makes them the single pinnacle of a particular characteristic; on this conception it is hard to see how two agents who do different things can both be acting out of virtue.[5] This conception of the virtues as extremes would result in a picture of the virtuous life that few, if any, could achieve. However, a conception of the virtues on which they are a mean between extremes results in a much less demanding and more realistic model of the virtuous life, which can incorporate and be sensitive to our social roles.

This sensitivity to our social roles can be extended from the moral virtues to the epistemic virtues.[6] Just as we take on specific moral roles we also take on epistemic roles. The most common example of this is in our choice of a profession. On deciding to become a doctor, an agent takes on many responsibilities, including the responsibility to be particularly epistemically careful in evaluating claims about the effectiveness of new drugs. An agent who does not take on the social role of a doctor still should be careful in evaluating such claims, but need not be as careful as one who has taken on a doctor's obligations. This is another example of there being different means between extremes for agents with different social roles. Between the extremes of being epistemically slipshod and being epistemically overcautious, we find the mean of epistemic carefulness. But epistemic carefulness is different for a doctor and a layperson, even if they find themselves in the same circumstance. If both a doctor and a layperson have read an article about a new drug in a popular magazine, the layperson acts virtuously by believing the drug stops heartburn, while the doctor acts epistemically virtuously by withholding judgment and looking for more information. Virtue epistemology offers a model on which the requirements on agents are sensitive to the epistemic social roles those agents choose. So tempered, these demands do not invite the charge that they are too demanding.

Epistemic Contextualism

Including some element of sensitivity to context is not a new tactic in epistemology. I will begin by considering two main versions of contextualism in epistemology, attributor contextualism and methodological contextualism. Both versions are introduced to do two jobs. The first is to undermine skeptical arguments of the form:

[5] The model of virtues as extremes seems to fit with versions of virtue epistemology that focus on reliability. Insofar as more reliability is always better, reliability is an extreme, rather than a mean. See Sosa 1991, Greco 1999, Goldman 1996.

[6] This extension of context-sensitivity fits well with the version of virtue epistemology offered by Linda Zagzebski (1996). First, since she intends to give an account of the epistemic virtues that is continuous with her account of the moral virtues, context-sensitivity should work the same for both types of virtues. Second, she offers a version of the virtues which takes them to be means between extremes, and she holds that the epistemic and moral virtues may require different things of different people (1996, 96–97).

I do not know that I am not a brain in a vat.
If I do not know that I am not a brain in a vat, then I don't know
that I have hands.

Therefore I don't know that I have hands.[7]

This is a counterintuitive and massively skeptical conclusion, which we
would like to avoid. Both types of contextualism respond by arguing that,
in the context of a skeptical argument, it is appropriate to say that I don't
know that I have hands. This does not imply, however, that in ordinary
contexts I don't know that I have hands. It is only when we engage in
philosophical discourse, particularly philosophical discourse of the skeptical sort, that we lose our knowledge. As David Lewis pithily puts it,
"Epistemology destroys knowledge" (Lewis 1996, 434). But not for good.
When we move out of skeptical contexts, our knowledge returns. The two
versions of contextualism agree about this much. They disagree about
what determines the context in question and how that context can be
changed. This difference is illustrated in the way that both theories handle
the second job for contextualism, which is to explain the changes in our
everyday use of the word "knows." It seems that our standards for
applying this word change fairly radically, depending on the topic we are
discussing. The standards I must meet to truthfully claim "I know that
John was at the scene of the crime" are radically different from the
standards I must meet to truthfully claim "I know John likes chocolate
cake." Epistemic theories of contextualism should give a mechanism to
explain this variation and should aim to produce results that fit, as well as
possible, our intuitions about the varying uses of "knows."

Attributor Contextualism

I will call the first type of contextualism "attributor contextualism."[8] This
type of contextualism takes its name from its focus on knowledge
attributions and the truth conditions for those attributions. Although
the context of the subject of the attribution is taken into account, what is
distinctive of this type of contextualism is that the context of the
attributor plays an important role in determining the meaning of the
contextually sensitive knowledge attribution.[9] This focus on attribution
entails that it is possible for two people, A and B, to both attribute
knowledge to the same third person, to both say, "John knows that his

---

[7] This formulation of the skeptical argument is from DeRose 1995. DeRose is simplifying and addressing the argument from chapter 1 of Unger 1975.
[8] Following DeRose (1999). This version of contextualism is also called semantic
contextualism by Pritchard (2002).
[9] The mechanism by which this occurs is different for different authors. Compare Lewis
(1996), DeRose (1995, 1999, 2002), and Cohen (1988, 1998, 1999). But all allow that changes
in the attributor's context can change the appropriate standards for knowledge.

bus has arrived," and for the knowledge attribution by A to be true while the knowledge attribution by B is false. In an ordinary context, the attributor A uses the term "know" in a way associated only with our everyday standards for knowledge. When, however, the attributor B uses the term "know" in a skeptical context, it has higher standards, perhaps impossible standards, associated with it. If John meets the ordinary standards but not the skeptical standards, then "John knows his bus has arrived" can be true when uttered by A and false when uttered by B. This is the distinctive feature of attributor contextualism, and a result that shows just how radical attributor contextualism is.

Having determined that the context of the attributor determines the meaning of the term "know," we still need to understand how features of the attributor's context affect this meaning. In the version of attributor contextualism offered by Keith DeRose (1995, 1999), the standards for knowledge in a particular conversational context depend on the propositions being considered as potential objects of knowledge. Expanding on Robert Nozick's tracking condition, DeRose argues that one requirement on knowing p be both that if p were not the case one would not believe that p and that if p were the case one would believe that p (Nozick 1981, chap. 3). To evaluate this subjunctive conditional, we are encouraged to focus not just on any way that p might be false but specifically on those ways p might be false which are closest to the way the world actually is. In terms of possible worlds, this means that a belief must track the truth at least as far from the actual world as the first non-p world. This tracking standard condition could be applied proposition by proposition, as is suggested by Nozick; however, DeRose's proposal is instead to provide a single standard for all the propositions considered within a conversational context. The proposition with the most stringent requirement for truth tracking then sets the standard for all the other propositions. Thus, all the possible worlds that must be considered for the most stringent standard must also be considered when evaluating the other propositions in that context.

These details provide attributor contextualism with its response to the skeptical argument. Evaluating the first premise, we must consider whether we would continue to believe that we were not brains in vats even in the first world in which we were so envatted. Since the brain-in-a-vat hypothesis is constructed so that our envatted experiences would be just like our current ones, even if we were envatted we would not believe that we were. Thus the belief that we are not brains in vats does not track the truth sufficiently far, and hence is not knowledge. DeRose accepts closure (within a context), and so he accepts the second premise of the skeptical argument.[10] What about the conclusion of this argument? DeRose holds that the conclusion is also true *in the context in which we are considering the skeptical brain-in-a-vat hypothesis*. When evaluating our belief that we have

---

[10] DeRose 1995 provides an extensive argument for accepting closure.

hands, we are forced to consider not just the first world in which we lack hands (a world in which we would believe that we do not have hands) but also the first world in which we are envatted. In that world, I would believe that I had hands, even though I would lack them. Thus my belief that I have hands does not track the truth *relative to skeptical standards*, and hence is not knowledge *relative to those standards*. But this result cannot be exported out of the skeptical context; in nonskeptical or ordinary contexts I do know that I have hands, because my belief does track the truth to the first world in which I lack hands. DeRose's analysis of the skeptical argument shows that it seems to prove more than it does prove. It does not prove that I never know I have hands, it proves only that I do not know that I have hands when the standards have been raised by the consideration of a skeptical hypothesis. Thus DeRose's version of attributor contextualism explains away the apparent force of the skeptical argument.

The same mechanism can be used to explain the ways that the meaning of "knows" shifts in nonskeptical contexts. How do we change contexts in ordinary conversation? Within a conversation the context can be changed by widening the focus to consider new propositions. The simplest way to do this is to introduce an alternative that has not been considered up to this point. We can do so by mentioning ways that reasoning may go wrong. One might point out that the arriving bus could be the #8 bus, not the #17 express bus that John wants to board. One might further point out that the signs on the bus could be mixed up. After bringing up these possibilities, it is inappropriate to continue to claim that John knows his bus has arrived. Attributor contextualism explains this by claiming that the standards for "knows" have shifted. Earlier we had to consider the first possible world in which the #17 express bus has not arrived. In that world John would not believe that his bus has arrived. With the introduction of new propositions to evaluate, the standards have been raised. John's beliefs must now track the truth out to the first world in which the bus signs have been switched. In that world, though the #17 express bus has not arrived, John would believe that it has arrived. Once the standards have been raised, John no longer meets the standards required for him to know that his bus has arrived. Attributor contextualism allows our epistemic standards to be shifted based on changes in the conversation alone, and it uses these shifts in standards to explain the ways in which our use of the word "knows" change over time.

Problems for Attributor Contextualism

The first objection to attributor contextualism is the worry that its hierarchical ranking of contexts grants too much to the skeptic.[11] If the epistemic standards given by different contexts are ranked, then we might

---

[11] This objection is developed in both Williams (1999, 2004) and Pritchard (2002).

rightly be concerned about what the "best" standard says. But the most stringent standard, the one that will be ranked highest, is the most skeptical possible context. For this is a context in which every possibility must be considered. So according to the highest-ranked epistemic standard, skepticism is true. And this seems like a victory for the skeptic. This ranking of contexts comes naturally within DeRose's framework, for the class of possible worlds in which one's belief must track the truth in a normal context is a proper subset of the class of possible worlds in which one's belief must track the truth in a skeptical context. Since the skeptical context forces the belief to track the truth in more worlds than the ordinary context, there is a clear sense in which the skeptical standards are higher than the ordinary standards.

Duncan Pritchard explains this worry by considering the way that the skeptical invariantist makes an analogy between absolute terms, such as "flat" and "straight," and "knows."[12] Absolute terms have a single absolute standard, and that standard is set by the entire absence of some things: bumps, curves, or doubts. Thus the absolute standard for flatness is something that a table (or a stomach) could never hope to achieve. However, the skeptical invariantist might allow that it is acceptable to use the term "flat" to describe tables (or stomachs) that approach the absolute standard, where closeness is determined by the context; but however appropriate it is to use "flat" in these contexts, these attributions of flatness are not really true, because they don't meet the highest standards of flatness. Application of a similar absolute standard to knowledge may be facilitated by attributor contextualism. Given a ranking of contexts, on which the skeptical context is the highest ranked, we might worry that while it is acceptable to say that I have hands in a normal context or that a table is flat in a normal context, in both cases there are higher standards that have not been met—so I don't *really* know, and the table isn't *really* flat. In either case, the highest standard is one that can never be met, and hence the existence of a hierarchy with placement of the strictest standard at the top leads to skepticism.

The second objection to attributor contextualism concerns the mechanism by which contexts are changed. Attributor contextualism is committed to the claim that changes in the attributor's conversational situation can make a change in the epistemic context, and hence in the truth of knowledge attributions. Yet contexts aren't always changeable in this way. An example here might be if a defense attorney were to ask a witness on the stand whether she really knew it was the defendant at the scene of the crime. After all, she might have been a brain in a vat and only thought that she was seeing the defendant.[13] In making this assertion the defense attorney is clearly drawing attention to a skeptical hypothesis in an attempt to make the standards for that skeptical proposition apply to

---

[12] Pritchard (2002, 45) characterizing the arguments in Unger (1971, 1975)
[13] This example is a variation of one raised in Kaplan (1991).

the context as a whole. But just as clearly, he is failing. It would be perfectly appropriate for the witness to say that in light of her long acquaintance with the defendant and the good lighting conditions at the scene of the crime, yes, she did know that the defendant was there. Thus she might properly ignore standards appropriate to the brain-in-a-vat proposition, even though she has been asked to evaluate it. It seems that sometimes, no matter how hard we try, conversation cannot change context; attributor contextualism cannot explain this fixity of standards.

Methodological Contextualism

Attributor contextualism can be contrasted with the type of contextualism held by Michael Williams, which I will call "methodological contextualism" because the contexts are determined by what he calls "methodological necessities."[14] This version of contextualism holds that it is context of the subject of knowledge attribution that matters, not the context of the knowledge attributor. This implies that it is not possible for one person to truly attribute knowledge to a subject while another person falsely attributes knowledge to the same subject. Furthermore, a mere change in conversation cannot change the context. Each of our methodological contexts carries with it certain parameters determining which things can be questioned and which must be taken as basic within that context. Those beliefs that must be taken as basic are the methodological necessities for that context. Take the methodological context for doing history. In such a context one might wonder if a particular document is authentic or not, or whether the date one has attributed to a found object is correct. But within the methodological context of doing history it is not appropriate to consider the skeptical scenario that the world was created five minutes ago. Although it might be reasonable to consider the Russellian hypothesis in other contexts, within the context of doing history even considering such a hypothesis is unreasonable. Our methodological contexts are determined by our interests. If we are interested in discovering the causes of a particular war, considering the Russellian hypothesis would only serve as a hindrance to that project. Since methodological contexts are connected to particular interests, we can only change those contexts by changing our interests and getting others to change theirs too (Williams 2004, 471). Thus for Williams it might be possible to change the context from that of doing history to that of skeptical worrying, but to make this change in context takes much more than simply asking others to consider a skeptical hypothesis; we must convince them to change their interests as well.

[14] Williams explains this concept in his 1992, 121–25, and uses this term throughout the rest of his arguments in that book and in his 2004. Williams does not have a special term for his own version of contextualism. Pritchard calls this version of contextualism "inferential contextualism" (2002, 35ff.).

This leads to the methodological contextualist's answer to the skeptical problem, which is similar to that proposed by the attributor contextualist; both focus on containing the skeptical results to the skeptical context alone. When one is in a normal context it is true that one knows that one has hands. When one is in a skeptical context it is true that one does not know that one is not a brain in a vat or that one has hands.[15] Epistemic skepticism is true, but only within skeptical contexts. As Williams puts it: "The most this amounts to is the discovery that we cannot justify any beliefs about the world under the (self-imposed) conditions of philosophical reflection. What it does not amount to is the discovery, under the conditions of philosophical reflection, that no such beliefs are ever justified" (1996, 60). Fortunately for those who want to avoid skepticism, there are many contexts in which we know any number of things. Skepticism in a skeptical context does not endanger our knowledge in other contexts.

Methodological contextualism also differs from attributor contextualism in rejecting a hierarchy of contexts (Williams 1992, 2004). Rather than thinking of one standard as being more demanding or rigorous than another, we are to think of the standards of each context as simply being the appropriate standards for the context. This lack of a hierarchy is a result of a very strong commitment to contextualism on Williams's part. All epistemic claims are to be judged within a specific epistemic context. This leaves no extracontextual ground from which to compare different epistemic contexts or the standards used within them (Williams 1999, 60). Of course, it is possible to compare two contexts within a third context, but this may not agree with evaluations in a fourth context. So no context can be used to give a definitive ranking of contexts. In particular, in the methodological contextualist framework, there is no way to rank the skeptical context as the highest epistemic context, so the comparison with absolute terms is not possible.

Methodological contexts are also more stable and harder to change than contexts based on the conversation of attributors. This fact can be beneficial in explaining situations like that of the skeptical lawyer where we cannot shift context through conversation alone. Methodological contextualism can explain this phenomenon by its contention that such a change requires a large shift from one methodological context to another. Rather than a small shift of attention, a total change of subject is required (Williams 2004, sec. 6). In a court of law, the methodological context is determined by explicitly stated rules about standards of admissibility and burdens of proof. Introducing skeptical worries cannot change this methodological context; it can only be changed by influencing the interests of those involved. There are, however, some conversational moves that might change this methodological context. For example, if

---

[15] Williams has recently argued that perhaps even in a skeptical context the demands of the skeptic are to be questioned, and hence the skeptical context may not be a legitimate one (2004).

someone runs into the courtroom yelling "Fire!" this changes the context from one of trying a case to one of evaluating a potential danger. It would be inappropriate to ask of the person yelling, "Do you know that there is fire beyond a reasonable doubt?" The methodological context has been changed, by completely changing the subject. So methodological contextualism can explain how it is possible for some dramatic conversational changes to result in changes in context. But these are all instances in which one is not just raising the standards but entirely changing the subject.

These considerations taken together give us good reasons to prefer methodological contextualism over attributor contextualism. Attributor contextualism grants too much to the skeptic by ordering the contexts in a hierarchy and placing the skeptical context at the top of that hierarchy; methodological contextualism offers no such hierarchy. In addition, attributor contextualism cannot explain why changes in conversation are often not enough to shift from one context to another; methodological contextualism can explain this fixity by insisting that our methodological contexts are rooted in our interests, which do not change so quickly.

Problems for Methodological Contextualism

One small puzzle facing methodological contextualism is a question of why we would choose to work in those methodological contexts with difficult standards. For if contexts are determined by our interests, and we often have an interest in expediency, why would we choose difficult contexts to work in? It would certainly be easier to switch to a context with more methodological necessities on which to depend. If the only thing keeping us in a particular methodological context is our interests, then it seems that our commitment to contexts should be as fickle as our interests are. Yet it seems that methodological contexts are far more stable than our interests. The context of doing history might change slowly over time; perhaps someone develops a database of genealogies that is eventually accepted as authoritative and no longer questioned. But this change is not anywhere near as fast as our changes of interest. What stops the historian, on a day when she is suffering from a headache, from abandoning her regular standards and accepting a new document without any question? To do so would be a way to satisfy her current interests, and interests are all that ground our methodological contexts.

A second, more profound question is generated by the idea that knowledge is valuable. This idea has driven many arguments in recent epistemology.[16] Yet it is unclear how it can be accommodated within methodological contextualism. If all knowledge is knowledge within a

---

[16] Riggs (2008) provides an excellent survey of recent debates about the value of knowledge and how to account for that value. While some have argued that not all knowledge is valuable (Sosa 2003), I will be assuming that the examples of knowledge I consider are ones that have value.

methodological context, what makes a methodological context a good one? Without an answer to this question, the value of knowledge within that context is in question. For if the context is not a good one, an achievement within it will not be good; such an achievement would be like the achievement of becoming a good thief. Relative to the standard *thief*, developing your skills with a picklock is valuable. Yet that does not ensure that developing picklock skills is valuable in itself. If thieving is a bad activity then perfecting it will be an overall bad development. As an epistemological example, consider the methodological context of blindly following a chosen cult leader. To do well in this context, one needs to develop the ability to ignore objections from others and ignore one's own misgivings about the teachings of one's chosen prophet. This ability is good relative to the standard *cult follower*, but is bad for one's overall standing as an epistemic agent.

This is a particularly pressing concern for Williams, for he allows that interests determine our methodological contexts. Yet some interests are good and others bad; it follows that some methodological contexts should also be good and others bad. What, then, makes a methodological context a good one, and such that knowledge found within it is valuable? This is a question that Williams's theory is ill equipped to answer; for Williams offers no extracontextual perspective from which to evaluate contexts. The lack of such a standpoint for comparison is essential to his antiskeptical arguments. He argues that there can be no pure epistemo-logical standpoint, as part of his overall argument that the skeptical context is a privileged one. But he offers no replacement standard on contexts; he avoids putting contexts in a hierarchy but in so doing eliminates any way to explain what makes a context good or bad.

Virtue Contextualism: Methodological Contextualism Supplemented with Social Roles

Having ascertained that methodological contextualism is preferable to attributor contextualism, I will now show how methodological contextu-alism can be supplemented by the robust relation to social roles we have already seen exhibited in the moral and epistemic virtues. This compar-ison will show that a virtue-based version of contextualism can take on all of the strengths of methodological contextualism and in addition give a more complete explanation both of our commitments to particular methodological contexts and of the value of knowledge.

What I will call "virtue contextualism" is a version of methodological contextualism supplemented with a specific grounding of the methodo-logical contexts.[17] Rather than being grounded in just any interests that

---

[17] This is quite different from, though perhaps complementary to, the version of virtue contextualism offered by Greco in his 2004, which holds not that the virtues themselves are

an agent might happen to have, these contexts are grounded in the social roles of that agent. The moral virtue theory of the Stoics insists that our lives and their embedded social roles are the materials with which we practice the moral virtues (Annas 2006, 522). A virtue epistemology following this same vein will make the same claim for the epistemic virtues. Without our social roles there would be no material with which to practice our epistemic virtues. Because virtue is a mean between extremes, and because the location of the mean depends on the social roles of the person who must act, there is no way to be a courageous person *simpliciter;* there is no mean in a vacuum. Similarly, there is no way to exhibit the epistemic virtues except within a social role. One is only courageous *in the role of a bystander*, or epistemically careful *in the role of a doctor*.

Virtue contextualism becomes more plausible when we remember that the social roles relevant to our virtues come in different degrees of specificity and can be either chosen or unchosen.[18] We have already seen how the role of doctor influences the way that the virtue of epistemic carefulness is manifested. The same sort of relation also holds with respect to social roles that I have not chosen and are an accident of birth. Being an American citizen, I am able to vote in certain elections. My role as a citizen will influence how I manifest my virtue of being appropriately epistemically trusting. Even though I might ordinarily trust the content of the evening news, when it concerns the effects of a referendum on which I will soon be asked to vote, I will appropriately be less trusting and more cautious. There are also social roles that I have because of the particular abilities I happened to be born with, not because of the place or situation in which I happened to have been born. Ordinarily we think that individuals ought to have a great deal of epistemic courage in defending their own perceptual experiences; they ought not to defer to the views of others too readily. If, however, I happen to be color blind, I should have more deference to others in the area of color judgments. Finally, the most general role we fall under is that of a rational human being. It is under this role that we can accommodate very general principles of reasoning, such as the requirement that we not violate rules of logic. But this commitment, while general, is not role free. For humans can only be expected to follow the rules of logic to the extent that human minds are capable of doing so; we are not required to see all the logical consequences of each of our beliefs, for example.

Like methodological contextualism in general, virtue contextualism can explain why it is sometimes the case that dramatic conversational changes can change the epistemic context. In these cases the conversation does this by making another of the agent's social roles salient. When someone shouts "Fire" in a courtroom, this brings salience to the social

---

sensitive to context but rather that context determines whether or not the truth of a belief is attributable to the epistemic virtue of the believer.

[18] In line with Cicero's four types of roles. (See footnote 2 above.)

role of a self-preserving member of society, and cues searches for exits and attempts to help others out of them in response to the epistemic and moral commitments of that role. Thus, conversion can change the context, but only by calling attention to an already existing social role of the agent; this implies that such changes are limited. We can explain why the skeptical lawyer fails to change the context to a skeptical one. The social roles we are playing with respect to the court of law are most salient in the courtroom, and are explicitly reinforced by the repeated explanation of the standards of proof in that context. This reinforcement stops the shift to a skeptical context, even if the participants in the court also have other social roles that would make them more skeptical.

The stability of our social roles also helps to explain why we take on epistemological burdens when we choose our contexts, by appealing to the costs and benefits associated with a social role. Sometimes we take on the burdens of a given social role because we want the benefits associated with that same social role and we cannot have one without the other. This is true in both the moral and the epistemic realm. When someone takes on the role of mother, she takes on an immense amount of responsibilities toward her child. Why would anyone take on these burdens voluntarily? Because the burdens are part of being a mother and having a child of one's own. In order to gain the benefits of being a mother, one must also take on the burdens, as they are both inseparable from the social role. The same phenomenon can occur in the epistemic realm. Why would a historian voluntarily put herself in the methodological context of doing history rather than the less demanding methodological context of a casual conversation? She takes on this burden because she wants to *be* a historian. In order to be a historian she needs to operate within a particular social-role context. Thus our desire to take on certain roles and to obtain the benefits associated with them can explain why we take on moral and epistemic burdens that we might otherwise avoid.

Once we have taken on these social roles, they influence which actions are virtuous for us. This is true both for our chosen and for our unchosen social roles. Sometimes we are forced into a particular social role, and we simply must work within it and fulfill it in the most virtuous way possible. We do not choose either to have parents or to have the particular parents that we do. Yet this role influences our moral and epistemic virtues. If our parents have a particular illness, we acquire an obligation to become more informed about that illness, and may also need to develop specialized knowledge about their dietary needs or medical care. Whether it is chosen or unbidden, once we have a social role it determines which actions are virtuous for us.

Virtues are by their very nature stable, since they are dispositions of the agent.[19] They can change over time, but cannot be put off and taken on at

---

[19] This is a standard characterization of the moral virtues. Zagzebski argues that they are a characteristic of the epistemic virtues as well in her 1996.

whim. Thus virtue contextualism can explain not only why we take on social roles in the first place but also why we hold ourselves to these standards after we have taken on the role. On a day when she has a headache, a historian might not want to hold herself to the standards of the methodological role of doing history. And yet, she does so. Why? If we think of methodological contexts as connected only to our current interests, or as something we can easily take on and abandon, this is hard to understand. If, however, we think of contexts as following from the social roles to which we have already committed ourselves, it is easier to explain why we hold ourselves to these standards even when it is not in our interest to do so.

Virtue contextualism can also explain why knowledge is valuable in general, even though each piece of knowledge will only be knowledge relative to a particular social-role context. We can see this clearly in the case of moral virtues. There are some social roles that are not valuable in themselves. Perfection of these social roles does not count as a virtue. One can develop the skills needed to become a good thief; yet this is not to develop a virtue. For virtues are part of *an overall good life*; they are excellences *of a person*. If a social role is compatible with living well, then we can develop virtues within that social role. But if a social role is incompatible with living a good life, developing an "excellence" within that social role will not count as a virtue. An excellent thief is not an excellent person. Similarly with the epistemic virtues. There are some epistemic social roles that we should not look to for developing excellence within, for they are not compatible with living an epistemically good life. Consider our example of the passive follower of a cult leader. One could develop one's ability to be a good cult follower; one could practice ignoring objections from others and even doubting one's own experiences. Yet this social role is not compatible with being a good believer, with having a good epistemic life. The extreme passivity of this role is problematic, for it is incompatible with our most basic social role of being a rational human. Thus, developing abilities relevant to the social role of cult follower will not count as developing virtues.

Given that virtue contextualism rules out some social-role contexts as being incompatible with a good life, we might wonder if this judgment on contexts will return us to a problematic hierarchical ranking of contexts. To address this concern we should note that limiting contexts to those based on social roles that are compatible with a good life still allows for a wide variety of acceptable ways to live our moral and epistemic lives. There is no single best life offered here; rather, there is a large range of social roles that are all compatible with living a good life. Although a virtue approach does allow for some ranking, by making a division between desirable and undesirable social roles, it does not provide the sort of hierarchical structure needed to give skeptical worries a toehold. In particular, the social-role context of the skeptic will not be more valuable than the epistemic context associated with the social roles of doctor, teacher, and parent. Each of these social roles will have subject matter appropriate to that social role, as well as standards of proof within and outside that subject matter. An agent will be more virtuously performing a social role insofar as she conforms to these standards. Of course, a person can be a better or a worse doctor or teacher. Furthermore, it may be true that for a particular person one social role is better than another. But this is because a particular person may be better suited to the demands of one role over another, and not because the social role itself, or the context associated with it, is more valuable. Thus by avoiding a hierarchy of social roles, virtue contextualism is not subject to the worry about conceding too much to the skeptic through giving a hierarchical ranking of contexts.

An Objection Considered

One objection that might be raised against virtue contextualism is a concern about attribution of knowledge to those who are in a social-role context different from that of the attributor. Since virtue contextualism is a version of methodological contextualism, and since methodological contextualism only takes into account the context of the subject to whom knowledge is attributed, virtue contextualism will focus only on the social-role context of the subject in explaining the variation in our standards of knowledge. Yet, sticking with the subject's context alone seems to violate some of our intuitions about particular cases in which someone in one social-role context is ascribing or denying knowledge to someone in another social-role context.

For example, consider a comparison between my sister, who is a doctor, and myself. Perhaps we both read an article in *Time* magazine stating that there is a new heartburn drug that is both effective and safe. In my social-role context as a layperson concerned with my health, this might be sufficient evidence for me to justifiably believe that the new drug is effective and safe. If the drug is in fact both effective and safe, and the way that *Time* gathered its evidence about this drug is unproblematic, then I know that the drug is effective and safe. But my sister, given her social role as a doctor, does not yet have sufficient evidence to reach the same conclusion. Reading about a medical advance in a popular magazine is not sufficient evidence for my sister; she should also check for information in the medical journals, and perhaps ask other doctors about their experiences with the drug. So, according to virtue contextualism, I know that the drug is safe and effective relative to my social-role context, while my sister does not know this relative to her social-role context. Even with the further stipulation that my sister and I understand completely our relative epistemic standings, still it seems wrong for my sister to say to her medical colleagues, "I don't know that this new drug is safe and effective, but my sister does." How can virtue contextualism explain this result, given that on its analysis my sister's statement is true?

There is a way to accommodate this intuition within virtue contextualism by paying attention to ways that the standards for warranted assertability sometimes differ from standards of truth.[20] In many conversational contexts it is not acceptable to assert *p* even though *p* is true; this is often because asserting *p* would mislead one's interlocutors. This type of accommodation is a version of what DeRose (1999, 2002) calls a "warranted assertability maneuver" (WAM). DeRose sees this mechanism as a possible objection to attributor contextualism; it would serve to cut attributor contextualism off from the support it receives from patterns of linguistic behavior. In defending attributor contextualism, he is concerned to address this type of argument and to show why it is not applicable. He agrees that some instances of arguments of this type are legitimate, but claims that others are not. A legitimate WAM is found in the fact that, while it is strictly speaking true to say "possibly P" when you know not P, this is a case where "possibly P" is often not warrantedly assertable. If I know that I have borrowed my neighbor's lawnmower, then I should not respond to his query about the location of his lawnmower with the evasive statement "It is possible that someone borrowed it." My statement is strictly speaking true; that I have actually borrowed the mower entails that it is possible that someone borrowed it. But my evasive answer would create the false implicature that I do not know that the mower has been borrowed. My assertion is unwarranted because it would, knowingly, create this false implicature.[21]

Working from this instance of a legitimate WAM, DeRose gives three criteria for distinguishing legitimate arguments of this type from illegitimate ones (1999, 198–200). First, we must have a case where it is unwarranted to assert either the proposition in question or the negation of that proposition. Second, a legitimate WAM must explain an apparent falsehood by appealing to the generation of a false conversational implicature. The appearance of truth as the result of a true implicature is more difficult explain. Third, the false implicature appealed to must be generated by a sufficiently general rule of conversation. Ad hoc special rules are not a sufficient basis on which to claim a legitimate WAM. DeRose argues that the WAM which applies to "possibly P" meets all three of these criteria. First, it is unwarranted for me to assert, "It is possible that someone borrowed your mower." But it is equally unwarranted for me to assert, "It is not possible that someone borrowed your mower," for, indeed, this is false. Second, we need to explain why it seems wrong to say, "It is possible that someone borrowed your mower," even though this

---

[20] The response mirrors, to some extent, the argument that Pritchard gives in his 2002 for treating attributor contextualism as a theory of pragmatics rather than as a theory of semantics.
[21] The use of conversational implicature in DeRose's standards for a good WAM is based on Grice 1989, especially the section "Logic and Conversation."

sentence expresses a truth. So it is an apparent falsehood that needs explaining by an appeal to conversational implicature. Finally, the false implicature is generated by general rule of conversation—namely, "assert the stronger." This rule helps to explain why a false implicature is generated by citing the fact that I am not saying all that I know (and that is relevant) in the conversation. By avoiding telling my neighbor that I know where his mower is, I imply that I do not know its location—a false implicature.

The WAM needed to explain our intuitions about cross-context attributions meets DeRose's three criteria.[22] First, while it seems wrong for my sister to say, "My sister knows that this drug is effective," it seems equally wrong for her to say, "My sister does not know that this drug is effective." To do so would be to imply that I have not sufficiently researched the effectiveness of the drug in question. But I have done research sufficient for my particular social-role context by consulting *Time* magazine. Thus the conditions on a WAM here imply that it is incorrect to assert either the knowledge claim or its negation. Second, the phenomenon to be explained is one in which there is a true statement that is not warrantedly assertable because of the false implicatures that it generates. Finally, the false implicature here is generated by a general rule of conversation. This rule is Grice's maxim "Be relevant" (Grice 1989, 27). When my sister is speaking in the social-role context of a doctor, her colleagues might well wonder why she is mentioning the knowledge of her nondoctor sister. In order to be relevant to the present conversation, my knowledge should somehow be related to the standards at hand. If all that is being claimed is simply that I meet my own social-role contextual standards for knowledge, this is not relevant to a discussion in a medical context. Bringing it up when not relevant gives the impression that it is relevant, which implies that I have knowledge relative to the medical context—a false implicature generated by a very general maxim of conversation. Thus the WAM used by virtue epistemology to explain cross-context attributions is successful by DeRose's three criteria and serves to insulate virtue contextualism from objections based on those attributions.

Conclusion

Virtue contextualism, then, serves as a useful supplement to methodological contextualism, and is superior to other versions of contextualism on a number of grounds. Virtue contextualism can use social roles and their

---

[22] DeRose argues that skeptical invariantism cannot avail itself of a WAM because it fails his three criteria (1999). It is not my place here to accept or reject this argument. We should note instead that virtue contextualism is neither skeptical nor invariantist; virtue contextualism allows for plenty of variation by subject's context, and it clearly makes a place for nonskeptical contexts. So, even if DeRose's arguments against skeptical invariantism's use of a WAM go through, it is possible that other theories, including virtue contextualism, can meet DeRose's criteria, and hence avoid his defense of attributor contextualism.

relationship to social-role context to explain why we would take on epistemic burdens that it might be possible to avoid. We cannot avoid the social-role context without also giving up the social role. Virtue contextualism can also explain the value of knowledge, even though each piece of knowledge is had within a context. Those social roles that are compatible with living a good life generate contexts such that the knowledge had within them is valuable. At the same time, virtue contextualism avoids the problems that beset attributor contextualism. Not only does it accommodate and correctly explain our practices of knowledge attribution, it also offers a robust response to skepticism. Virtue contextualism is thus the best way to include sensitivity to context in our epistemology.

Acknowledgments

Many thanks to Keith Lehrer, Terry Horgan, Justin Fisher, Cara Nine, Guy Axtell, Heather Battaly, and John Turri for each providing me with detailed comments and suggesting important improvements to earlier drafts of this chapter. I presented drafts at the Northwest Philosophy Conference and the Central Division APA, and received very constructive comments from those audiences, as well as very detailed and instructive feedback from Noah Lemos's commentary on my presentation at the Central APA.

References

Annas, Julia. 2002. "My Station and Its Duties: Ideals and the Social Embeddedness of Virtue." *Proceedings of the Aristotelian Society* 102:109–23.
———. 2006. "Virtue Ethics." In the *Oxford Handbook of Ethical Theory*, edited by David Copp, 515–36. Oxford: Oxford University Press.
Aristotle. 1984. *Nicomachean Ethics,* volume 2 of *The Complete Works of Aristotle.* Edited by Jonathan Barnes, translated by W. D. Ross, revised by J. O. Urmson. Princeton: Princeton University Press.
Cicero. 1991. *On Duties.* Edited by M. T. Griffin and E. M. Atkins, translated by E. M. Atkins. Cambridge: Cambridge University Press.
Cohen, Stewart. 1988. "How to Be a Fallibilist." *Philosophical Perspectives: Epistemology* 2:91–123.
———. 1998. "Contextualist Solutions to Epistemological Problems: Scepticism, Gettier, and the Lottery." *Australasian Journal of Philosophy* 762:289–306.
———. 1999. "Contextualism, Skepticism, and Structure of Reasons." *Philosophical Perspectives: Epistemology* 13:57–89.
DeRose, Keith. 1995. "Solving the Skeptical Problem." *Philosophical Review* 1041:1–52.

————. 1999. "Contextualism: An Explanation and a Defense." In *The Blackwell Guide to Epistemology*, edited by John Greco and Ernest Sosa, 187–205. Malden, Mass.: Blackwell.

————. 2002. "Assertion, Knowledge, and Context." *Philosophical Review* 111:167–203.

Epictetus. 1995. *The Discourses, the Handbook, Fragments of Epictetus* Edited by Christopher Gill, translated by Robin Hard. London: Everyman.

Goldman, Alvin. 1996. "Epistemic Folkways and Scientific Epistemology." In *Empirical Knowledge: Readings in Contemporary Epistemology*, edited by Paul Moser, 423–46. Lanham, Md.: Rowman and Littlefield.

Greco, John. 1999. "Agent Reliabilism." *Philosophical Perspectives: Epistemology* 13:273–96.

————. 2004. "A Different Sort of Contextualism." *Erkenntnis* 61:383–400.

Grice, Paul. 1989. *Studies in the Way of Words*. Cambridge, Mass.: Harvard University Press.

Kaplan, Mark. 1991. "Epistemology on Holiday." *Journal of Philosophy* 88:132–54.

Lewis, David. 1996. "Elusive Knowledge." *Australasian Journal of Philosophy* 744:549–67.

Long, A. A. 2002. *Epictetus: A Stoic and Socratic Guide to Life*. Oxford: Oxford University Press.

Nozick, Robert. 1981. *Philosophical Explanations*. Cambridge, Mass.: Harvard University Press.

Pritchard, Duncan. 2002. "Two Forms of Epistemological Contextualism." *Grazer Philosophische Studien* 64:19–55.

Riggs, Wayne. 2008. "The Value Turn in Epistemology." In *New Waves in Epistemology*, edited by Vincent Hendricks and Duncan Pritchard, 300–323. Basingstoke: Palgrave Macmillan.

Sosa, Ernest. 1991. "Reliabilism and Intellectual Virtue." In *Knowledge in Perspective*, 131–45. Cambridge: Cambridge University Press.

————. 2003. "The Place of Truth in Epistemology." In *Intellectual Virtue: Perspectives from Ethics and Epistemology*, edited by Michael DePaul and Linda Zagzebski, 155–79. Oxford: Oxford University Press.

Unger, Peter. 1971. "A Defense of Skepticism." *Philosophical Review* 80:198–219.

————. 1975. *Ignorance: A Case for Skepticism*. Oxford: Oxford University Press.

Williams, Michael. 1992. *Unnatural Doubts: Epistemological Realism and the Basis of Scepticism*. Cambridge, Mass.: Blackwell.

————. 1999. "Skepticism." In *The Blackwell Guide to Epistemology*, edited by John Greco and Ernest Sosa, 35–69. Malden, Mass.: Blackwell.

————. 2004. "Scepticism and the Context of Philosophy." *Philosophical Issues* 14:456–75.

Zagzebski, Linda. 1996. *Virtues of the Mind*. Cambridge: Cambridge University Press.

7

VIRTUE, EMOTION, AND ATTENTION

MICHAEL S. BRADY

The *perceptual model* of emotions maintains that emotions involve, or are at least analogous to, perceptions of value. On this account, emotions purport to tell us about the evaluative realm, in much the same way that sensory perceptions inform us about the sensible world. An important development of this position, prominent in recent work by Peter Goldie amongst others, concerns the essential role that virtuous habits of attention play in enabling us to gain perceptual and evaluative knowledge. I think that there are good reasons to be sceptical about this picture of virtue. In this chapter I set out these reasons, and explain the consequences this scepticism has for our understanding of the relation between virtue, emotion, and attention. In particular, I argue that our primary capacity for recognizing value is in fact a non-emotional capacity.

1

According to the perceptual model of emotions, fear involves perceiving something as dangerous, anger involves perceiving something as insulting, shame involves perceiving something as shameful, and so on, for other central cases of emotion.[1] Proponents of the perceptual model support their views by listing a number of ways in which emotional reactions are similar to sensory perceptions, where sensory perceptions are taken to be the *paradigm* of perceptual experiences.[2] For instance, they claim that both emotions and sensory perceptions possess phenom-

---

[1] Supporters of perceptual models of the emotions include Elgin (1996 and 2008), Döring (2003), Johnston (2001), de Sousa (1987), Nussbaum (2001), Prinz (2004), Roberts (2003), Tappolet (forthcoming), and Zagzebski (2004).

[2] If we think that sensory perceptions exhaust the class of perceptual experiences, then we will deny that emotions literally involve perceptions of value. But even if we accept this and thus reject a more liberal understanding of perception, we can still *call* the relevant models of emotions "perceptual models" if they propose that there are important and interesting similarities between emotions and sensations, and hence (given the assumption) between emotions and perceptions.

enal properties; both are "passive" responses, in that the experiences are things that "happen" to the person, rather than things that the person "does"; both are (typically) caused by features of the subject's environment; both (typically) represent such features, suggesting that both have similar "correctness conditions"; and both can diverge or come apart from their associated judgments or beliefs, and as a result are not to be thought of as involving judgments or beliefs.[3]

Supporters of the perceptual model claim that there is another important point of similarity between sensory perceptions and emotional experiences, which is that perceptions and emotions play similar *epistemic* roles in the justification of empirical and evaluative beliefs, and as a result enable us to attain (respectively) empirical and evaluative knowledge.[4] To see this in more detail, note that it is intuitively plausible to suppose that perceptual experiences provide or constitute *reasons* or *evidence* for empirical beliefs, at least in the absence of defeating conditions (see, e.g., Brewer 1999, 18). That is, we often appeal to our perceptual experiences in order to explain *why* we believe what we do, and in order to *justify* our believing as we do. Thus, as John McDowell writes, "[S]uppose one asks an ordinary subject why she holds some observational belief, say that an object within her field of view is square. An unsurprising reply might be 'Because it looks that way'" (1994, 165). In normal circumstances, then, we take the deliverances of our perceptual apparatus as prima facie reasons or evidence for our empirical beliefs. Such reasons are *defeasible*, since there are conditions that undermine the deliverances of our senses and defeat the rationalizing potential of our experiences. Our senses can, after all, deceive us, and when they do it is no longer true to say that our seeing something as thus-and-so is a reason to believe that it is thus-and-so.[5]

Those who favour the perceptual model hold that the epistemic role of emotions mirrors that of perceptual experiences. Here too the standard picture maintains that emotions provide prima facie reasons for evaluative beliefs: my fear of a neighbour's dog, for example, is a prima facie reason to think that the dog is dangerous. As Catherine Elgin writes, "Fear is evidence of danger; trust is evidence of reliability" (2008, 33). As

---

[3] Perceptions diverge from the relevant perceptual beliefs in the case of known visual illusions and hallucinations; emotions diverge from the relevant evaluative beliefs in the case of "recalcitrant" emotions—for instance, in cases of fear where someone knows that the object of fear is harmless.

[4] See, e.g., Elgin (1996 and 2008), Döring (2003), and Tappolet (forthcoming).

[5] In so far as perceptual experiences are internal states, this might be taken to support internalism about reasons. However, I am not committed to internalism, at least if this is interpreted as the thesis that the *only* things relevant to justification are suitably internal to the subject's perspective. I can maintain that perceptual experiences are reasons whilst holding that what makes them reasons is something potentially external to the subject, such as their standing in an appropriate causal relationship with the relevant belief.

with perceptual experiences, however, the reasons provided by our emotional responses are *defeasible*, since there are conditions that undermine and defeat the deliverances of our emotional mechanisms or faculties. Emotions such as fear can, after all, lead us astray, by presenting as dangerous something that we know to be perfectly safe: it is a common experience, for instance, for people to be afraid of harmless house-spiders. In such circumstances, emotional appearance and evaluative reality diverge, and it is no longer true to say that our emotional experience of something as evaluatively thus-and-so is a reason to believe that it is evaluatively thus and so.

In light of the possibility of divergence between emotional experience and evaluative reality, the supporter of the perceptual model owes us an explanation as to how we can gain evaluative knowledge on the basis of our emotional experiences. Here I want to focus on views expressed by Peter Goldie (2004), who develops the idea that virtuous habits of attention enable us to close the gap between emotional appearance and evaluative reality, and thus enable us to attain evaluative knowledge. According to Goldie, the virtuous person has a disposition to pay attention to, consciously reflect upon, and (if necessary) regulate the operation of his belief-forming mechanisms when, and only when, there is good reason to check up on their operation. In this he follows Christopher Hookway, who stresses that effective deliberation in general requires that "issues enter into our conscious deliberations if and only if their doing so is important for the success of [the] activities" (Hookway 2000, 64; see also Hookway 2003 and 2006). On this general account, the virtuous person is someone who pays attention to and checks up on his belief-forming mechanisms only when such attention and reflection is warranted. An important corollary of this idea is that in the absence of such attentional focus, the virtuous subject can *trust* that his belief-forming mechanisms provide him with accurate information about himself and his environment, and so can rely on such mechanisms as sources of knowledge. Virtuous habits of attention therefore involve dispositions to check up on and regulate our emotional, perceptual, and other mechanisms when, and only when, there is good reason to do so. When attention is not drawn to the operation of these mechanisms, then the virtuous person is right to trust that appearance matches reality.

To see this picture in more detail, consider first the defeasibility of perceptual experiences. It does not follow, from the fact that our perceptions *can* diverge from reality, that the virtuous person is under an obligation to, or is motivated to, pay attention to all of her perceptual experiences and constantly check to see whether such experiences result from the proper functioning of her perceptual systems. Virtue does not require, as Goldie puts it, that "the content of each particular perceptual experience should be held in suspense pending a check on one's perceptual mechanisms or any other sort of second-order reflective endorsement"

(2004, 251). One reason that virtue does not require that we constantly check our perceptual mechanisms is that such attentional focus will be impossible, given the sheer number of our perceptual experiences. We would not be able to achieve any form of success in navigating around the world if we had to constantly check to determine whether appearance lines up with reality. Goldie continues: "The epistemic requirement, rather, is the commonsense one that we need only consciously seek to satisfy ourselves that the deliverances of a particular perceptual experience are as they should be if there is good reason to do so on that occasion" (2004, 251). Intellectual virtue therefore involves virtuous habits of attention, which enable us to exert what Karen Jones calls "regulative guidance" over our perceptual mechanisms, facilitating conscious reflection about their operation when this is required, and leading us to discount their deliverances or decide that the appearances are indeed veridical (Jones 2003, 196). In the absence of attention being drawn to the operation of our perceptual mechanisms, the virtuous person is right to trust her perceptual experiences, and to regard them as providing her with information about how things really are. Virtuous habits of attention are therefore essential in the story of how our perceptions provide us with information and knowledge about the sensory world, since virtuous habits of attention are required for the proper functioning and regulation of our perceptual systems.

Something similar can be said about virtuous attention to our emotional systems, and so provides an account of how attention plays a role in enabling emotional experience to provide us with evaluative knowledge. The standard picture, as we saw, maintains that emotions provide prima facie reasons for evaluative beliefs: my fear of a neighbour's dog, for example, is a prima facie reason to think that the dog is dangerous. And although what is emotionally salient might on occasion diverge from reality, here too it is not necessary for the virtuous person to pay attention to each and every emotional occurrence in order to check on the operation of her emotional systems, and in order to reflectively endorse or reject how things emotionally appear to her. Rather, "it is part of being intellectually virtuous to check, when (and only when) the occasion requires, whether our emotions are distorting perception and reason" (Goldie 2004, 250). In the absence of attentional focus on the operation of her emotional mechanisms, however, the virtuous person is right to trust the deliverances of such mechanisms, and to regard her emotions as providing her with genuine information about how things are in the evaluative world.[6] As a result, our emotions "can help us to find our way around the world, without our constantly having to consciously reflect on our reasons for our responses on each and every occasion" (Goldie 2004,

[6] Goldie writes that if one is virtuous, "and if there are no other undue influences on one's thinking, then one will see things as they really are" (2004, 258).

258). So the thought is that in the absence of focused attention on and reflection about the mechanisms giving rise to emotional experience, the emotional responses of the virtuous subject can constitute conclusive reasons for evaluative judgments and beliefs. Emotions, in so far as they are suitably attuned to the world around us, enable us to see evaluative reality.

This picture of virtuous monitoring and regulation of our emotional experiences strikes me as suspect, however, for reasons I'll now explain.

2

I want to argue that Goldie's view of the virtuous governance of emotional capacities is mistaken, on the grounds that emotions and perceptions have quite different effects on our attention. In particular, I want to argue that whereas emotional experiences typically persist and capture our attention, perceptual experiences do not. This suggests that emotions are unlike perceptions in their epistemic role; very roughly, it suggests that whereas perceptual experiences can be conclusive reasons for empirical beliefs, emotional experiences are not conclusive reasons for evaluative beliefs. Indeed, I want to argue that on a certain view of evaluative concepts, emotional experiences fail to provide any kind of reason for evaluative beliefs. As a result, we can doubt that the virtuous person is someone who trusts that her emotional capacities can, by themselves, tell her about the evaluative world. The different relations between emotion, perception, and attention cast doubt on the idea that the virtuous person is someone who, in normal circumstances, gets evaluative knowledge *via* her emotional responses.

The first point to make in order to establish this is that it is a common feature of emotional life that emotions direct and focus our attention on to objects and events of potential significance or importance to us. As Aaron Ben Ze'ev puts it, "[L]ike burglar alarms going off when an intruder appears, emotions signal that something needs attention" (2000, 13). But emotions do not just direct or capture our attention; they also *consume* our attention. That is, emotional objects and events often hold sway over us, and when they do our attention remains fixed on the object or event, so much so that it is sometimes difficult for us to disengage our attention and shift focus elsewhere. When this occurs, the emotional object or event remains the focus of our consciousness, and our attention is concentrated on that object or event. So fear, anger, jealousy, shame, and guilt are not simply reflexive, automatic, and short-term interruptions to our mental life, in virtue of which we notice certain things. Instead, such emotions very often persist and dominate that life: we remain focused on and attentive to danger, infidelity, wrongdoing, insults, and loss.

Now it is plausible to think that the point or function of emotional focusing of attention is to alert us, quickly, automatically, and at little mental cost, to objects of potential importance or significance. Emotions enable us to quickly and efficiently *notice* things that might be important to us (Vuilleumier, Armony, and Dolan 2003, 419). What, then, is the point of attentional capture and consumption? Here I want to propose that a central function of the capture and consumption of attention in emotional experience is to make us consciously aware of, and facilitate conscious reflection about, the emotional object or event. Moreover, I propose that the point of such conscious reflection and deliberation is to enable the emotional subject to arrive at a judgment as to whether emotional appearance in this instance really does match evaluative reality, or as to whether there really is a gap between how things emotionally appear and how things evaluatively are. On this picture, the persistence of emotional experience enables the subject to determine whether what appears to be dangerous or shameful really is dangerous or shameful, and as a result facilitates an enhanced representation of the emotional object or event. Since ordinary sensory perceptions do *not* persist, they do not capture and consume our attention in this way, and hence do not facilitate the search for reasons that bear on the question of whether sensory appearance matches empirical reality.

The view that emotions often involve persistent attentional focus, and that this leads to enhanced higher-level or conscious processing of emotional stimuli, will no doubt be controversial, since it runs counter to a tradition which claims that persistence of emotion undermines reflection. However, my proposal is supported by empirical evidence, and in particular by evidence indicating that emotions involve increased *cortical arousal*. Thus, Joseph LeDoux writes that "it has long been believed that the difference between being awake and alert, on the one hand, and drowsy or asleep on the other is related to the arousal level of the cortex. When you are alert and paying attention to something important, your cortex is aroused. When you are drowsy and not focusing on anything, the cortex is in the unaroused state" (1996, 287). For LeDoux, "Emotional reactions are typically accompanied by intense cortical arousal. . . . This high level of arousal is, in part, the explanation for why it is hard to concentrate on other things and work efficiently when you are in an emotional state" (1996, 289). Now increased arousal is in part a matter of increased sensitivity of cells in the cortical and thalamic regions, resulting in increased processing of emotional stimuli. LeDoux continues: "While much of the cortex is potentially hypersensitive to inputs during arousal, the systems that are processing information are able to make the most use of this effect. For example, if arousal is triggered by the sight of a snake, the neurons that are actively involved in processing the snake, retrieving long-term memories about snakes, and creating working memory representations of the snake are going to be especially affected by arousal. Other neurons are inactive at this point and don't reap the benefits" (1996, 287–88). Moreover, additional sensitivity of cells in the cortical and thalamic regions results in a "feedback loop" of arousal, since sensitivity of such cells triggers further arousal of the amygdala, the area of the brain that initially activates arousal systems in response to emotional stimuli. As a result, writes LeDoux, "arousal locks you into whatever emotional state you are in when arousal occurs" (1996, 290). This is the neurophysiological perspective on what happens in attentional capture and consumption. Consequently, we can say that emotions involve the mobilization and direction of attentional mechanisms in order to "provoke a more detailed stimulus analysis [and] enhance the representation of the relevant stimuli" (Vuilleumier, Armony, and Dolan 2003, 432). We thus have empirical support for the idea that the persistence of cortical arousal which accompanies attentional focus serves to facilitate a better evaluation of our emotional situation, through promoting conscious awareness of, and reflection about, our emotional circumstances. Moreover, as LeDoux notes, even novel visual stimuli fail to hold our attention for long in the absence of some emotional element or factor to trigger cortical arousal. So ordinary sensory perceptions do not have this effect on attention.

This supports our second point, which is that emotions are unlike sensory perceptions on an *epistemic* dimension: for whereas the latter typically constitute conclusive reasons for perceptual beliefs, at least in the absence of defeating conditions, it is rarely if ever the case that our emotions *themselves* serve to justify an evaluative judgment. Instead, as we have seen, what normally happens in emotional experience is that we (more or less) reflectively and consciously *seek out* reasons which either support or count against our initial emotional appraisal or take on our situation. So whereas my having a perceptual experience as of a football on my lawn will suffice, absent defeating conditions, to justify my belief that there is a football on my lawn, my feeling of guilt the morning after a departmental party will not, by itself, constitute a conclusive reason to believe that I behaved badly at the party. Instead, the persistence of guilt will incline me to reflect on the events of the evening and look for reasons that bear on the question of whether I did anything wrong. In the usual course of events, we *feel the need* to seek out reasons that either back up or disconfirm our emotional take on some object or event, and thus feel the need to seek out considerations that have a bearing on the accuracy of our initial emotional response. In so far as the persistence of attention motivates this search, it functions to promote conscious reflection on such reasons, and enables us to gain an enhanced representation of our evaluative situation.[7]

---

[7] It might be argued that emotion is only correlated with higher-level reasoning, and facilitates the search for and discovery of reasons, in subjects who are already virtuous. As a

Indeed, we might go further than this and claim that whereas perceptions are prima facie reasons for empirical beliefs, emotions *cannot* be reasons, even prima facie reasons, for evaluative beliefs. For a plausible position in metaethics holds that evaluative concepts like "dangerous," "insulting," "disgusting," "amusing," and so forth, are best understood along *sentimentalist* lines. At least, many prominent philosophers have maintained that these evaluative concepts can only be understood in terms of particular human emotions or sentiments. Sentimentalist accounts propose that we are to understand what it is for something to be dangerous or shameful, let's say, in terms of its eliciting or meriting certain emotional responses, namely, fear and shame. As a result, "sentimentalism . . . is the thesis that evaluative concepts are *response-invoking*: they cannot be analyzed or elucidated without appeal to subjective responses" (D'Arms and Jacobson 2006, 190). Now the most plausible versions of sentimentalism about value are second-order accounts, according to which "to apply a response-dependent concept Φ to an object X (i.e. to think that X is Φ) is to think it *appropriate* (merited, rational, justified, warranted) to feel an associated sentiment F towards X" (D'Arms 2005, 3). These are the kinds of accounts favoured by *sensibility theorists* such as John McDowell, David Wiggins, and David McNaughton, who reject dispositionalist theories of evaluative concepts. (Noncognitivists, such as Simon Blackburn and Allan Gibbard, hold similar views.) That is, sensibility theorists deny that an evaluative concept Φ is to be understood in terms of the sentiments that people are disposed to feel under "normal" conditions. Instead, sensibility theorists maintain that we must understand evaluative concepts in terms of appropriate or fitting or merited emotional responses. On this account, then, to *judge* that X is Φ is to judge that it is rational or appropriate to feel F in response to X; to say that some object is dangerous is, therefore, to say that it *merits* fear, or that fear in this instance would be rationally appropriate, correct, warranted, or fitting. If sentimentalism is correct, however, then our emotional responses cannot be reasons or evidence for the associated evaluative judgments. My fear of the dog, for instance, cannot be a reason to judge that the dog is dangerous, for then my fear would be a reason to judge that fear in these circumstances is appropriate or merited or fitting—and we have good reason to doubt that fear can justify itself in this way. The very fact that I am afraid of the dog cannot, by itself, be evidence that it is fitting or appropriate to be afraid of the

result, virtue, rather than emotion, might be responsible for facilitating reflection on our reasons. However, the phenomenon of rationalization—where subjects often "invent" reasons in order to justify their emotional appraisals—counts against this argument. I take it that rationalization is one instance of a widespread need to justify how we feel, to ourselves and to others, and hence that the search for and reflection upon reasons is not restricted to the virtuous—at least on the assumption that the virtuous do not engage in rationalization and invention of reasons.

dog. On a sentimentalist account of evaluative concepts, therefore, emotions do not and cannot provide evidence or reasons for evaluative judgments.

If these arguments are correct, then we should acknowledge that there is a significant difference between the epistemic roles of emotions and perceptions, a difference that is highlighted by the different effects emotions and perceptions have on our attention. In so far as emotions have the function of bringing things to our attention and, through the capture and consumption of our attention, facilitating conscious awareness, reflection, and deliberation about the relevant events or objects, then emotions facilitate their *own* appraisal through the search for reasons which bear on emotional accuracy. The persistence of an emotional experience is, on this line, *itself* a way of checking whether the evaluation that is partly constitutive of the emotional experience is accurate. So emotions, by bringing things to our reflective consciousness, contain in part the means for their own regulation; the problem of possible divergence between emotional appearance and reality is one that emotions themselves have the function of solving.[8] If so, then the fact that I feel fear is not, by itself, a reason to believe that the object of my fear is dangerous, and hence my emotion does not, by itself, provide me with information about the evaluative realm. Instead, my fear promotes the search for reasons which bear on the question of whether I really am in danger, and hence on the question of whether my experience of fear is warranted.

In the following section, I consider the implications of this difference between emotions and perceptions for our understanding of the relation between virtue, emotion, and attention.

3

According to Goldie, the intellectually virtuous person pays attention to and reflects upon her belief-forming mechanisms when (and only when) she has good reason to do so. On this picture, the virtuous person will be someone who pays attention to the operation and outputs of her perceptual and emotional systems when (and only when) this is necessary: for instance, when there is a possibility of divergence between how things appear in perceptual or emotional experience and how things really are. If so, reflection and deliberation will only be needed in cases where perceptual and emotional experiences do not, by themselves, constitute or provide good reasons for the relevant empirical and evaluative beliefs:

---

[8] This is not to imply that the emotions can perform this regulatory function by themselves, without the input of any other capacities. As we'll see in the following section, the virtuous person is someone with a *non-emotional* capacity to identify and recognize reasons that bear on the question of the accuracy of her emotional experiences. Without the capacity to discover genuine reasons, our emotions will not be regulated in the right way.

when, that is, it is an open or live question whether what appears to be the case, either perceptually or emotionally, really is the case.

However, in the previous section I claimed that one of the central functions of emotions is to promote and facilitate reflection and deliberation. If this is correct, then the above picture of intellectual virtue with respect to our *emotional* experiences is one that we have good reason to reject. In so far as emotional experience promotes attentional focus and conscious reflection aimed at discovering reasons which bear on the accuracy of the experience itself, then emotional experience seems to be incompatible with trusting that *this very experience* provides answers to our questions or gives us information about the evaluative world. The fact that emotions promote and facilitate conscious, thoughtful reflection aimed at determining the accuracy of our emotional experiences would seem to *prevent* our having confidence in the capacity of such experiences to rationalize and justify our evaluative beliefs. Instead, since emotional experience will prompt us to look elsewhere for considerations that bear on the accuracy of our emotional responses, it is *these* considerations that provide us with information about the evaluative realm. Reasons for evaluative beliefs are thus considerations that emotional experiences enable us to discover, rather than emotional experiences themselves.

This suggests that the actual relation between emotion, virtue, and attention is significantly different to that proposed by the defender of the perceptual model. On that model, the virtuous person is someone who is confident that his emotional experiences provide him with information about the evaluative realm, and who only consciously reflects on the possibility of divergence between emotional appearance and evaluative reality when his attention is drawn to his current emotion. On the account that I favour, however, the virtuous person will not trust that his emotional experiences by themselves give him information about the evaluative world. Instead, he will be confident in his capacity to recognize value because he is confident in his *non-emotional* capacity to recognize and identify the kinds of considerations that bear on the accuracy of his emotional responses: considerations, that is, that speak to whether his situation genuinely is dangerous or shameful, and so on. Moreover, on my account this non-emotional capacity to recognize and identify reasons does not require conscious and continuous reflection on the subject's part; instead, the virtuous subject is someone who has learned to directly recognize the emotion-relevant features in a wide variety of circumstances. As a result, there is no *epistemic* point to the virtuous person's being emotionally engaged in such circumstances, since there is no point to his consciously reflecting on his reasons in such circumstances. This has the following implication: on the rival perceptual model, attention is drawn *to* the operation of our emotional experiences only in situations where there is good reason to reflect on their operation. On the model that I favour, attention will be drawn *by* the operation of our emotional mechanisms only in situations where there is good reason to reflect on the operation of one's *non-emotional* capacity to recognize value. On my view, the normal circumstances in which the virtuous person is sensitive to values are non-emotional circumstances, where he relies on his non-emotional capacity to recognize that these features are signs of danger, these features are evidence of wrongdoing, and the like. The presence of an emotional response or reaction signals, by contrast, that circumstances are *abnormal* or *surprising*: in such circumstances, the virtuous person cannot take it for granted that he is sensitive to the relevant values, but instead is motivated to reflect upon and deliberate about his evaluative situation. I propose, then, that we understand the virtuous person's sensitivity to value—his capacity to notice what needs to be noticed, to recognize what is important or significant in his situation—as a non-emotional sensitivity. The virtuous person does not "see the world by feeling," a phrase suggested by Daniel Jacobson (2005, 387), although her emotional responses might be vital in the *development* of her capacity to recognize reasons for fear, shame, guilt, and so on.

As an illustration, consider the development of a capacity to recognize and identify reasons and values when driving a car. In order to drive safely and effectively, one has to develop a large number of skills. These might include, for instance, the capacities to negotiate roundabouts, to merge into heavy traffic on a motorway, to engage the clutch to change gear, to judge distances quickly and accurately, and so on. It is clearly important, when learning how to do such things, that the person be emotionally engaged and thereby consciously focused on the task in hand. Some level of anxiety when doing these things would seem, if not essential, then highly desirable in keeping one's attention focused on what is going on. The learner driver is thus emotionally engaged and consciously attentive to a very large number of things—which is part of the explanation for why learning how to drive is so mentally draining. An experienced driver, on the other hand, will be confident in her abilities to do all of these things and more, and with little in the way of conscious attention. The experienced driver doesn't have to consciously focus on or think about changing gear, nor is she emotionally engaged or anxious about negotiating roundabouts or merging into heavy motorway traffic. This is because the experienced driver no longer has any *need* for emotional assistance in performing such tasks: these operations are now habitual or second-nature to her. Instead, the experienced driver is confident in her *non-emotional* abilities to recognize and identify what is significant in her driving environment—such as the distance between her car and the cars around her when merging on to the motorway, or the right time for her to change gear, or the amount of room that she should give to the cyclist as she overtakes. The skilful driver relies upon her non-emotional capacity to identify what is important for her when driving, rather than "seeing by feeling." Note that on this account, too, the presence of an emotional response for the experienced driver signals that circumstances are abnormal or surprising: in freezing fog or heavy snow, even an experienced driver needs to be consciously focused upon and attentive to her driving, and hence there is a point to her being emotionally engaged in these circumstances. In normal circumstances, however, the capacity of the experienced driver to notice what needs to be noticed, and to recognize what she ought to recognize, is, plausibly, a non-emotional capacity.

4

In this section I consider a number of objections to my proposal, and argue that none is ultimately convincing.

The first objection is that emotions *can* constitute reasons or evidence for evaluative beliefs, since a subject can be aware of reliable correlations between emotional responses and values. Earlier I noted that emotions have the function of making certain objects and events salient for us, thereby alerting us to things of potential significance. But of course, emotions can do this more or less reliably. Indeed, we might think that certain emotions have evolved to co-occur with values; and it hardly needs pointing out that emotions can be trained or calibrated so that they function more efficiently in bringing to our attention important aspects of our environment. If so, then although my fear (say) might not be an infallible indicator of danger, it might nevertheless be a *reliable* indicator of danger. Since this is something of which I can be aware, my fear can function as a reason for me to believe that I am in danger. As Catherine Elgin points out, we commonly "take ourselves to be able to reliably correlate emotions with circumstances" (2008, 37). That is, "we can often tell which emotional reactions reflect the presence of emotional [evaluative] properties. So under certain recognizable circumstances, an emotional reaction affords epistemic access to such properties" (2008, 40–41).

This is a serious objection but one that ought to be resisted, since it presupposes the operation of a recognitional capacity that is independent of, and normatively prior to, our emotional experience. It is this recognitional capacity, rather than our emotional experience, that is central to justifying our evaluative beliefs. Let me explain. The idea that we can use reliable emotional experiences as indicators of genuine value is expressed nicely by Elgin, who writes that "the epistemic yield of emotions, like the epistemic yield of perceptions depends not on taking all deliverances at face value, but on a sophisticated understanding of when and to what extent they are trustworthy" (2008, 37). But what is involved in coming to understand when and to what extent my fear, for instance, is trustworthy? Presumably, this is a matter of sufficient experience of and suitable training in recognizing the *circumstances* in which fear is reliable and unreliable. We learn, for instance, that fear in these circumstances co-occurs with genuine danger, whereas fear in these other circumstances is phobic. However, the capacity to recognize circumstances in which fear is reliable (or unreliable) would seem to involve the capacity to recognize *features* or *properties* of those circumstances that speak in favour of (or against) taking one's emotional appraisal seriously. After all, there must be something about the relevant circumstances that indicates to us that fear is trustworthy (or untrustworthy), and it is difficult to see what this could be apart from the features or properties of the circumstances. But since the features or properties that speak in favour of (or against) taking an emotional experience seriously are reasons in favour of (or against) the relevant evaluative judgment, then a sophisticated understanding of when and to what extent our emotions are trustworthy presupposes a capacity to identify reasons and evidence for our evaluative judgments. In other words, a sophisticated understanding of the reliability of our emotional responses presupposes a capacity to recognize considerations that bear on the accuracy of our emotional responses, and hence a capacity to recognize *value*. The fact that taking an emotional response to be a reliable indicator of value presupposes a prior sensitivity to that very value therefore renders the emotional response otiose. The objection gets things the wrong way around. It is not our awareness of the reliability of fear in these circumstances that gives us reason to believe that we are in danger. Instead, it is our sensitivity to and sophisticated understanding of danger that grounds our awareness that fear in these circumstances is reliable. It is our recognitional capacity, rather than our emotional experience, that therefore justifies our evaluative beliefs.

A second objection to my account is that it is committed to an unattractive picture of the virtuous subject. On my account, emotional experience promotes attentional focus and conscious reflection aimed at discovering reasons which bear on the accuracy of the emotional experience itself. But if, as on a standard Aristotelian account, the virtuous person must have the appropriate emotions, then the virtuous person will be reflectively checking the accuracy of his emotional appraisals far too often. Indeed, he might be accused of having the intellectual vice of being unduly thorough or unduly suspicious. This is not all. For in so far as emotion (and hence reflection) is pervasive, my account makes the conditions for evaluative knowledge too stringent—at least if we think that constant monitoring and continuous reflection are a bar to evaluative knowledge. So a standard Aristotelian view of the virtuous person raises a serious problem for my account of the relation between virtue, emotion, and attention.[9]

This objection too can be resisted. The objection assumes that the standard Aristotelian position is correct, and that the virtuous person must have the appropriate emotions in order to count as virtuous. It then

---

[9] This objection, and a version of the previous objection, are due to Heather Battaly.

assumes that the Aristotelian position, combined with my account of the role and function of emotional experience, entails that the virtuous person will be checking the accuracy of her emotional appraisals far too often. But it is not clear to me that this entailment holds. This is because the Aristotelian claim about the pervasiveness of emotions is plausible only if emotions are thought to be operating, for the most part, *subconsciously* in the background of the virtuous person's experiences. To see this, recall that the virtuous person is more like an experienced driver than a learner: the virtuous person is akin to someone who does not *feel* anxious or afraid in situations where it is appropriate for a learner to feel afraid (such as when merging on to a busy motorway). Indeed, in normal circumstances the experienced driver will attain evaluative knowledge (e.g., that it is safe to merge now) in the absence of emotional feelings and attentional focus, and hence in the absence of reflection and deliberation about the accuracy of one's emotional experience. If, then, emotions are held to be pervasive and necessary for evaluative knowledge, in normal circumstances emotions will be operating subconsciously and in the background.

On my account, however, attention is captured and consumed by *conscious* emotional experiences: it is our conscious emotional *feelings* that motivate reflection and deliberation, since it is our conscious emotional feelings which capture and consume our attention. As a result, the Aristotelian idea that emotions are pervasive and operating subconsciously does not entail that the virtuous person will be constantly checking up on the accuracy of his emotional appraisals, if such reflection and checking is motivated—as I maintain—by conscious emotional experiences. By the same token, my view that conscious emotional experience promotes reflection and deliberation does not, even when combined with the Aristotelian view of the pervasiveness of emotion, make the conditions for evaluative knowledge too stringent. Although constant monitoring and continuous reflection is a bar to evaluative knowledge, my account isn't committed to the idea that the virtuous person will be constantly monitoring or reflecting on the operation of her belief-forming mechanisms, since neither my account nor the Aristotelian account is committed to the idea that *conscious* emotional feelings are pervasive in the life of the virtuous person. So I can accept, for the sake of argument, the Aristotelian commitment to the pervasiveness of emotion, without accepting that this renders my account of the virtuous person unattractive, or that I make the conditions for evaluative knowledge too stringent.

A third potential problem with my account is that it seems to suggest that the virtuous person will be unemotional, or that a lack of emotion ought to be an ideal that we should strive to reach. This, as has often been said, would hardly be an attractive picture of the virtuous person. But I don't think that anything I have said thus far constitutes an attack on the value of and need for the emotions in our virtuous life. For one thing, the most that follows from the above account would be that the virtuous person will be relatively unemotional, *in normal circumstances*, when it comes to his recognition of and sensitivity to genuine value. But as we have seen, emotions will be essential in the life of the virtuous person when circumstances are abnormal or surprising, precisely because they alert the virtuous person to the fact that he needs to pay attention to and reflect on his evaluative situation. For another, emotions clearly have a role to play in the development and maintenance of the capacity to recognize what is genuinely valuable, in those who are less than fully virtuous. Even if emotions do not by themselves constitute a sensitivity to value, they would seem to be essential in the development of non-emotional capacities to identify considerations that constitute genuine signs of danger, insult, infidelity, and the like. As I have stressed, emotions bring potential reasons and values into our reflective consciousness, facilitate reflection as to whether emotional appraisals in these circumstances are accurate, and as a result familiarize us with features and properties that constitute genuine reasons for our evaluative beliefs and judgments. Finally, emotions are clearly important for *action* related to the virtuous life. In particular, they would seem to play an essential motivating role in getting us to do what we have good reason to do. As a result, nothing I have said above commits me to the view that virtue requires us to get rid of or temper our emotions *tout court*. I maintain, nevertheless, that in normal circumstances a virtuous person gains knowledge of value through his non-emotional capacities to recognize reasons and evidence, and that in normal circumstances emotional reactions are *epistemically* unnecessary.

To deny that virtuous sensitivity to value is a form of emotional sensitivity is not, therefore, to downplay the vital roles that emotions play in enabling us to achieve evaluative knowledge. But it is to claim that supporters of the perceptual model have been too optimistic in thinking that emotions themselves constitute reasons for belief and action, and that in the absence of attention being drawn to the operation of our emotional mechanisms we can trust our emotional responses to provide us with evaluative knowledge. If I am right, emotions themselves are not ways of seeing, although they can help us, through their influence on attention, to see what we need to see.

Acknowledgments

An earlier version of this chapter was presented at the 2008 Fullerton International Philosophy Conference entitled "Virtue and Vice: Moral and Epistemic." I would like to thank the organisers of the conference, Heather Battaly and Amy Coplan, the conference delegates, Ryan Nichols, and Fiona Macpherson for helpful comments and feedback on the chapter. I am particularly grateful to Heather Battaly for pushing me to answer a host of excellent objections, and for her sterling editorial work.

References

Ben Ze'ev, Aaron. 2000. *The Subtlety of Emotions.* Cambridge, Mass.: MIT Press.

Brewer, Bill. 1999. *Perception and Reason.* Oxford: Clarendon Press.

D'Arms, Justin. 2005. "Two Arguments for Sentimentalism." *Philosophical Issues* 15:1–21.

D'Arms, Justin, and Daniel Jacobson. 2006. "Sensibility Theory and Projectivism." In *The Oxford Handbook of Ethical Theory,* edited by David Copp, 186–218. New York: Oxford University Press.

de Sousa, Ronald. 1987. *The Rationality of Emotion.* Cambridge, Mass.: MIT Press.

Döring, Sabine. 2003. "Explaining Action by Emotion." *Philosophical Quarterly* 53:214–30.

Elgin, Catherine. 1996. *Considered Judgement.* Princeton: Princeton University Press.

———. 2008. "Emotion and Understanding." In *Epistemology and Emotions,* edited by Georg Brun, Ulvi Doguoglu, and Dominique Kuenzle, 33–49. Aldershot: Ashgate.

Goldie, Peter. 2004. "Emotion, Reason and Virtue." In *Emotion, Evolution, and Rationality,* edited by Dylan Evans and Pierre Cruse, 249–69. Oxford: Oxford University Press.

Hookway, Christopher. 2000. "Epistemic Norms and Theoretical Deliberation." In *Normativity,* edited by Jonathan Dancy, 60–77. Oxford: Blackwell.

———. 2003. "Affective States and Epistemic Immediacy." *Metaphilosophy* 34:78–96.

———. 2006. "Reasons for Belief, Reasoning, Virtues." *Philosophical Studies* 130:47–70.

Jacobson, Daniel. 2005. "Seeing by Feeling: Virtues, Skills, and Moral Perception." *Ethical Theory and Moral Practice* 8:387–409.

Johnston, Mark. 2001. "The Authority of Affect." *Philosophy and Phenomenological Research* 53:181–214.

Jones, Karen. 2003. "Emotion, Weakness of Will, and the Normative Conception of Agency." In *Philosophy and the Emotions,* edited by Anthony Hatzimoysis, 181–200. Cambridge: Cambridge University Press.

LeDoux, Joseph. 1996. *The Emotional Brain.* New York: Simon and Schuster.

McDowell, John. 1994. *Mind and World.* Cambridge, Mass.: Harvard University Press.

Nussbaum, Martha. 2001. *Upheavals of Thought.* Cambridge: Cambridge University Press.

Prinz, Jesse. 2004. *Gut Reactions.* New York: Oxford University Press.

Roberts, Robert C. 2003. *Emotions: An Essay in Aid of Moral Psychology.* Cambridge: Cambridge University Press.

Tappolet, Christine. Forthcoming. The Irrationality of Emotions." In *Philosophical Perspectives on Irrationality,* edited by Daniel Weinstock.

Vuilleumier, Patrik, Jorge Armony, and Ray Dolan. 2003. "Reciprocal Links Between Emotion and Attention." In *Human Brain Function,* 2nd edition, edited by Richard Frackowiak et al., 419–44. San Diego: Academic Press.

Zagzebski, Linda. 2004. *Divine Motivation Theory.* Cambridge: Cambridge University Press.

8

FEELING WITHOUT THINKING:
LESSONS FROM THE ANCIENTS ON EMOTION AND
VIRTUE-ACQUISITION

AMY COPLAN

I believe that the examination of things good and evil, of ends and of virtues, depends on the correct examination of the emotions.
—Posidonius of Apamea (qtd. Galen 1981, v. 469, 12–16, fr. 30)

In ancient Greek philosophy questions about the nature of virtue were often directly tied to questions about the nature of emotion. In contemporary philosophy of mind and moral psychology, these questions are usually addressed separately. Those who debate the nature of emotion today have little to say about the implications of the debate for theories of virtue and moral education. They offer arguments in favor of characterizing emotion in particular ways but tell us little about why these characterizations matter. I suspect that it is in part due to their silence on this issue that the debate on the nature of emotion is often considered a waste of time that amounts to nothing more than an argument about labels. In this chapter, I show that it matters a great deal how we characterize emotion. Indeed, if we care about coming up with successful strategies for acquiring virtue, then we must get clear about the nature of emotion.

By briefly sketching some important ancient accounts of the connections between psychology and moral education, I hope to illuminate the significance of the contemporary debate on the nature of emotion and to reveal its stakes. I begin the chapter with a brief discussion of intellectualism in Socrates and the Stoics, and Plato's and Posidonius's respective attacks against it. Next, I examine the two leading philosophical accounts of emotion: the cognitive theory and the noncognitive theory. I maintain that the noncognitive theory better explains human behavior and experience and has more empirical support than the cognitive theory. In the third section of the chapter I argue that recent empirical research on emotional contagion and mirroring processes provides important new evidence for the noncognitive theory. In the final section, I draw some preliminary conclusions about moral education and the acquisition of virtue.

1. Intellectualism: Is Knowledge the Path to Virtue?

Intellectualism is the view that knowledge is sufficient for or identical to virtue. Intellectualists argue that if one has knowledge of the good, one will necessarily do what is good. Weakness of will (*akrasia*) is therefore an impossibility, since intellectualists deny that one can know the right thing to do and yet not do it. According to the intellectualist picture, reason is all powerful, and rational understanding guarantees virtue. Provided that one reasons well, emotion poses no threat to one's virtue; either emotion is no match for reason, which will always overrule it, or it is a species of reason and can be regulated by reasoned argument.

Intellectualism originates in ancient Greek philosophy with Socrates and the early Stoics, especially Chrysippus, who seems to have been influenced by Socrates in his understanding of virtue (Schofield 1984; Brown 2006). In the *Protagoras*, Socrates argues against the common view that knowledge fails to motivate action and is insufficient for virtue, claiming that "knowledge is a fine thing capable of ruling a person, and if someone were to know what is good and bad, then he would not be forced by anything to act otherwise than knowledge dictates and intelligence would be enough to save a person" (1997b, 352c). According to Socrates, knowledge cannot be overcome by desire, pleasure, pain, fear, or love and is therefore sufficient to motivate action and sufficient for virtue.

According to the intellectualist view, our emotions and behavior follow directly from our knowledge or ignorance. For example, in Plato's *Apology* Socrates considers the fear of death to be a direct result of ignorance. It is because we mistakenly believe that death is a great evil that we fear it. Were we to learn the truth about death—that it is nothing evil at all but is either a dreamless sleep or the relocation of the soul to another place—then we would no longer fear it (Plato 1997a, 40c–41c). As Gregory Vlastos points out, Socrates' entire philosophical method is based on an intellectualist view of moral knowledge. Through the *elenchus*, Socrates tests his interlocutors' knowledge, believing that by helping them to see errors in their reasoning and to correct false beliefs, he is helping to inculcate them with virtue. Socrates believes himself to be aiding his interlocutors in the pursuit of virtue and yet he does not combine the *elenchus* with an examination of the interlocutors' actions, behaviors, or habits (Vlastos 1957). Virtue is a property of the intellect.

For the Stoics, virtue is "nothing other than the mind disposed in a certain way" (Seneca 1969, 113.2; L&S 29B). This disposition is the perfection of one's reason, which is achieved through living in accordance with nature, which we do by exercising our rational capacities. There is no separate irrational capacity in the soul capable of unseating reason. The Stoic sage possesses genuine knowledge of good and evil and possesses a firm and consistent rationality. His knowledge and "right reason" guarantee his virtue. The early Stoics' intellectualism is in part based on their understanding of emotion as a type of judgment. Emotions can be regulated by knowledge and argument because they are types of judgments themselves.

Plato famously rejects Socratic intellectualism in the *Republic*, where he develops a faculty psychology with three distinct and independent capacities, or powers. The tripartite soul explains weakness of will, psychological conflict, and vice. According to Plato, it is possible and not uncommon for emotion or appetite to overwhelm reason, causing us to act against our reasoned judgment. Appetite and emotion can both be difficult to control. They require a particular type of nonrational training appropriate to their nature, which includes a regimen of certain types of poetry and music, physical exercise, and diet. Since the nonrational parts of the soul are fully independent of reason, they can oppose it and are cognitively impenetrable, that is, not subject to reason's control. To acquire virtue we therefore need more than just knowledge. We need a way to train the nonrational elements of our soul.

Following Plato and adopting his faculty psychology, the Middle Stoic Posidonius (c. 135–c. 51 B.C.) rejects the intellectualism of Chrysippus due to what he considers to be its inadequate account of human psychology and emotion and the relevance of this psychology to moral education.[1] Posidonius maintains that Chrysippus's monistic psychology cannot explain the irrational forces within the soul that often work against our reasoned judgments, and that Chrysippus's identification of emotion with judgment creates insurmountable difficulties. He argues in favor of Plato's tripartite model of the soul, which makes the irrational capacities of the soul irreducible to judgments and is therefore able to account for psychological conflict, vice, and the fact that judgments often have little or no influence on emotion.

Posidonius develops a number of important objections to Chrysippus's theory of emotion and reformulates Stoic ethics to make it better fit the empirical facts (Galen 1981, v. 459–65, fr. 169; see also Kidd 1971; Edelstein 1936, 1966; Long 1986). In this way, Posidonius is much like the contemporary noncognitive theorists of emotion. In fact, several of Posidonius's arguments against Chrysippus closely resemble contemporary arguments against cognitive theories of emotion.[2] A number of empirical facts work against Chrysippus's account, according to Posido-

---

[1] For a fuller discussion of Posidonius's view, see Sorabji 2000, esp. 93–132, Kidd 1971, 1988, and Edelstein 1936, 1966. For arguments against the standard interpretation of Posidonius, including the extent to which his views on emotion were influenced by Plato, see Cooper 1999 and Gill 1998.

[2] Posidonius's attack on Chrysippus is much more developed and complex than my brief discussion here suggests. Sorabji 2000 provides a nice discussion of Posidonius's objections and develops some objections of his own. I will only discuss two of Posidonius's objections here.

nius. One of these concerns the changing nature of emotion. Posidonius observes that emotion often diminishes over time, but the judgments that are supposed to constitute the emotion do not change. If emotions are identical to judgments, then how can they change when their constitutive judgments do not?[3]

Another problem Posidonius identifies with the view that emotions are judgments is that rational argument often fails to elicit an emotional response without some sort of vivid imagery to accompany it: "For I think you are quite familiar with the way people are without fear or distress when they have been rationally persuaded that something bad for them is present or approaching, but they have these passions when they get an impression of those things themselves. How could anyone activate the irrational by means of reason, unless he set before it a picture like a perceptual impression? Thus some people have their appetite roused by a description, and when someone vividly tells them to flee the approaching lion, they are frightened without having seen it" (qtd. Galen 1981, 5.6., 22–26, fr. 162). In the first sort of case Posidonius characterizes in this passage, we are logically persuaded that something bad is going to happen yet do not respond with fear. How is this possible if emotion is nothing other than judgment? And why does vivid imagery make a difference? In the second sort of case Posidonius offers in this passage, we respond emotionally to another's description because of the description's vivacity. The cognitivist who takes a Chrysippean view of emotion is hard pressed to explain this. Posidonius has no such difficulty. He argues that the irrational element of the soul is not moved by the rational, just as the rational is not moved by the irrational. Images are something nonrational and thus can activate the nonrational element of the soul.

Posidonius's divergence from the orthodox Stoic view has important implications for how he conceptualizes moral education and the pursuit of virtue. Due to the nature and structure of the soul, we cannot use reason or argument to gain complete control over our internal states and thus cannot rely on reason alone for virtue. The nonrational powers in the soul must be treated in some way other than through the cognitive therapy prescribed by Chrysippus. Posidonius's alternative is a therapy of "measuring" and "disciplining," which features irrational movements such as music and rhythms, and habituation. Together these two measures temper the passions, and allow for the cultivation of virtue by restoring order to the soul. They are essential for moral education, since they prevent the irrational powers from seizing control of the soul and causing us to behave in ways we rationally judge to be wrong. Unlike the cognitive therapy of the intellectualists, Posidonius's regimen for moral

---

[3] See Sorabji 2000, 109–14, for a discussion of how Chrysippus anticipates this objection and Posidonius's alternative solution.

education functions by soothing, calming, cajoling, urging, and exhausting the irrational elements of our soul.[4]

As should be clear from my discussion so far, the position one takes in the debate over intellectualism hinges to a large extent on one's view of emotion and whether emotions are considered to be, or to essentially involve, cognitive judgments or to be controlled by such judgments, or are considered to be independent of reason, primarily nonrational, and not subject to rational control. How does this relate to virtue and intellectualism? If virtue requires appropriate emotion, and emotion cannot be made appropriate by knowledge alone, then knowledge is insufficient for virtue.

The ancient debates on intellectualism and emotion show that how one understands the nature of emotion and its relationship to reason has significant implications for one's theory of virtue. It will in part determine how one understands virtue and the strategies one will devise to achieve it. Intellectualists will seek virtue through rational pursuits alone, attempting to shape the emotions by correcting false beliefs and acquiring knowledge, that is, through methods such as the Socratic *elenchus* or the cognitive therapy of the Stoics. Those who consider emotion to be a psychological faculty independent of reason will consider the pursuit of and possession of knowledge and rational understanding to be insufficient to determine one's actions. Emotions require their own type of training through strategies capable of influencing them. These strategies must involve more than the pursuit of knowledge and the correction of false beliefs.

If we fast forward to the twentieth and twenty-first centuries, we find that certain features of the ancient debate over intellectualism and emotion have resurfaced in contemporary philosophy and psychology of emotion where there remains a sharp divide between those who take emotions to be a type of cognitive judgment and those who define emotions as fundamentally noncognitive and thus not fully controllable by reason. Although the contemporary debate mirrors the ancient debate in several respects, philosophers and psychologists today have far less to say about the relevance of one's definition of emotion to one's theories of virtue and moral education. Thus, as I explained above, it will be instructive to keep the ancient debate in mind as we consider the arguments being offered today.

2. Contemporary Philosophy of Emotion: How Should We Define Emotion?

A principal question in contemporary philosophy of emotion concerns the nature of emotion—more specifically, whether it is essentially cognitive or noncognitive. Thus, there is the cognitive theory of emotion (also

---

[4] Galen argues that Posidonius gets the idea for this training from the regimen Plato develops in the *Republic*, which is specifically designed to train all three parts of the soul so that the nonrational parts will be attuned to reason, which is required for virtue.

sometimes referred to as the judgment theory, propositional attitude theory, or cognitive appraisal theory), and the noncognitive theory of emotion (also sometimes referred to as the feeling theory or the sensation theory).

The cognitive theory, which has many variations, has been the dominant view in philosophy and psychology for the past several decades. Its central claim is that some type of thought or judgment is essential to or identical to emotion, whereas patterns of bodily change and feelings are considered nonessential. For example, if my beloved dog dies, I will judge this to be a tremendous loss and will be sad. Cognitivists would argue that the core of my sadness is my judgment that I have experienced a loss. Certain physiological changes and feelings may accompany this judgment, but they are nonessential. If they failed to occur, I would still be sad. What matters is the evaluative judgment, not bodily upset or sensations. Therefore, emotions are fundamentally cognitive.

Noncognitivists contend that the defining feature of emotion is an affective or embodied appraisal, which they define as a noncognitive bodily evaluation of the relationship between the organism's well-being and some stimulus or event. Appraisals carry meaning, but the meaning is bodily rather than conceptual or propositional. Jenefer Robinson (2005) characterizes appraisals as "rough-and-ready" and as "instinctive." They work extremely quickly and below the level of consciousness to generate physiological changes, motor changes, changes in facial and vocal expression, and action tendencies, and they focus attention on whatever feature of the stimulus or situation is most significant to the organism's well-being. The function of appraisals is to enable us to respond adaptively to a wide range of situations that bear on our survival or well-being.[5] According to noncognitivists, appraisals require no deliberation, inference, or high-level processing. Emotions, therefore, are fundamentally noncognitive.

In the literature on emotion there has been confusion about what different philosophers mean when they use the term "cognitive"—confusion that has been exacerbated by the fact that, for most psychologists, all neural activity is considered "cognitive activity" (Griffiths 1997, 24; see also Debes 2009). Paul Griffiths (1997) explains that the debate among different philosophers and psychologists is really over what sort or level of mental processing is taking place when an emotion occurs. In the philosophical literature on emotion, the term "cognitive" almost always refers to one of the following features: (1) high-level processing; (2) involvement of the

---

[5] See Robinson 2005, 41–47; Prinz 2004b, 52–78; and LeDoux 1996, 49–51. Robinson, Prinz, and LeDoux all argue on the basis of empirical data that appraisals can be noncognitive. However, it should be pointed out that appraisal theorists in psychology almost always consider appraisals to be cognitive. For an overview of appraisal theory, see Scherer 1999.

neocortex; (3) associated with problem solving, thought, or conceptualization; (4) more or less voluntary, and thus within our control. The term "noncognitive," on the other hand, almost always refers to a different set of features: (1) low-level processing; (2) subcortical (that is, does not involve the neocortex); (3) associated with reflexive responses and not with propositional thought or deliberation; (4) fast and immediate; (5) more or less involuntary, and thus minimally within our control, if at all.

It may appear to some that the problem of how to define emotion is not a genuine problem. In fact, it has been suggested in recent years that the cognitivists and the noncognitivists are not as far apart as they seem, especially now that they seem to have been influenced by one another's arguments. For example, many cognitivists now grant that emotions often have characteristic bodily states and feelings, and noncognitivists acknowledge that cognition can be an eliciting condition of emotion, or, in some cases, a stage in the unfolding of an emotion episode.

Nevertheless, I maintain that the differences between cognitivists and noncognitivists are substantial and that we should avoid collapsing the distinction between them. One view considers judgment to be a necessary condition of emotion; the other does not. One view considers physiological arousal and the perception of bodily changes to be necessary conditions of emotion; the other does not. These differences are not merely terminological, and they have real-world implications for how one conceives of virtue and its cultivation. How we conceptualize emotion will directly influence how we go about attempting to acquire virtue.

The ancients understood the extent to which one's theory of virtue depends on one's account of emotion, which is why we see a clear dividing line between the intellectualists and the anti-intellectualists on the issue of emotion. Socrates and the Stoics both have a monistic psychology in which emotion is not truly independent of reason and therefore is not an independent source of conduct. This psychology enables them to argue for intellectualism. If emotion poses no real challenge to reason, then knowledge of the good will be enough to ensure virtuous action. Cultivating virtue will be a process of cognitive therapy through which false beliefs are corrected and new knowledge is sought.

In contrast, Plato and Posidonius both consider the correction of false beliefs and increased understanding to be critical for virtue, but not sufficient for it. The reason for this is human nature. If emotion is fully independent of reason, as Plato and Posidonius claim, then it can cause us to go against our rational beliefs, performing actions we understand to be irrational or immoral. Thus, due to the nature of emotion as a psychologically distinct capacity, virtue requires not only the perfection of reason but also a distinctive type of emotional conditioning that will regulate emotions and train them to be aligned with reason. This training cannot be purely cognitive if it is to have any effect. It must operate at a noncognitive level as well.

The ancient debate is instructive because it reveals the stakes of the contemporary debate on how to classify emotion. If we get our descriptions and theories of emotion wrong, we will get our descriptions and theories of virtue wrong. Keeping that in mind, let us now turn to the major arguments of the cognitivists and the noncognitivists.

Robert Solomon and Martha Nussbaum are two of the most prominent cognitive theorists of emotion (see Solomon 1976, 2003, 2004, 2007; Nussbaum 1994, 2001, 2004). For decades Solomon has written about the importance of emotion, rejecting the longstanding view in the history of philosophy that characterizes emotions as largely unimportant and meaningless, or as fundamentally detrimental due to their interference with reason. Solomon defends emotion in part through his characterization of it as a type of judgment. Arguing against the traditional view, he insists that emotions are intelligent, purposive, and what give our lives meaning. Through emotion, we motivate, guide, and influence our own actions and attitudes and the actions and attitudes of others (2004, 2007). Emotions thus function as "strategies for getting along in the world."

Solomon supports these claims by arguing that emotions are constituted and structured by evaluative judgments, which are based on beliefs, which express attitudes, and for which we have reasons (2007, 206). We engage with the world through our emotions, and they "essentially involve the ability to conceptualize and evaluate" (2007, 204). Take anger, for example. Anger is the judgment that one has been wronged. This judgment is what makes anger what it is. Although Solomon acknowledges that it may typically be accompanied by certain physiological changes and sensations, he says that these are merely accidental features and are not part of anger's content. What is essential in anger, as in all emotions, is how one's thoughts and judgments engage the world (2004, 2007).[6]

Since Solomon defines emotions as intelligent and as structured by judgments, he is able to argue that we are responsible for our emotions and that they are susceptible to criticism. If a judgment can be right or wrong, and we are accountable for the judgments we make, then emotions can be right or wrong, and we are accountable for the emotions we experience. Moreover, insofar as we have control over our judgments, we have control over our emotions. We can choose our emotions by modifying our judgments. It may not always be easy to do this, but it is possible given the nature of emotion.

---

[6] Since Solomon first published his theory of emotion in the 1970s, a great deal of philosophical and empirical work has occurred. He has modified his view over the years; it was much stronger in his earlier work. He has taken empirical work and the work of his critics into account. Nevertheless, he still conceives of emotion as essentially constituted by judgments, though admittedly he now construes judgments more broadly than he once did.

Nussbaum holds a view of emotion very similar to Solomon's, though whereas Solomon's theory is inspired by Continental thinkers such as Jean-Paul Sartre, Nussbaum's is inspired by the Stoics, so much so that she describes it as neo-Stoic. Nussbaum's is one of the strongest versions of the cognitive theory; she claims that "emotions can be defined in terms of judgment alone" (2004, 196). More specifically, she argues that emotions are judgments about important things, or judgments of value (see also Nussbaum 1994, 2001).

According to Nussbaum, emotions are much like thoughts. They take intentional objects, and are an active way of seeing and interpreting these objects. They also embody beliefs about the intentional object—beliefs that are often highly complex (2004, 188). As for bodily changes and sensations, Nussbaum, like Solomon, denies that they play an essential role in emotion. Physiological changes and the perception of them may or may not occur during an emotion. Either way, such changes are neither necessary nor essential (2004, 195). Moreover, while it may be the case that emotions are usually accompanied by bodily sensations, nothing follows from this. If for some reason one experiences no bodily changes or sensations but makes the relevant sort of judgment, one will still be experiencing emotion, according to Nussbaum. This is the case because what constitutes emotion and is necessary for it are particular sorts of judgments about one's well-being (2004, 195). Thus, Nussbaum, like the Stoics, conceives of emotion as a function of reason (2004, 193).

Solomon and Nussbaum both intend to challenge the long-held view that reason alone is what makes us human and gives our lives meaning and that it is the only faculty we can trust. They are right to recognize the importance of emotion and to affirm it as meaningful, but in doing this they end up overintellectualizing it. In their attempts to find a place for emotion in a well-lived life, they transform it into a species of reason, arguing that characterizations of emotion as noncognitive render it primitive, unintelligent, and meaningless.

We need only accept this conclusion if it is impossible for noncognitive experiences to be meaningful and important. On the other hand, if it is possible for bodily feelings and patterns of bodily change to register information and communicate something about the world and our relationship to it, then emotion can be meaningful and significant without needing to be cognitive. Moreover, if one of our goals in theorizing emotion is a richer and more complex understanding of our psychology and how it works, then it makes little sense to explain emotion in terms of thoughts or judgments. What about emotional meaning will be emotional if emotions are reducible to judgments?

Recent noncognitive theories of emotion proposed by Jenefer Robinson (1995, 2004, 2005, forthcoming) and Jesse Prinz (2004a, 2004b, 2007) provide a more complex picture of human psychology, explaining what emotion is and how it works at both the personal and the subpersonal levels. Naturalist in approach, Robinson and Prinz construct their accounts of emotion on the basis of empirical research in neuroscience and psychology, focusing less on the analysis of concepts and intuitions than on developing the clearest and most precise model of emotion that the current empirical data will allow.[7]

Robinson's and Prinz's respective accounts are both inspired by the work of William James, who famously held that common sense about emotion gets it backwards. We do not cry because we are sad but are sad because we cry. James defines emotions as felt perceptions of bodily change, which help to prepare one to respond to the environment (1984). Like James, Robinson and Prinz emphasize the bodily dimensions of emotion. Appealing to empirical research, they maintain that the body can appraise situations and the environment on its own, in the absence of any judgment or thought.

This places Robinson and Prinz in direct opposition to the cognitivists. The heart of emotion on their view is an affective appraisal. As explained above, an affective appraisal involves a series of bodily changes that gauge how some stimulus or situation bears on the organism's well-being and prepare the organism to respond accordingly. No high-level cognitive activity is required. The appraisal is nonconceptual, which is to say that it is unmediated by judgment or thought.[8] Cognitive activity may occur prior to the affective appraisal and may be the stimulus that elicits the affective appraisal, but the appraisal itself is noncognitive. It is essential to point out that although the noncognitivists deny that emotion is a species of thought or reason, they do not deny that it is meaningful. Embodied appraisals have a meaning of their own, independent of the meaning bestowed by reason. They are *the body's way* of communicating how one is faring in relation to the world.

Robinson defines emotion first and foremost as a process—a complex and dynamic process which changes as it unfolds, at the center of which is an affective appraisal. Affective appraisals can occur in response both to simple stimuli to which we are predisposed to respond, such as loud and sudden sounds or slithery motion, and to more cognitively complex stimuli, such as judgments or inferences. However, as explained above, the appraisal itself, the sine qua non of the emotion, is itself noncognitive.

According to Robinson, affective appraisals are relatively coarse-grained. They respond to stimuli in a very basic way, registering a given stimulus as good or bad, or familiar or unfamiliar. The appraisal happens extremely quickly and does not require one to recognize or conceptualize

---

[7] Robinson and Prinz both draw on a wide range of empirical research, which I will not attempt to detail here. Some of the most critical data comes from the work of neuroscientists Joseph LeDoux (1996) and Antonio Damasio (1994, 1999, 2003); and psychologists Paul Ekman (1982, 2003) and Robert Zajonc (2000).

[8] Zajonc's experiments on affective priming, mere exposure effects, and subception (2000) and LeDoux's research on fear (1996) provide strong evidence for Robinson's and Prinz's conclusions about the independence of affect from cognition.

the stimulus that sets it off. It is a series of bodily changes that fixes one's attention and prepares the body to react appropriately to the environment. The feeling of these changes is how we experience the emotion.

Robinson does not deny that cognitive activity can be part of an emotion episode, but she says that if it is, it will occur either prior to the onset of the emotion or after the affective appraisal has already initiated the emotion episode. In the latter case, the cognitive activity is a type of cognitive monitoring or a cognitive reappraisal. Once the emotion process has been set off by an affective appraisal and one's attention is focused on the relevant stimulus, one is then in an emotional state. At that point, the individual can cognitively monitor or reappraise the situation, which usually results in either the minimizing or the intensifying of the emotional response.

Suppose, for example, that I have fallen asleep on my sofa and am abruptly awakened by a strange tapping sound. Immediately my body affectively appraises this stimulus, and I feel afraid. Now in a state of fear, I become hyper alert and strain to listen to the sound. When I hear it again, I realize that it is coming from the front door. It sounds as though someone is right outside, possibly attempting to get inside. These thoughts that occur to me are examples of cognitive monitoring.

Once I become afraid, my emotion fixes my attention on the sound, the source of my fear, which I then try to figure out. When I realize that the sound is coming from my front door and that it could be someone trying to get inside, I cognitively monitor the stimulus. This cognitive reappraisal leads to an increase in my fear. I am now wide awake, my heart pounding in my chest. I continue to listen for the sound, as I contemplate how I will escape and wonder why my dogs are not barking. In my alert state, I notice the sound of the wind picking up. The strange sound outside the door gets louder as the wind blows. Afraid to move, I continue to listen to the sound and then notice that I only hear it when the wind is blowing. I conclude that it is more likely that the wind is blowing something against the door than that a crazed maniac is trying to break in. This would explain why the sound changes with the wind and why my dogs are unconcerned. After reaching this conclusion, my heart rate begins to return to normal, and my feelings of fear begin to subside.

This description shows how Robinson's theory allows for cognitive activity during emotion episodes. In the scenario, I attempted to determine the source of the strange tapping sound, I considered the possibility that it was coming from a crazed maniac trying to break into my house, I contemplated how I would escape, I questioned why my dogs were not barking at the sound, I realized that the sound occurred when the wind was blowing, and so on. In short, I did a lot of cognitive monitoring and cognitive reappraising of the sound and the situation. However, this cognitive monitoring was not necessary for me to experience emotion, and it only began after my initial affective appraisal put me into a state of fear. The identical cognitive activity would not be part of an emotion had I not made the initial affective appraisal. This is a key point. The affective appraisal is what makes the experience an emotion. Without it, there is no emotion. Robinson's view is the converse of Solomon's and Nussbaum's. For Robinson, cognitive activity may be part of an emotion episode and may play a role in how we label emotion, but it is nonessential.

Like Robinson, Prinz rejects the cognitive theory of emotion. He makes no room for cognitive activity as part of the emotion proper. Cognitive activity may cause an emotion, but when it does, it occurs prior to the emotion; it is not a constitutive element. Prinz defines emotions as embodied appraisals. They are somatic signals that represent concerns, but without being conceptual, propositional, or cognitive. They are less like concepts than like percepts. In fact, Prinz often describes emotion as a form of perception that represents how some stimulus or event matters to the organism.

How is it possible for emotions to represent our concerns if they are noncognitive? Take fear, for example, which is said to represent danger. How can a noncognitive state represent danger? Because fear has the function of representing or detecting danger. In other words, it was evolutionarily selected for to detect danger, because fear increased the fitness of those who experienced it. Although fear evolved to be set off by danger, it does not *describe* danger. Drawing on Fred Dretske's notion of representation, Prinz explains that fear represents danger in the same way that the beeping of a smoke alarm represents smoke. The smoke alarm was designed to beep when smoke is present, and yet the beeping does not describe smoke. Still, representing or detecting smoke is what the alarm does, which is why it can represent without describing (Prinz 2007, 60–64; 2004, 52–60).

Embodied appraisals represent concerns nonconceptually and noncognitively. In the case of fear, embodied appraisals can be triggered by several different stimuli: a loud noise, the sight of a snake or spider, the judgment that one is in danger. Prinz calls the stimulus, which may be cognitive or noncognitive, a calibration file; it calibrates fear to danger, but the calibration file is not part of the emotion itself. It is an eliciting condition that occurs before the emotion. In order to get the emotion of fear, there must be (1) an embodied appraisal, which represents the stimulus as dangerous through bodily changes, and (2) the perception of those changes, which is what we feel as fear.

The appraisal's bodily registration of concern can take place extremely quickly, before one has time to fully process a given stimulus. Thus, if one encounters a coiled snake, it can trigger a fear response before any judgment, even a perceptual one, is made. Not all emotions will be triggered in such an immediate way, but the fact that they can, means it is possible for us to experience emotions in the absence of any thought or judgment whatsoever, not even as a cause.

3. Emotional Contagion and Mirroring Processes

There is an additional line of evidence that seems to support a non-cognitive theory of emotion that so far has not been brought to bear on the debate: the data on emotional contagion, mirroring processes, and mirror neurons.[9] Emotional contagion is defined by psychologists Elaine Hatfield, John Cacioppo, and Richard Rapson as the "tendency to automatically mimic and synchronize expressions, vocalizations, postures, and movements with those of another person, and, consequently, to converge emotionally" (Hatfield et al. 1992, 153–54). As Stephen Davies explains, this "involves the transmission from A to B of a given affect such that B's affect is the same as A's but does not take A's state or any other thing as its emotional object" (forthcoming). Contagion happens extremely quickly and is typically below the threshold of awareness. The main processes involved in it are motor mimicry and the activation and feedback from mimicry, all of which are automatic and involuntary.[10]

Emotional contagion is not a higher-order cognitive process, which explains why we see it occur in numerous species, most of which are not thought to possess the capacity for self-knowledge. Stephanie Preston and Frans de Waal hypothesize that emotional contagion developed before more complex emotional processes such as empathy, and involves fast and reflexive subcortical processes that go directly from sensory cortices to thalamus to amygdala to response (Preston and de Waal 2002). The research on emotional contagion shows that due to our hardwired ability to "catch" one another's emotions, our emotional experiences can be directly and immediately affected by others' emotions and need not depend on any conscious evaluation or interpretation of the other's emotions or external events. This is highly significant for the theory of emotion debate, as it provides clear and robust evidence of emotions occurring through automatic, unconscious processes.

Related to the work on emotional contagion is a new and growing body of research on mirror neurons and mirroring processes. This research provides additional evidence for a noncognitive theory of emotion. Discovered in the early 1990s, mirror neurons are a special class of neurons that fire both when we observe another performing an action and when we perform the action ourselves. They are a mechanism for shared experience through which the mere perception of another's experience activates the same experience in an observer.

---

[9] An important exception is a forthcoming paper by Stephen Davies on emotional contagion and music entitled "Infectious Music: Music Listener Emotional Contagion." In the paper, Davies discusses the research on emotional contagion, provides a revised definition of it, and briefly argues that it raises problems for the cognitive theory of emotion.

[10] See Dimberg 1988, 1990; Adelman and Zajonc 1989; Levenson, Ekman, and Friesen 1990; Bavelas et al. 1987; and Hatfield et al. 1994, 53–62.

The early work on mirror neurons concentrated on motor action, but clinical data and brain imaging studies now indicate that there is a mirror system for emotion as well.[11] The strongest evidence is for fear and disgust, and it indicates that there is a common neural substrate for the experience and the perception of these emotions. Neuroscientist Marco Iacoboni explains how the emotional mirror system works:

> Mirror neurons provide an unreflective, automatic simulation (or "inner imitation," as I have sometimes called it) of the facial expressions of other people, and this process of simulation does not require explicit, deliberate recognition of the expression mimicked. Simultaneously, mirror neurons send signals to the emotional centers located in the limbic system of the brain. The neural activity in the limbic system triggered by these signals from mirror neurons allows us to feel the emotions associated with the observed facial expressions—the happiness associated with a smile, the sadness associated with a frown. (2008, 111–12)

In this passage, Iacoboni describes how the mirror system allows us effortlessly and automatically to code sensory information in directly emotional terms.

This research has significant implications for the debate between cognitivists and noncognitivists. It reveals how and why it is possible for us to have emotions purely as a result of perceiving another person having emotions. There can be little doubt that emotion generated by mirroring or emotional contagion is an "outside-in" process. Upon witnessing another person expressing an emotion, we automatically, involuntarily, and prereflectively mirror that emotion. It follows that at least some of the time we do not choose our emotions through our thoughts, judgments, or beliefs; our emotions do not reflect our personal values, commitments, and goals; and we can go from not experiencing an emotion to experiencing one without any cognitive activity.

4. Why Do Definitions Matter?

In the third section of this chapter I argued for a noncognitive theory of emotion, such as the ones proposed by Robinson and Prinz. But why does it really matter how we categorize emotions? Why should we not simply say that cognitive emotions are one thing, and noncognitive emotions another? Drawing the line this way will not settle the debate and will leave us with problems. First, the cognitive theory is misleading. It over-intellectualizes emotion and emotional experience, and, as is clear from the ancient debate over intellectualism, this has consequences for how one constructs a moral theory, including one's strategies for developing virtue. Second, even if we were to distinguish emotions triggered by judgments from those that occur as an immediate response to some

---

[11] See Iacoboni 2008; Goldman 2006; and Rizzolatti and Sinigaglia 2007.

sensory stimulus, the purely noncognitive emotions would still warrant serious attention. It would not do to characterize them as bodily reflexes and leave them out of our moral theorizing.

Purely noncognitive emotions influence our thinking, our behavior, and our social and moral lives.[12] Thus moral theorists must address them, and must treat them both as genuine emotions and as noncognitive. Being noncognitive does not make emotions meaningless or unimportant. On the contrary, it suggests that they have a distinctive meaning that is tied to bodily experience and is irreducible to judgments or thoughts.

In all likelihood, classifying the purely noncognitive emotions as something other than emotion would lead philosophers to continue to ignore them, concentrating on reason alone, since they could argue that genuine emotions are susceptible to rational argument. They could defend intellectualism since knowledge would be enough to control their emotions and thus sufficient for virtue.

I suspect that cognitive theories have been motivated, at least in part, by philosophers' desire to conceive of emotions as something completely within our control and something more mental than bodily. Peter Goldie (2000) says that philosophers have attempted to force emotion into the mold of rationalizing explanations when the best that we can hope for is to make them intelligible. To the cognitivists' credit, they take emotion seriously and acknowledge its importance. Yet to do this, they turn it into a species of reason. If emotion is a species of reason, then it poses no threat to our idea of ourselves as rational and reflective beings who deliberately and consciously choose what to think, what to respond to, and what to value.

This is the promise of Stoic intellectualism. If knowledge is sufficient for virtue and nothing in the outside world counts as a genuine evil, then one can insulate oneself from suffering and vice through the pursuit of knowledge and the elimination of false beliefs. So, provided our judgments are correct, emotion will not interfere with our rational goals and pursuits. We will have self-control and self-sufficiency. We will be the sole determiners of our happiness, not subject to irrational forces and unexpected events in the outside world or to the emotions of those around us.

It is understandable that philosophers would aspire to this. Self-sufficiency and self-control are both highly appealing. Yet once we appreciate the nature of emotion, it becomes obvious that this sort of control is impossible for creatures that are social and embodied, as we are. Ironically, understanding the extent to which we lack full control of our emotions will give us greater control of them than we would have if

---

[12] For discussion of the ways in which noncognitive affect influences cognition, including memory, attention, and cognitive flexibility, see Davidson 1994; Blascovich and Mendes 2000; and Leary 2000.

we accepted the inaccurate cognitive model, because it will enable us to employ appropriate strategies for dealing with them. Plato and Posidonius understood this, which is why they insisted that knowledge is not sufficient for virtue and that, since emotions and desires are sometimes impervious to reason, moral education must include more than learning what is right and wrong. It must include the training and habituation of our emotions so that they can be conditioned, through practice and experience, to track the appropriate things. Our education, including the stories we are told and the music we listen to, our environment, and the company we keep all matter greatly, according to Plato and Posidonius, since they can prevent or encourage virtue.

If we have any hope of figuring out how to theorize about moral psychology and how to cultivate virtue, we must take more seriously the facts of our embodiedness and sociality, and come to terms with the ways in which our sensory experiences and social interactions influence our emotions, and thus our behavior, our thoughts, and our values. Although we should never give up on the pursuit of knowledge, it is time to face the fact that knowledge is not enough to make us virtuous, that intellectualism is an illusion, and that we do not have full control over our emotions.

References

Adelman, Pamela K., and R. B. Zajonc. 1989. "Facial Efference and the Experience of Emotion." *Annual Review of Psychology* 40:249–80.
Annas, Julia. 1992. *Hellenistic Philosophy of Mind*. Berkeley: University of California Press.
Bavelas, Janet Beavin, et al. 1987. "Motor Mimicry as Primitive Empathy." In *Empathy and Its Development*, edited by Nancy Eisenberg and Janet Strayer, 317–38. Cambridge: Cambridge University Press.
Blascovich, Jim, and Wendy Berry Mendes. 2000. "Challenge and Threat Appraisals: The Role of Affective Cues." In *Feeling and Thinking: The Role of Affect in Social Cognition*, edited by Joseph P. Forgas, 59–82. Cambridge: Cambridge University Press.
Brown, Eric. 2006. "Socrates in the Stoa." In *A Companion to Socrates*, edited by Sara Ahbel-Rappe and Rachana Kamtekar, 275–84. Malden, Mass.: Blackwell.
Cooper, John M. 1999. *Reason and Emotion: Essays on Ancient Moral Psychology and Ethical Theory*. Princeton: Princeton University Press.
Damasio, Antonio R. 1994. *Descartes' Error: Emotion, Reason, and the Human Brain*. New York: G. P. Putnam.
———. 1999. *The Feeling of What Happens: Body and Emotion in the Making of Consciousness*. New York: Harcourt Brace.
———. 2003. *Looking for Spinoza: Joy, Sorrow, and the Feeling Brain*. New York: Harcourt, Brace.

Davidson, Richard J. 1994. "On Emotion, Mood, and Related Affective Constructs." In *The Nature of Emotion: Fundamental Questions*, edited by Paul Ekman and Richard J. Davidson, 51–55. New York: Oxford University Press.

Davies, Stephen. Forthcoming. Infectious Music: Music Listener Emotional Contagion." In *Empathy: Philosophical and Psychological Perspectives*, edited by Amy Coplan and Peter Goldie. Oxford: Oxford University Press.

Debes, Remy. 2009. "Neither Here Nor There: The Cognitive Nature of Emotion." *Philosophical Studies* 146, no. 1:1–27.

Dimberg, Ulf. 1990. "Facial Electromyographic Reactions and Autonomic Activity to Auditory Stimuli." *Biological Psychology* 31, no. 2:137–47.

———. 1988. "Facial Electromyography and the Experience of Emotion." *Journal of Psychophysiology* 2, no. 4:277–82.

Edelstein, Ludwig. 1936. "The Philosophical System of Posidonius." *American Journal of Philology* 57, no. 3:286–325.

———. 1966. *The Meaning of Stoicism*. Cambridge, Mass.: Harvard University Press.

Ekman, Paul. 1982. *Emotion in the Human Face*. Cambridge: Cambridge University Press.

———. 2003. *Emotions Revealed: Recognizing Faces and Feelings to Improve Communication and Emotional Life*. New York: Times Books.

Galen. 1981. *On the Doctrines of Hippocrates and Plato*, edited and translated by Phillip De Lacy. 2nd ed. Corpus Medicorum Graecorum 5.4, 1–2. Berlin: Akademie-Verlag.

Gill, Christopher. 1998. "Did Galen Understand Platonic and Stoic Thinking on Emotions?" In *The Emotions in Hellenistic Philosophy*, edited by Juha Sihvola and Troels Engberg-Pedersen, 113–48. Dordrecht: Kluwer.

Goldie, Peter. 2000. *The Emotions: A Philosophical Exploration*. Oxford: Oxford University Press.

Goldman, Alvin I. 2006. *Simulating Minds: The Philosophy, Psychology, and Neuroscience of Mindreading*. Oxford: Oxford University Press.

Griffiths, Paul E. 1997. *What Emotions Really Are: The Problem of Psychological Categories*. Science and Its Conceptual Foundations series. Chicago: University of Chicago Press.

Hatfield, Elaine, John T. Cacioppo, and Richard L. Rapson. 1994. *Emotional Contagion*. Cambridge: Cambridge University Press.

Iacoboni, Marco. 2008. *Mirroring People: The New Science of How We Connect with Others*. New York: Farrar, Straus and Giroux.

James, William. 2003. "What Is Emotion?" In *What Is an Emotion?: Classic and Contemporary Readings*, second edition, edited by Robert C. Solomon, 65–76. New York: Oxford University Press.

Kidd, I. G. 1971. "Posidonius on Emotion." In *Problems in Stoicism*, edited by A. A. Long, 200–15. London: Athlone Press.

———, ed. 1988. *Posidonius*, volume 2, *The Commentary*. Cambridge: Cambridge University Press.

Leary, Mark R. 2000. "Affect, Cognition, and the Social Emotions." In *Feeling and Thinking: The Role of Affect in Social Cognition*, edited by Joseph P. Forgas, 331–56. Cambridge: Cambridge University Press.

LeDoux, Joseph E. 1996. *The Emotional Brain: The Mysterious Underpinnings of Emotional Life*. New York: Simon and Schuster.

Levenson, Robert W., Paul Ekman, and Wallace V. Friesen. 1990. "Voluntary Facial Action Generates Emotion-Specific Autonomic Nervous System Activity." *Psychophysiology* 27, no. 4:363–84.

Long, A. A. 1986. *Hellenistic Philosophy: Stoics, Epicureans, Sceptics*. Second edition. Berkeley: University of California Press.

Nussbaum, Martha. 1994. *The Therapy of Desire: Theory and Practice in Hellenistic Ethics*. Princeton: Princeton University Press.

———. 2001. *Upheavals of Thought: The Intelligence of Emotions*. Cambridge: Cambridge University Press.

———. 2004. "Emotions as Judgments of Value and Importance." In *Thinking About Feeling: Contemporary Philosophers on Emotions*, edited by Robert C. Solomon, 183–99. New York: Oxford University Press.

Plato. 1997a. *Apology*. Translated by G. M. A. Grube. In *Complete Works*, edited by John M. Cooper and D. S. Hutchinson. Indianapolis: Hackett.

———. 1997b. *Protagoras*. Translated by Stanley Lombardo and Karen Bell. In *Complete Works*, edited by John M. Cooper and D. S. Hutchinson. Indianapolis: Hackett.

Preston, Stephane D., and Frans B. M. de Waal. 2002. "Empathy: Its Ultimate and Proximate Bases." *Behavioral and Brain Sciences* 25, no. 1:1–20.

Prinz, Jesse. 2004a. "Embodied Emotions." In *Thinking About Feeling: Contemporary Philosophers on Emotions*, edited by Robert C. Solomon, 44–58. New York: Oxford University Press.

———. 2004b. *Gut Reactions: A Perceptual Theory of Emotion*. New York: Oxford University Press.

———. 2007. *The Emotional Construction of Morals*. Oxford: Oxford University Press.

Rizzolatti, Giacomo, and Corrado Sinigaglia. 2007. *Mirrors in the Brain: How Our Minds Share Actions, Emotions, and Experience*. Translated by Frances Anderson. New York: Oxford University Press.

Robinson, Jenefer. 1995. "Startle." *Journal of Philosophy* 92, no. 2: 53–74.

———. 2004. "Emotion: Biological Fact or Social Construction?" In *Thinking About Feeling: Contemporary Philosophers on Emotions*, edited by Robert C. Solomon, 28–43. New York: Oxford University Press.

———. 2005. *Deeper Than Reason: Emotion and Its Role in Literature, Music, and Art*. Oxford: Clarendon Press.

———. Forthcoming. "Emotion." In *The Handbook of Philosophy of Psychology*, edited by Jesse Prinz. Oxford: Oxford University Press.

Scherer, Klaus R. 1999. "Appraisal Theory." In *Handbook of Cognition and Emotion*, edited by Tim Dalgleish and Mick J. Power, 637–63. New York: John Wiley and Sons.

Schofield, Malcolm. 1984. "Ariston of Chios and the Unity of Virtue." *Ancient Philosophy* 4:83–96.

Seneca. 1969. *Letters from a Stoic*. Translated by Robin Campbell. London: Penguin.

Solomon, Robert C. 1976. *The Passions*. Garden City, N.Y.: Anchor Press/Doubleday.

———. 2003. *Not Passion's Slave: Emotions and Choice*. New York: Oxford University Press.

———. 2004. "Emotions, Thoughts, and Feelings: Emotions as Engagements with the World." In *Thinking About Feeling: Contemporary Philosophers on Emotions*, edited by Robert C. Solomon, 76–88. New York: Oxford University Press.

———. 2007. *True to Our Feelings: What Our Emotions Are Really Telling Us*. New York: Oxford University Press.

Sorabji, Richard. 2000. *Emotion and Peace of Mind: From Stoic Agitation to Christian Temptation*. Oxford: Oxford University Press.

Vlastos, Gregory. 1957. "Socratic Knowledge and Platonic Pessimism." *Philosophical Review* 66, no. 2:226–38.

Zajonc, Robert B. 2000. "Feeling and Thinking: Closing the Debate over the Independence of Affect." In *Feeling and Thinking: The Role of Affect in Social Cognition*, edited by Joseph P. Forgas, 31–58. Cambridge: Cambridge University Press.

9

A CHALLENGE TO INTELLECTUAL VIRTUE
FROM MORAL VIRTUE:
THE CASE OF UNIVERSAL LOVE

CHRISTINE SWANTON

1. Introduction

On the Aristotelian picture of virtue, moral virtue has at its core intellectual virtue in the form of practical wisdom. Unlike some, such as Julia Driver (2001), I agree with this view of virtue. But an interesting challenge to the Aristotelian orthodoxy is provided by the case of universal love and its associated virtues, such as the disposition to exhibit grace, to forgive, and to be merciful, where appropriate.

I shall not in this chapter answer this challenge by showing that universal love can be a virtue in so far as it has practical wisdom, since the concept of practical wisdom itself is extremely complex and would require a full chapter for its analysis. Rather, I shall argue that certain problems in understanding universal love as rational can be overcome. Overcoming these problems is a necessary condition of conceiving universal love as capable of exhibiting practical wisdom and as being a virtue in an Aristotelian sense.

What, then, is universal love? Understood as a virtue, universal love can be thought of as a virtue described at a high level of abstraction, by contrast with associated more specific virtues of universal love, such as grace, human kindness, benevolence, and forgiveness. As a virtue, universal love is constituted by a preparedness to be, for example, beneficent, gracious, forgiving, merciful to *anyone* where appropriate, and a manifesting of that preparedness to assignable individuals, as appropriate. That preparedness, and its manifestation where appropriate, is not to be withdrawn on the basis of lack of virtue or other merits in the object of love, the unattractiveness of the object, or lack of affection for the object.

Here in broad outline is the problem discussed in this chapter. It may be difficult to find a property in the object of such love, in virtue of which the grace, forgiveness, or mercy, for example, ought to be bestowed. Where a disposition to forgive, for example, is said to be a virtue of universal love, it may arguably be virtuously manifested even where the person forgiven has not shown remorse for wrongs done.[1] She need not merit the forgiveness. Indeed, it may be thought that universal love, far from exhibiting practical wisdom, exhibits a vice of excess because it does not discriminate between those who merit love and those who do not. In reply, it is claimed that universal love is not a merit-based form of love, and indeed is a different form of love from partialistic forms of love such as friendship, as I indicate below (see Lewis 1977). It may be thought, however, that people merit the forgiveness founded on universal love, for example, by their possession of universal properties such as humanity or dignity. Yet, as Gregory Vlastos has shown in his distinction between merit and worth, these are not merit-conferring properties.[2] Finally, forgiveness and grace may be rationalized by their being good for the agent, but this seems to locate the reason (or the principal reason) for the grace or forgiveness in the wrong place. It is still unclear, then, *for what reasons* we should bestow universal love.

Perhaps love in general, including universal love, is not necessarily exhibited *for reasons*. This is the view I shall defend. The problem is to show how, despite this, the manifestation of universal love in the specific (putative) virtues of universal love can nonetheless be seen as rational. Showing this is the task of the chapter. As I stated earlier, I do not complete the larger task of showing exactly how universal love can be understood as practically wise and as a virtue.

Many actions, expressive of love, such as ruffling one's son's hair out of affection, do not seem to be done for a reason. To say that there is no reason for, say, the dispensing of grace on an occasion could in one sense of "for a reason" mean:

(a) There is no intention with which the grace is dispensed.

As Rosalind Hursthouse (1991) puts it, there is no "desired upshot" of the behavior. In short, in this kind of case an agent's actions are not done for *that agent's* reasons. Following Hursthouse, I call actions without reasons in this sense "arational."

Perhaps, however, there is a reason for such an action even if it is not the agent's reason. Such a reason is a normative reason: a reason that provides a justification for the agent's action. Such a reason makes the action fitting in some way: it justifies the action as permitted, required,

---

[1] This view is by no means uncontroversial: Charles Griswold (2007), for example, believes that forgiveness, though a virtue, requires for its manifestation, at least in its best form, an interdependence between the forgiver and the one forgiven, such that the latter as well as the former are transformed in some way.

[2] Vlastos showed this a long time ago in a classic paper (Vlastos 1962). However, even if such factors as human worth and dignity are not merit conferring, some, such as Eve Garrard (2002), claim that "common human nature" provides a "weak reason" for forgiveness.

appropriate, desirable, admirable, and so forth. To say that an action is not done for a reason in this sense is to say that there is no (normative) reason for it. To say that there is no reason for, say, the dispensing of grace on a particular occasion in this sense would mean:

> (b) There is no *reason* which would justify the action as fitting in some way.

I call actions without reasons in this (second) sense "reasonless." A basic notion of a reason in this normative sense is Jonathan Dancy's concept of a contributory reason. This is the notion to be employed in this chapter. Dancy defines "contributory reason" as follows: "A contributory reason for action is a feature whose presence makes something of a case for acting, but in such a way that the overall case for doing that action can be improved or strengthened by the addition of a second feature playing a similar role" (2004, 15).[3]

I shall argue that:

> (a) Acts of grace, for example, may be *expressions* of love, and as such may be arational in Hursthouse's sense, but nonetheless rational.
>
> (b) Acts of grace may be reasonless in Dancy's sense, but nonetheless rational.

To show that universal love in its various manifestations may be rational even if arational and reasonless, I first need to show what it is and how it is possible. That is the task of the next two sections. Section 4 introduces the notion of grace, which is then used for illustrative purposes in the remainder of the chapter. Section 5 shows how grace can be rational while being arational in Hursthouse's sense, while section 6 shows how grace can be rational while being reasonless.

2. The Possibility of Universal Love

The notion of universal love has been thought incoherent precisely because (it is thought) it cannot possess both of the following features attributed to universal love. These features are:

> (a) It is not love of humanity as such but love of *particular* individuals in their particularity.
>
> (b) It is *universal* love, by contrast with the partialistic affections of friendship, romantic love, love of one's own children, and so on.

The combination of universality and particularity has not been thought problematic for universal respect, but it has rendered the ideal of

---

[3] Contributory reasons are thus features in the world, such as the fact that a book was borrowed is a contributory reason for returning it to its owner.

universal love suspect. Kant's distinction between love and respect illustrates the problem (see Kant 1996; see further Swanton 2003). For Kant, respect fundamentally is keeping one's distance, whereas love is at its heart forms of "coming close." Given that we are not talking about a generalized love of humanity when speaking of universal love, as (a) claims, it would seem impossible for love to be both a coming close and universal. Universal love, like universal respect, is owed to all human beings merely as humans, but universal respect merely demands that we keep our distance. We can satisfy this demand in the case of each and every individual by our refraining from actions that violate dignity. But how can one come close to each and every individual? Furthermore, it may be thought, love cannot be both particular and universal since love of individuals is surely partialistic. By its very nature it involves favouring certain people.

To resolve these problems, it is necessary to understand the way that universal love is universal and particular, in both a formal and a substantive sense. Formally, universal love as a virtue is universal in the sense that it is a *preparedness* to come close (on Kant's analysis) to *any* individual regardless of personal relations, merits, and so forth; and it is particular in that it requires (on Kant's view, for example) an actual coming close in ways that are appropriate to circumstances and opportunity. Also, the virtue of universal love (unlike other forms of love, such as friendship, romantic love, love of close blood relatives) is impartial in the sense that it is not withdrawn or withheld on the basis of the absence of partialistic relation. For example, if an enemy or a criminal lies bleeding at one's doorstep, a virtue of universal love (basic human kindness or charity) requires that one come to his aid and not, out of malice, hatred, indifference, or callousness, leave him there bleeding.

In the next section I make substantive sense of the notion of universal love by distinguishing between love as a relation between individuals and "lovingness" as a basic emotional attunement to the world at large. As we have seen, the virtue of universal love is a *preparedness* to manifest love towards *any* human individual regardless of attractiveness, merits, and so forth, and is expressed by actual manifestations where appropriate. But what is the nature of the preparedness? Employing Heidegger's notion of a *Grundstimmung* (fundamental attunement or "mood"), I shall claim that the preparedness is an emotional orientation to the world at large. This I shall call a "totalizing" attunement of *lovingness* (the Grundstimmung of lovingness). The attunement of lovingness is manifested in action through the operation of the *virtues* of universal love, such as grace, benevolence expressive of lovingness, and dispositions to be forgiving and merciful. Thus, at the emotional core of such virtues is the attunement of lovingness.

In more detail, I ask: How can we deploy Heidegger's notion of attunement to solve in a substantive way the problem of alleged incoherence in the idea of universal love? My answer can be summarized as follows.

(1) The "preparedness" constituting the virtue of universal love is a background *emotional* orientation or attunement to the world *as a whole*. On this account one can forgive in perhaps a formal way, without that forgiveness being an expression of universal love. Similarly, one can be beneficent to a stranger without that beneficence being an expression of universal love.

(2) One might describe such an emotional orientation as being open to the world at large, and being close, or coming close to it (in Kant's words), or to "uniting" with it (in Hume's words). More specifically, lovingness is an emotional *closeness*, in an *open* way, to the world at large. (Contrast pathological fear, shyness, selfishness, and profound boredom, which inhibit the coming close; and totalizing hate and anger, which inhibit the open-ness). I shall not have space in this chapter to discuss the properties of coming close and openness.

(3) Lovingness as a general emotional orientation has several forms, notably benevolence as a general desire for another's good (Hume), or a disposition to make others' non-immoral ends one's own (Kant); hope as a disposition to be open to the future and to come close to it by not seeing it as persecutory or to be feared; wonder as a disposition to be open to the wonders of nature and to come close to nature (though in a respectful way); joy as a disposition to take delight in the world and what it has to offer.

(4) Of most relevance to the general virtue of *universal* love as *agape* or *caritas* is a totalizing attunement of benevolence. However, since the virtue of universal love *as manifested* is a relationship between assignable individuals, the Grundstimmung of benevolence cannot be *actually expressed* to *all* individuals. As is the case with virtue in general, where it is not expressed universal love is constituted by a preparedness only. One might even think of such a situation as analogous to Hume's "virtue in rags" being still virtue, except that the impossibility of expressing universal love to all is constituted by our finitude.

(5) The background "totalizing" orientation of benevolence in a more or less developed form is at the core of the various more specific virtues of universal love that give content to the idea of a preparedness to express forms of universal love to individuals.[4]

---

[4] The qualification "more or less developed form" is meant to indicate a conception of virtue that is a threshold concept, and thus non-ideal. Otherwise, on certain theological views, even Jesus may fail to possess virtues of universal love, given that he was less than perfect in this area on occasion.

(6) Universal love is appropriately manifested or expressed if one or other of the virtues of universal love is manifested, for example, grace, forgiveness, mercy, and what Hume calls general benevolence.

3. Lovingness and Heidegger's Notion of a Grundstimmung

To understand the conception of the virtue of universal love just outlined, we need to explain Heidegger's notion of a fundamental emotional attunement, and apply it to the notion of lovingness. This is the task of the present section.

A fundamental emotional attunement, or Grundstimmung, has several basic features.

(a) A Grundstimmung is an *emotional* orientation to the world. According to Heidegger, the world is made meaningful or significant by, inter alia, *emotional* attunements, though this investing with significance is not planful, or even self-conscious. There are many types of attunement shaping our perspective on the world: "Attunements—joy, contentment, bliss, sadness, melancholy, anger—are after all something psychological, or better, psychic; they are emotional states" (Heidegger 1995, 64).

(b) A Grundstimmung is an occurrent emotional state: a kind of mood. Indeed, "Grundstimmung" is often translated as "mood." Though occurrent, it can have different emotional qualities and intensities at different times, ranging from what Daniel Goleman calls an emotional "hum"[5] to what Heidegger calls "irruptions," which may be intense and overwhelming. The background attunement of lovingness, for example, is capable of "irrupting" in intense emotion resulting in grace, forgiveness, unexpected kindness, and so on. A background attunement can manifest itself suddenly in an overpowering way; it can "occur out of the blue" and "precisely whenever we do not expect it at all"; "it irrupts" (Heidegger 1995, 135). Such "irruptions" of an emotional attunement, says Heidegger, are not things one can simply undertake, like "picking a flower" (1995, 69), but that is not to say we have no control of these manifestations at all.

(c) A Grundstimmung is pervasive. Unlike some attunements, which may be "like the utterly fleeting and ungraspable shadows of clouds flitting across the landscape" (Heidegger 1995, 64), a

---

[5] For example, Goleman talks of "a steady hum of anxiety" (2004, 65). Like Heidegger, Goleman claims that we are always in some mood or other; there is a "constant emotional hum" (57).

fundamental attunement "pervades" us (Heidegger 1995, 69). The notion of pervasiveness suggests that the attunement is not a mere disposition that is activated when appropriate, it is not only an occurrent but also an enduring or relatively enduring emotional state. As stated above, however, it need not endure in an intense way but rather persist as an emotional hum in, for example, a state of background anxiety or fear, a loving peaceable attitude towards the world, a dull sadness left over from grief perhaps, and so on.

There is, however, a question about how "pervasive" is "pervasive." Should a virtue of universal love as an excellence proper to human nature allow for uncharacteristic moments where hate, anger, hostility, drive out the background attunement of lovingness?[6] In this case, lovingness would be analogous to a match which has the disposition to strike when struck, but which will not manifest this disposition when, uncharacteristically, it has become wet. In reply to this problem, two things should be noted. (i) On the classic conception of universal love, anger at the sin should not drive out the attunement of lovingness and thus a preparedness towards, for example, loving-kindness towards a particular wrongdoer. (ii) It may be necessary in the human being to experience attunements driving out lovingness on the way to full virtue, if we are to understand the nature of love. This is not, however, to say that, if or when virtue as a *perfection* is attained, lovingness is not pervasive in the sense of omnipresent. Nor is it to say that virtue as a perfection is even attainable by human beings. Indeed, we may lower our sights for what counts as virtue, understanding it as a threshold concept, as I do.[7]

(d) A Grundstimmung is a *Grund*stimmung; that is, it structures our orientation to the world. It does not just colour it; it determines in quite fundamental ways the way we see things. Consider the following passage in Heidegger: "[A]nger ... 'blows over' as we say. Hate does not. Once it germinates, it grows and solidifies, eating its way inward and consuming our very being. But the permanent cohesion that comes to human existence through hate does not close it off and bind it. Rather, it makes us perceptive [*sehend*] and deliberative [*überlegend*]. The angry man loses the power of reflection. He who hates

---

[6] I thank my student Robert Hulse for drawing my attention to this issue, particularly in relation to Heidegger.

[7] On this conception, less than ideal states may count as virtues, though where the threshold is set in relation to various aspects of virtue will vary according to context, and may well be quite vague.

increases refection and deliberation to the point of 'hard-boiled' malice. Hate is never blind: it is perspicacious [*hellsichtig*]. Only anger is blind. Love is never blind: it is perspicacious. Only infatuation is blind, fickle and susceptible—an affect not a passion. To passion belongs a reaching out and an opening up of oneself. . . . Passion: the perspicacious gathering grip [*der hellsichtig sammelnde Ausgriff*] on beings."[8] For Heidegger, then, hate and love, unlike anger and infatuation, are *Grundstimmungen* in the above sense.

(e) A Grundstimmung may structure our view of the world in a way that is relatively deep or profound, relatively superficial, or in a way that is more seriously distorting.[9] In Heidegger's terms, an attunement can "disclose" the world more richly or less richly (or radiantly, as Heidegger sometimes puts it). There are two ways in which an attunement can be deep for Heidegger. The first is indirect. Some attunements may characteristically close off or dim down a potentially rich disclosure of reality, such as profound boredom or crippling angst, were they to endure for a long time in an intense way. However, if such an attunement assails us at certain times, it may provide for what Heidegger calls "moments of vision" allowing us to adopt a deeper orientation to the world. The second way in which an attunement can be deep is direct. As we have noted, a *Grund*stimmung is a kind of attunement that structures our orientation to the world in a stable and enduring manner. It may thereby directly facilitate a rich disclosure of the world. Such an attunement may be lovingness, as opposed to profound boredom.

(f) A Grundstimmung is "totalizing." That is to say, it organizes our orientation to the world so that the world *as a whole* is made meaningful, in one or other of its aspects. Following David Weberman (1996), I shall call such an attunement "totalizing." Weberman puts the point this way: "For Heidegger . . . moods [*Grundstimmungen*] are intentional, but rather than not being about anything in particular, they are in a sense about *everything*" (1996, 386). What counts as the "world as a whole" is contextual. For example, wonder may be a disposition directed at nature in general—indeed, the universe; hopefulness to the future as such; benevolence to all beings having a good.

---

[8] Heidegger, *Nietzsche*, vols. 1 and 2, trans. David Farrell Krell (San Francisco: Harper, 1991), 58f., quoted in Weberman 1996, 389.

[9] For Heidegger, one form of distortion is an "absolutizing" form of disclosure, such as science seeing itself as *the* theory of the real, thinking it can disclose the world in *all* its aspects (including the ethical and the poetic). The "mood" of science is thus for Heidegger dry and monotonous.

How is the idea of a totalizing attunement to be understood in relation to the emotions? Fundamentally for Heidegger, although emotional attunements are "feelings" they are ways of "being in the world" and "being with others"; they are not something purely private or inner. We say, for example, that a person of "good humour brings a lively atmosphere with them" (Heidegger 1995, 66). Thus Grundstimmungen make the world intelligible in various ways in a *social* context: this is necessary if they are to structure our view of the world.

The idea of a *totalizing* Grundstimmung may be explicated with the help of Amelie Rorty. In "Explaining Emotions," Rorty introduces the concept of "magnetizing dispositions," which are "dispositions to gravitate toward and to create conditions that spring other dispositions" (1980, 106). Such dispositions "determine actions and reactions by determining the *selective* range of a person's beliefs and desires," and they explain "tendencies to structure experience in ways that will elicit [a] characteristic response" (1980, 107). Rorty distinguishes beliefs that can be understood in propositional form, with well-defined truth conditions, from "intentional sets," which are "patterns of discrimination and attention" (1980, 113). A magnetizing disposition is intentional in so far as it predisposes to such patterns, and if such a magnetizing disposition is about "everything" (understood contextually as we have seen), it is totalizing. In Heidegger's terms, a magnetizing disposition is a "gathering," and the more the disposition gathers, the closer it is to being totalizing.

Magnetizing dispositions can be emotional. Rorty gives the following example: "A magnetized disposition to irascibility not only involves a set of specific low thresholds (e.g. to frustration or betrayal) but also involves looking for frustrating conditions, perceiving situations as frustrating. It not only involves wearing a chip on one's shoulder but involves looking for someone to knock that chip off" (1980, 107).

I have outlined several features of Grundstimmungen. Let us now apply the notion of a Grundstimmung to lovingness, in terms of which we have defined the emotional preparedness characterizing universal love. Given that a Grundstimmung predisposes one to patterns of attention, emotional response, motivation, and so forth, to what sort of patterns does lovingness predispose one? Where we are speaking of that form of lovingness as universal love or agape, it involves a readiness to be helpful, kind, gracious, forgiving, and beneficent in a large range of circumstances, so one is not easily derailed from beneficent, kind, or helpful acts by such factors as being in a hurry, stressed, or harassed. It therefore also involves patience.

As we saw under feature (b) of Grundstimmung, sometimes this emotional preparedness or readiness takes the form of what Heidegger calls an irruption. Overwhelming or intense emotion can precipitate acts of difficult forgiveness, or one may feel powerful charitable love for needy or vulnerable individuals, precipitating acts of great generosity or courage. This feature of universal love, and the distinction between a powerful feeling and background emotional hums, allows for a resolution of a problem with the idea of lovingness as a Grundstimmung as a deep rather than relatively shallow structuring of the world. Here is the problem. Consider the notions of superficiality or profundity in relation to the aspect of the Grundstimmung of lovingness that is the preparedness characterizing the virtue of universal love. One relatively superficial totalizing form of lovingness is a "love of humanity," rather than a preparedness to manifest love towards determinate beings (any of them as individuals). Where lovingness as love of humanity replaces attention to individuals in, for example, Iris Murdoch's sense (Murdoch 1970), there is a bland superficiality, marked by niceness, superficial friendliness, a generalized philanthropy, a benign benevolence. It could even be described in Heidegger's terms as an "obstructive casualness" akin to Heidegger's example of being bored at a dinner party while nonetheless "chatting away," preventing a deeper understanding where beings could be enticing to one in a way that is not mere curiosity.

By contrast, universal love in, for example, the Christian tradition is founded on a lovingness that is the exact opposite of Heidegger's "profound boredom." Such boredom is described as a way of being in the world oneself where beings as a whole "withdraw," because they are no longer enticing to one. In stark contrast, "profound" lovingness is an emotion where the world, in Heidegger's language, is disclosed richly (or radiantly): beings are enticing and seen in their individuality, in a deep way. This is arguably not true of Kant's universal practical love, which, like Hume's general benevolence, is nonetheless a love of individuals, and as such differs from love of humanity. However, there is a dilemma for the deeper kind of lovingness as a totalizing attunement. On the one hand we may think that, unlike profound boredom, lovingness should be pervasive or omnipresent as a background emotion. However, it may be claimed, surely love cannot be both deep and totalizing in this way? Would not such a form of love be crippling, if possible at all?

Heidegger's analysis of Grundstimmungen shows how this dilemma can be resolved. Though "pervasive" and occurrent, they are standardly in the background as a kind of emotional hum. This does not imply actual "engrossment," to use Nel Noddings's term (Noddings 1984), in all individuals, let alone an intense engrossment.[10] Indeed, this would be impossible, of course. However, at times this background attunement may irrupt, come to the foreground in intense ways. This is possible because one has it in one to love *particular* human beings, even strangers, in a profound manner. This more intense manifestation may, for example, be an act of profound generosity, grace, or forgiveness when the wrongdoer is unrepentant.

---

[10] Noddings herself denies that engrossment need be "intense" or "pervasive" in the life of the carer (1984, 17).

4. Grace

What is the relation between the Grundstimmung of lovingness and the virtues of universal love, such as forgiveness, mercy, grace, and what Hume calls general benevolence? My suggestion is: a loving act *from* one of these virtues *expresses*, in a manner appropriate to the relevant virtue, the totalizing attunement of lovingness in a relatively profound way. Acts of grace, for example, would be expressive of that attunement. Indeed, some of those expressions could be described as the attunement irrupting in those acts. In order to illustrate how such expressions of love can be seen as rational, even though "arational" in Hursthouse's sense, and "reasonless" in the sense elaborated above, we need to describe, albeit briefly, one of the virtues of universal love. I shall focus on grace.

The idea of grace as a virtue in a secular tradition may be thought puzzling. Although grace in the Christian theological tradition is taken to be a free and unmerited favour manifested as a gift from God, it is also possible to think of it as a secular virtue. That it can be a *virtue* is suggested by the notion of *hanan* in the Hebrew scriptures, a notion explicated by Stephen J. Duffy as "kindness expressed as a gift" (1993, 18). On this account, grace can denote both the gift itself and a virtue of which the gift is an expression. Grace as a virtue is a species of kindness, itself a virtue of universal love.

A number of features attest to grace as a specific form of kindness. In the translation of the Hebrew scriptures into Greek, claims Duffy, *hen* (favour) was translated as *charis*, which has different connotations, still associated with grace as a secular virtue, and which makes it more specific than kindness as such. In particular, it connotes "attractiveness, grace, charm, elegance" (Duffy 1993, 24), so that a person with the virtue of grace also exhibits the right dispositions in relation to the *manner* of expressing the gift of grace. Thus charity is to be expressed in a gracious delightful manner, as opposed to a way that discomfits, humiliates, or accentuates one's superiority in relation to the recipient.

Two other features of grace differentiate it from kindness as a more general virtue. First, in the form of *hesed*, according to Duffy, grace "points to unpredictable, surprising acts of kindness" that can be "overwhelming, astonishing graciousness" exhibiting overflowing abundance (1993, 20–21). Secondly, an action expressive of grace is often conceived as a "downward motion." As the pastor and Bible scholar Donald Barnhouse claimed, "Love that goes upward is worship; love that goes outward is affection; love that stoops is grace."[11]

This latter feature clearly attests to the theological notion of grace, but can we make sense of it in a secular context? I believe so. Very

---

[11] Barnhouse 1952, 72, quoted in Charles R. Swindoll, *The Grace Awakening* (Nashville, Tenn.: W Publishing Group, 1990), 9.

schematically, grace is a form of love that is expressed by someone in a superior position, to someone in an inferior position. This downward orientation of grace may or may not presuppose hierarchy, such as a legitimate authority structure. Even where the hierarchy is an illegitimate one, grace may be dispensed: in the case of slavery, a slave may dispense grace to his owner when the latter, through injury, say, is in a temporarily weak position.[12] Thirdly, there may be a dynamic element to the "stooping" quality of grace. Consider a speaker's graciously answering a hostile question at a conference. Originally the speaker is in a superior position in a sense; the hostile questioner attempts to reverse that position, but instead of the speaker aggressively retaking the higher ground with retaliatory hostility, she shows no interest in this, offering instead "love that stoops."[13] Finally, the downward movement of grace can be manifested when the dispenser, though not in a superior position now, is able to place himself there but refrains from doing so. For example, someone may refuse to take offence and refuse to embarrass or discommode a person who might have given offence. (See my example of Bruce* below.)

The basis for the downward orientation of grace is that the person to whom grace is shown does not deserve it. It is not necessarily the case that she deserves *not* to be shown it, but there is no desert by virtue of which grace is deserved. It seems that for Philip Yancey (1997), however, grace can be rightfully bestowed to someone *un*deserving.

Yancey replies to this difficulty, in relation to the parable of the landowner: "None of us gets paid according to merit, for none of us comes close to satisfying God's requirements for a perfect life. If paid on the basis of fairness, we would all end up in hell" (1997, 62). Regardless of whether this reply is good theology, it does not help in an understanding of grace as a secular virtue. A better reply involves the appreciation of the pluralistic nature of the criteria of justice.[14] We are inclined to say that though someone has a right to bestow a favour, it is unjust for him to do so when the recipient is undeserving (lacking appropriate merits). This apparently leaves no room for the kind of grace described in the parable of the landowner, where in response to the above view the landowner claims a right to bestow favour with her own assets. The solution to the problem is to recognize the plural elements of justice, so that it may be appropriate to claim that a favour is not or (more weakly) may not be unjust when the benefactor has a right to bestow it. Given a context in which desert or merit does not apply or is overridden by other elements of justice, the problem is not a problem of injustice, it is a problem of when is

---

[12] Thanks to Julian Swanton for this example.
[13] I owe this rather nice example to Heather Battaly (though I am unsure whether she would agree with the analysis).
[14] Here I follow David Schmidtz (2006).

the grace "cheap grace"?[15] Has the favour or gift exhibited wisdom, or a weak failure to recognize a need for tough love, for example?

"Grace" that by contrast usurps rules of justice, grace that one has no right to bestow, or that clearly violates rules of worthwhile institutions designed to preserve their integrity (such as passing with a C – a student who clearly deserves to fail) not only is unwise, and for that reason not expressive of virtue, but also exhibits other vices, such as arrogance, inappropriate partialism, cowardice, and so on. On this account, then, grace as a virtue of character is not a virtue incompatible with justice as a virtue of character, it is only opposed to forms of "justice to excess," namely, dispositions to exhibit excessively or inappropriately the "book-keeping" forms of rigoristic or legalistic justice.[16] (A homely example is that of a well-off person quibbling over every cent when the account for a group meal is being divided.)[17] These are vices routinely excoriated by Christian apologists of grace such as Philip Yancey and Charles Swindoll, as well as Nietzsche. As a result, grace as a gift is described as "free," but to say that it is free is not to say that it is capricious.

The features of grace described above have correlative vices the understanding of which helps us grasp the elusive concept of grace. Let me itemize some.

(a) Grace as a virtue is contrasted with legalism as a vice. Not surprisingly, since grace as a virtue is the antithesis of legalism as a vice, there are no rules for the expression of grace. How this can work in a way that makes grace rational is the topic of the remaining sections of this chapter.

(b) Grace as a virtue is contrasted with condescension. Although there is downward motion to grace in the sense specified above, that cannot be condescending. Condescension stems from a basic disposition to compare, which results in several types of tendency to condescension: contempt and a sense of superiority, and a tendency to be censorious and judgmental.

(c) Grace as a virtue is similarly contrasted with pride as a vice. In such pride one's sense of self-worth is dependent on comparisons with others: in particular, it is *dependent* on thinking of oneself as superior to others, and on judging oneself to be superior to others, in general or in relevant respects (even if those judgments are correct).

---

[15] Cheap grace is grace that is unmindful of the importance of various forms of merit and is bestowed too readily, in the wrong way, and so on. It is thus a vice of excess. See Bonhoeffer 1959.

[16] This subtlety is not manifested where the thick concept "just" is applied to acts. A just act can be expressive of legalistic rigoristic justice as a vice: hence, although an act can properly be described as just, it may nonetheless be wrong, as I argue in Swanton 2003.

[17] Thanks to Heather Battaly for this example.

(d) Grace as a virtue is contrasted with blind charity. Although grace is charitable, it need not be blind. The avoiding of inappropriate self-referential comparisons is not tantamount to ignorance or even excusing others' faults.

(e) Grace as a virtue is contrasted with humility as a vice.[18] Humility as a *virtue* focuses on one's beliefs about one's relative weakness, lack of talent, lack of moral fibre and so forth (this is the field of the virtue), and involves various dispositions of dealing properly with those beliefs, and right attitudes in relation to them. Humility as a *vice* consists in improper ways of dealing with and attitudes towards those beliefs, notably indulging in inappropriate self-referential comparisons where a person's self-worth is dependent on comparing herself to others, and she thinks she is worthless because she believes herself to be inferior to them in various ways. (Her beliefs about inferiority in respect of various merits, such as skill on the violin, may or may not be true, though in some forms of humility as a vice her beliefs about her own merits are routinely false, since she underestimates them.)

(f) Grace as a virtue is contrasted with cheap grace. One might think that someone must merit grace, and because grace is not dependent on merits, it is precisely the ill-desert of the recipient of grace that merits the grace. But grace is not a reward for ill-merit. It must be compatible with taking responsibility, just punishment, and so on.

(g) Grace as a virtue is contrasted with failure to let be. The mark of receiving grace is not to feel indebted, not to feel that one must pay back the favourer in some way. Advice can be dispensed with argument, but the mark of grace is to know when to let things be. The grace-giver knows when argument is invasive, unproductive. He may know that the receiver of grace will eventually understand the advice, and take it on board.

5. Universal Love as Arational

Let us turn now to the rationality of universal love as manifested in action, with grace as an example. In line with a modern secular understanding of grace, derived from *charis*, as being "too mundane to express the religious heights and depths of *hesed*" (Duffy 1993, 24), I offer the following ultra-mundane example. An ex-president of a car club, Wayne, recently celebrated his eightieth birthday. The celebration consisted of a

---

[18] Both pride and humility can be virtues. In the former, one's sense of self-worth is not dependent on self-referential comparisons of superiority. In the latter, one's sense of one's proper place in a greater world is not coupled with self-contempt.

restaurant meal for various friends, for which he paid. He invited only one club committee member, John, who had recently relieved him of the very onerous task of producing the club magazine. He did not invite the club captain, Bruce. Bruce was offended and hurt. He had been a club member for much longer than John had, and his relationship with Wayne was of much greater duration. Bruce takes umbrage in a rather public way, behind Wayne's back. Nor does he let the matter rest. Bruce does not accept his non-invitation with grace. Consider now a hypothetical Bruce with grace: we call him Bruce*. Out of lovingness Bruce* graciously accepts the non-invitation. It does not crop up in conversation at all. He would have loved to have been invited, but there is not a trace of hurt or bitterness in his soul. He may have thoughts that Wayne harbours petty resentments directed at the committee in general, and that Wayne is not wealthy and had to have a restricted invitation list, but he does not need to struggle to turn these thoughts into excuses for his non-invitation. He certainly does not dwell on negative speculations that are not well supported by evidence. A range of actions and non-actions attests to the presence of grace in Bruce*. Bruce*'s expressions of grace are expressions of universal love as lovingness: it is not just reserved for friends and family. He is ready to see the world in general in a gracious way.

We begin with the problem of the putative arationality of expressions of grace. As we have seen, arational actions are actions that, though voluntary, are not actions with a desired upshot: there is no intention with which the action is done. In this sense the action is not done *for* a reason. Hursthouse gives as examples of arational actions throwing the recalcitrant tin opener out of the window and ruffling one's child's hair. Nonetheless, it does seem that the two actions differ, in that one seems rational, while the other does not. The latter seems rational on the grounds that it is good to show affection, and this is an appropriate way to show it here and now. In short, to use a term of J. L. Austin's, some arational actions may be "felicitous" and others not (Austin 1962). Though purely expressive actions are uncalculated, not end directed, spontaneous, and an "epiphenomenon" of underlying character, as A. H. Maslow (1949) claims, they can be assessed as felicitous or unfelicitous. There are several modes of infelicity in expressive behaviour: an expression may be "false" in the sense of insincere or exaggerated, it can be inapt in the circumstances, it may be expressive of undesirable emotions, character, or motivations.

It may be argued, however, that for arational actions to be rational they must be *guided* by one's reasons. Nonetheless I would argue that the fact that one does not ruffle one's son's hair for a reason, the fact that the action is *expressive* of affection does not entail that the action is not reason responsive. Imagine that in the course of ruffling my son's hair my other son says, "That's embarrassing." I see his point and desist immediately. Or later he says I should not have done that in front of his brother's friends. I resolve to extirpate my tendencies to such spontaneous acts of affection when friends are around. Reason responsiveness does not entail acting *for* reasons but rather entails being responsive to reasons. An act can be rational when it is reason responsive, even if not done for reasons.

Let us apply the above considerations to Bruce*'s expressions of grace. First, are they arational? Consider Bruce*'s failure to complain about the non-invitation, his smiling pleasantly and making kind remarks when Wayne's faults are mentioned, and so on. Such behaviour comes naturally and spontaneously to Bruce*: there is no intention with which he makes the kind remarks and fails to complain. His actions and non-actions are expressive of underlying character structure. On the face of it we may say that these expressions of grace, like ruffling one's child's hair out of affection, are felicitous, though arational.

My claim raises now the next issue: whether actions expressing universal love in the form of grace, for example, are reasonless. I have suggested that actions can be reason responsive even if not done *for* reasons, but surely that suggests there are contributory reasons for the actions. In that case they would not be reasonless in the sense defined above. Let us now investigate this claim.

6. Universal Love as Reasonless

The question arises: How do we assess Bruce*'s actions as grounded in contributory reasons, even if arational? The following kind of features may be thought to provide *contributory* reasons for such expressions of grace.

(a) Grace properly understood is a virtue: it is good to show grace to people and to have graciousness as a character trait.

(b) It is the case that this act of grace is an appropriate way to dispense or show grace in this particular circumstance.

(c) This action that appears or may appear to be an act of grace is indeed expressive of grace, and not of some vice that masquerades as the virtue of grace.

(d) The act is part of a network of what Robert Solomon (2002) calls Aristophanic reasons. These are reasons that are relationship centred.

The question now is: Are considerations of types (a) to (d) contributory reasons for Bruce*'s acts of putative grace, such as

P: Bruce*'s refraining to complain about his non-invitation?

According to Dancy's notion of a reason, a reason is a feature in virtue of which some normative property such as rightness is attributable. Reasons are features that make or help to make an act right, or to be done, for example. As Dancy claims, these features are part of the "resultance base" of such normative properties. A resultance base is somewhat restrictive in its domain: not all features of an action, for example the absence of defeaters, play the role of *making* an act right or wrong, for example (see Dancy 2004, 89–90).[19]

Are features of types (a) to (d) contributory reasons for an act? Consider features of type (a). As I understand Dancy, that grace is a virtue is not a feature that makes something of a case for an act such as P. It is not therefore a reason; rather, it may be an "enabling condition." A feature is an enabling condition if, were it not to obtain, reasons for the action would not be reasons. So, if grace were not a virtue, putative reasons for the act, such as the failure to complain is gracious, would not be contributory reasons for performing the act.

Consider now (b). According to Dancy, the absence of defeaters, such as my promise was not given under duress and friends are not around, is not part of the resultance base of the rightness of an act of keeping a promise, or abstaining from ruffling my son's hair, respectively. Putative reasons of type (b) are also enabling conditions rather than reasons. The same point applies to (c): the absence of defeaters, such as vice-related features, are not part of the resultance base of the rightness of P.

Consider (d). It has been claimed that locating "reasons" for love in properties of the beloved is a mistake. Rather, such reasons should be seen as Aristophanic. As Solomon puts it, "A reason for love, then, has to do with the way two people 'fit' together, not with the features either of them might have, nor even with features they might share" (2002, 19). However, what is the relation of "has to do with"? Furthering or fostering the loving relationship which is one that "fits" is an odd intention with which to love a person. Perhaps contributory reasons can be found lurking here. Are your expressions of love right *in virtue of* the fact that you have met your beloved at a rugby match, discovered that he loves Auckland rugby, frequents with you the lovely French restaurant near the ground after the match, and so on? These features, in Solomon's terms, "spell out" the love, put it in narrative context, and make it intelligible. But features that make a relationship a fitting one will not act as contributory reasons for an act expressing love in that relationship.

It may be thought that the above points, if valid, would tell against the rationality of expressive acts of grace. For they would be reasonless. At best, we would have enabling considerations for such acts, we would not have reasons. However, in Dancy's own terms, enabling conditions do

---

[19] I am not concerned here to defend Dancy's account and his distinction between reasons and enabling conditions, though I find these persuasive. I am concerned to show that even if true, the apparent problems his account poses for the rationality of virtues of universal love can be resolved.

make a "rational difference" even if they do not count as reasons (Dancy 2004, 40). The *rationality* of expressive acts of grace could be secured by appeal to features (a) to (d), even if such acts are reasonless. The following problem arises, however. If there are no contributory reasons for an arational act of grace at all, how can there be enabling conditions, since by hypothesis there are no reasons that are enabled? Technically, considerations of types (a) to (d) cannot be enablers in Dancy's sense for arational actions. In reply, I say that even if this is correct, such considerations do make a rational difference in the assessment of the felicity of the expression of (arational) acts of grace.

Let us see how such considerations can make such an expression rational. Recall the point made in section 3: an arational action may be rational in the sense of being reason responsive even if not done for reasons of the agent. An analogous point can now be made in relation to reasonless actions: it is possible for actions that are reasonless to be assessable in terms of features that make rational differences, such as those described in (a) to (d). For example, consider again Bruce*'s manifestations of grace. Bruce argues that these actions are not really manifestations of a virtue at all but displays of blind charity, the vice Bruce* is accused of possessing. Bruce* argues lucidly against this claim (he is not only a saint but an intelligent one), subtly explaining the difference between blind charity and loving grace, the connection between a tendency to be uncomplaining and grace, and so on. Bruce* has been rational consideration responsive, and outsiders can assess his behaviour as rational.

In this chapter, then, I have met some of the challenges posed to thinking of universal love as a virtue from the intellectual requirements of virtue. In the course of showing this I have given an account of universal love employing Heidegger's notion of a Grundstimmung. I have not definitively shown that universal love is in fact a virtue, but its potential status as such is now both more comprehensible and more persuasive than it might otherwise have been.

Acknowledgments

I thank Heather Battaly for her extremely useful and thorough editorial comments.

References

Austin, J. L. 1962. *How to Do Things with Words*. Edited by J. O. Urmson. Oxford: Clarendon Press.
Barnhouse, Donald Grey. 1952. *Romans, Man's Ruin*, vol 1. Grand Rapids, Mich.: Wm. B. Eerdman's.
Bonhoeffer, Dietrich. 1959. *The Cost of Discipleship*. London: SCM Press.

Dancy, Jonathan. 2004. *Ethics Without Principles*. Oxford: Clarendon Press.
Driver, Julia. 2001. *Uneasy Virtue*. Cambridge: Cambridge University Press.
Duffy, Stephen J. 1993. *The Dynamics of Grace: Perspectives in Theological Anthropology*. Collegeville, Minn.: Liturgical Press.
Garrard, Eve. 2002. "Forgiveness and the Holocaust." *Ethical Theory and Moral Practice* 5:147–65.
Goleman, Daniel. 2004. *Emotional Intelligence and Working with Emotional Intelligence*. London: Bloomsbury.
Griswold, Charles. 2007. *Forgiveness: A Philosophical Exploration*. Cambridge: Cambridge University Press.
Heidegger, Martin. 1995. *The Fundamental Concepts of Metaphysics: World, Finitude, Solitude*. Translated by William McNeill and Nicholas Walker. Bloomington: Indiana University Press.
Hursthouse, Rosalind. 1991. "Arational Actions." *Journal of Philosophy* 88:57–68.
Kant, Immanuel. 1996. *The Doctrine of Virtue: The Metaphysics of Morals*. Translated and edited by Mary Gregor. Cambridge: Cambridge University Press.
Lewis, C. S. 1977. *The Four Loves*. London: Fount.
Maslow, A. H. 1949. "The Expressive Component of Behavior." *Psychological Review* 56:261–72.
Murdoch, Iris. 1970. "The Idea of Perfection." In *The Sovereignty of Good*, 1–45. London: Routledge.
Noddings, Nel. 1984. *Caring: A Feminine Approach to Ethics and Moral Education*. Berkeley: University of California Press.
Rorty, Amelie. 1980. "Explaining Emotions." In *Explaining Emotions*, edited by Amelie Rorty, 103–26. Berkeley: University of California Press.
Schmidtz, David. 2006. *Elements of Justice*. Cambridge: Cambridge University Press.
Solomon, Robert. 2002. "Reasons for Love." *Journal for the Theory of Social Behavior* 32:1–28.
Swanton, Christine. 2003. *Virtue Ethics: A Pluralistic View*. Oxford: Oxford University Press.
Vlastos, Gregory. 1962. "Justice and Equality." In *Social Justice*, edited by Richard B. Brandt, 31–72. Englewood Cliffs, N.J.: Prentice Hall.
Weberman, David. 1996. "Heidegger and the Disclosive Character of the Emotions." *Southern Journal of Philosophy* 34:379–410.
Yancey, Philip. 1997. *What's So Amazing About Grace?* Grand Rapids, Mich.: Zondervan.

10

OPEN-MINDEDNESS

WAYNE RIGGS

Why Talk About Open-Mindedness?

One reason to talk about open-mindedness is that there has been a lot of recent interest in the so-called epistemic or intellectual virtues. It is still early going, but there are already disputes about what these virtues amount to, whether they actually exist, what implications they have for other issues and commitments in epistemology, and so on. Indeed, many of the standard problematics and disputes one finds in virtue ethics are being recapitulated in the much newer field of virtue epistemology.

One reason for this recent interest in virtue epistemology is that it seems to hold some promise to help us gain a better understanding of some areas of epistemology that have been neglected for a long time but are now coming back into fashion. Virtues are properties of agents, not of propositions, or beliefs, or belief-forming processes, and forth. Insofar as one thinks that epistemology should tell us something about ourselves as cognitive agents, rather than merely help us classify (after the fact) whether our beliefs officially count as knowledge or not, virtue epistemology looks like a promising line of inquiry.

But why talk about *open-mindedness* in particular? It is a common practice for virtue epistemologists to offer a list of some of the specifically *epistemic* virtues they have in mind, to help the uninitiated get a grip on what they are talking about. It is striking how often open-mindedness is at the very top of that list. One might conclude from this sociological fact that open-mindedness is generally understood to be either (a) the most important of the epistemic virtues or (b) the least controversial example of an epistemic virtue. Either of these conclusions, if true, would make it particularly interesting to talk about open-mindedness. However, I'm not convinced of (a), and I am suspicious of the significance of (b).

As for (a), I strongly suspect that these lists of epistemic virtues are constrained by the fact that we have a somewhat impoverished and confusing vocabulary with which to refer to them. The main problem seems to be that many traits we might naturally count as epistemic virtues have analogues that are moral virtues (or perhaps the same trait is both an epistemic and a moral virtue). Examples of this are intellectual courage, intellectual charity, and so on. While these also usually make the lists, one could imagine that when one is trying to specify and articulate a set of virtues that are peculiarly relevant to epistemology, one would rather lead with something that doesn't wear its complicity with ethics on its sleeve. Though, as I discuss later, I believe that open-mindedness has deep ethical significance, it does not present itself initially as a moral virtue. This makes open-mindedness an easy choice to top one's list. Thus, I rather doubt that it is a general estimation of the greater importance of open-mindedness relative to the other intellectual virtues that is responsible for its pride of place in most lists of such virtues.

As for its controversiality, this is hard to judge because so little has been written about the specific nature of any of the intellectual virtues. Most of the work in virtue epistemology has been at a very abstract level, with very little attention paid to understanding individual virtues.[1] This is a problem, because we don't have as firm or precise a prephilosophical grip, I would submit, on the specifically intellectual virtues as we do on the ethical virtues. This makes it hard to judge the relative significance of various specific proposed virtues. It also makes it hard to judge whether the more abstract accounts of intellectual virtue are on the mark, since we can't easily judge whether the abstract theories count the right traits as virtues.

So this line of thought has led to a reason to talk about specific intellectual virtues. Abstract and theoretical virtue theory of any sort needs to be informed by a clear understanding of the individual specific virtues one means to be giving an account of. I hope to make some headway on this project here.

But still, why open-mindedness particularly? I find open-mindedness uniquely interesting because several puzzles arise about it almost as soon as one begins to think about it. For example, why should anyone *want to be* open-minded? Doesn't open-mindedness imply a lack of commitment to one's own beliefs? But surely being open-minded must be compatible with full commitment to what one takes to be true at the moment. As we shall see, this problem is even more acute for people who embody all the other epistemic virtues. Is there any reason at all for such people to be open-minded?

Some of these and other puzzles I shall discuss raise deep worries about the coherence of the notion of open-mindedness as a virtue, while others raise serious questions about whether being open-minded is a good thing from the perspective of improving one's own or anyone else's epistemic lot. This is surely a worry for any trait that aspires to be an epistemic virtue.

I shall take up the issue of these puzzles shortly, but first I want to say what I take to be some desiderata for an account of open-mindedness that is sufficient to address the motivations I have given for providing such an

---

[1] For important exceptions to this claim, see Roberts and Wood 2007 and Fricker 2007.

account in the first place. These desiderata are somewhat tendentious, but for the following reason: I want to know if it is possible to provide an account of open-mindedness that is plausible *and* makes open-mindedness *interesting in its own right*. What do I mean by this? An account of a specific virtue is interesting in its own right if it provides us with a unique way of expressing a worthwhile evaluation of our ethical or cognitive practice. This is completely independent of whether it is possible to provide a definition of any other important evaluative concept in terms of that virtue or any other. My interest in the virtues is in their specificity and distinctness. I value the richness of vocabulary and the precision of expression that one gets from employing the language of individual virtues. Thus, the only accounts of individual virtues that are satisfactory to me are those that preserve these features. If it turns out that open-mindedness cannot be given such an account that remains plausible, then it would not follow that open-mindedness is not a virtue, but simply that it is not a virtue that is interesting in its own right.

The desiderata listed in the following section are motivated by these considerations. Solving the various puzzles I will raise for an account of open-mindedness is, naturally, among those desiderata as well.

Desiderata for an Account of Open-Mindedness

Desideratum 1: "Open-Mindedness" Should Be a "Thick" Concept

I hesitate to use the notion of "thick" concepts, because there seems to be much dispute over what precisely that means, and I do not want to become an interested party in such a debate. Let me be clear that in what I say here I do not mean to be taking a stand on the proper understanding of "thick concept." Yet it does seem to offer a way to describe the features that I think a good account of open-mindedness should have. Some of the properties often associated with "thickness" are the following: simultaneous descriptive and normative content, richness of detail or specificity, fairly straightforward application to the way we live our lives. These properties tend to come together anyway. If a concept is both specific and has descriptive content in addition to normative content, it is likely to be easy to see what would count in the real world as falling under it. Contrast this with the concept "the good," or even "virtue." The latter is a bit more specific and applicable to real life than the former, but neither goes very far in that respect. But individual virtues can and should be articulated in much finer detail. An account of a specific virtue should provide a rich description of the features of someone who embodies that virtue. Consequently, it will be easier to recognize someone who has that specific virtue on the basis of such an account than it would be to recognize someone who is virtuous on the basis of an abstract and "thin" account of virtue.

A related point is that the resulting description of the virtue should pick out something distinctive. One of the attractions of virtue theories in either ethics or epistemology is that they claim to provide us with a much richer vocabulary for describing and understanding our ethical or epistemological lives. "Virtue talk" allows us to pick out and refer to a variety of uniquely important ways of being good, or doing well, or whatever it is you think virtues are indicative and/or constitutive of. For a virtue theory to meet this desideratum, the individual virtues must be genuinely distinct as well as sufficiently specific. An account of the virtues according to which each of the individual virtues really just amounts to the same thing would be inadequate on this measure. So would be an account of some individual virtue according to which being virtuous in that particular way was no more than meeting the conditions for being good in some very general way. Such a result would render the virtue uninteresting in itself.

Desideratum 2: Virtues as Traits of Persons

As should be clear by now, I am treating intellectual virtues in much the way that virtue ethicists treat ethical virtues. This is not without its problems. There is a deep divide among those who calls themselves virtue epistemologists over precisely this point. On the one hand are those who envision intellectual virtues as simply abilities, competencies or perfections of a cognitive sort. For these epistemologists, nearly any process that contributes fairly immediately to consistent true belief formation, for example, eyesight, counts as a virtue. I don't mean to exaggerate here; there are restrictions as to what can count as a virtue on such views. John Greco, for example, requires that the relevant processes be "integrated" into one's "cognitive character" (see, e.g., Greco 2002). But this restriction is largely meant to eliminate the possibility of fairly arcane processes that usually appear only in philosophy papers. Guy Axtell (1997) calls this position "virtue reliabilism," and Greco and Ernest Sosa (2007) are prominent examples of proponents of such views.

On the other hand are those virtue epistemologists who take intellectual virtues to be deeply analogous to ethical virtues. Linda Zagzebski, for example, argues that intellectual and ethical virtues are not merely analogous but intellectual virtues are in fact a subset of the moral virtues (1996, 166ff.). Such virtues tend to require much more from the virtuous agent than those of the virtue reliabilist. Zagzebski's (1996) theory, for example, requires reliability just as virtue reliabilism does, but also requires that the intellectually virtuous agent have the right standing motivations, and that such motivations be present and causally active in the production of belief. James Montmarquet requires that one be "epistemically conscientious" in the production of belief in order to be intellectually virtuous (1993, 19ff.).

Axtell (1997) calls theories that impose and emphasize these kinds of agential requirements "virtue responsibilist" theories.

I am not committed to any particular account of intellectual virtue in the abstract. But for the purposes of this chapter, I am going to assume that hard-core virtue reliabilism is not correct, and that some degree of agential involvement is necessary for significant cognitive virtue. That is because if hard-core reliabilism is correct, then the individual virtues are not particularly interesting in their own right. The individual features of different virtues play no important role in such theories. Indeed, the only feature of individual virtues that matters in such theories is their truth conduciveness.

It is important to note that the purposes of hard-core reliabilists are not necessarily aligned with my own. Their primary interest tends to be providing an adequate account of knowledge. It may very well turn out that what the virtue reliabilists call "virtue" really is a necessary condition for knowledge, yet there is a richer, more agent-involved notion of virtue that is not necessary for most knowledge (though it may be sufficient), but is quite relevant to being an excellent cognizer. So long as I am not committed to providing an account of knowledge in terms of the kinds of virtues I am interested in, there need not even be a conflict between my project and that of the hard-core reliabilists. So it is not so much that I am assuming hard-core reliabilism is false as that I am assuming that something a little closer to virtue responsibilism is (at least also) true.

Desideratum 3: The Puzzles of Open-Mindedness

This brings me to the puzzles that arise very quickly once one begins to think about open-mindedness as a virtue. Any satisfactory theory of open-mindedness must dispel the air of paradox arising from worries such as the following:

a. Why should anyone *want to* be open-minded?
b. Why should a(n otherwise) virtuous person be open-minded?
c. How is it possible to be open-minded? (For example, How is open-mindedness consistent with full-blooded, confident belief?)
d. How do we determine when and with regard to what we should expend resources in our pursuit of open-mindedness?

(Admittedly, the last of these is not really so much a puzzle as it is a difficult question for any account of open-mindedness. But, as we shall see, it arises naturally from attempts to resolve the first three puzzles.)

These puzzles are related, at least in the sense that a consideration of one leads naturally to a consideration of the others. Let us begin with (a). Why should anyone want to be open-minded? In ordinary usage, being open-minded implies being prepared to take seriously the views of others, especially when those views are in conflict with one's own. But what would motivate such an attitude? It would seem that only a lack of full confidence in one's beliefs would lead one to spend any time or effort considering views that conflict with one's own. Indeed, full confidence in one's beliefs would seem to render the attitude of open-mindedness irrational, at least insofar as being open-minded required any effort at all, which it generally does. The obvious immediate response to this worry is to say that we all recognize that we are fallible, and that even our most strongly held beliefs could be false. Thus, paying attention to alternative views is a good strategy to discover our mistaken beliefs.

This leads us to wonder whether open-mindedness is even consistent with the possibility of full, confident belief. This worry is discussed by Jonathan Adler (2004). Echoing claims commonly made in the literature in the philosophy of education, he acknowledges the appearance that "open-mindedness toward a specific belief is not compatible with holding that belief" (2004, 128). Yet it seems that open-mindedness, if it is appropriate at all, is appropriate with regard even to those beliefs we hold most strongly. Indeed, we often think that it is with respect to just such beliefs that open-mindedness is *most* important. I have in mind here religious and political beliefs, and beliefs in the correctness of social norms. These are typically held very strongly, and yet it is often with respect to these beliefs that we take the charge of closed-mindedness to be most damning. But, if we are not to be so open-minded that our brains fall out, we must still be capable of strong belief. Yet this seems impossible if we are to be open-minded with regard to those strongly held beliefs.

All of this is even more problematic when we consider someone who is an exemplary epistemic agent in every way save being open-minded. Here the puzzle of motivation is especially daunting. Recall that the initial response to the motivation problem was a recognition that one's beliefs could be wrong, even when one is confident in them. But a highly epistemically virtuous agent has no reason to expect that anyone in her epistemic community is likelier to get to the truth than she is. Obviously, there will be exceptions with regard to highly specialized fields in which the virtuous agent has no expertise, but otherwise she has every reason to think that her own views are much more likely to be true than any other views she is likely to find represented among those around her. Why should she be open-minded? Indeed, why would it be a good thing for her to be open-minded? It doesn't look as if being open-minded is a good way to improve her epistemic situation.

So we have two distinct problems here, one of which comes in two different varieties. There is the problem of motivation, both for normal believers and for otherwise epistemically virtuous believers. Then there is the problem of the compatibility of open-mindedness and strongly held belief. A solution to the motivation problem requires showing that it is worthwhile for us to be open-minded. More specifically, it must be shown that being open-minded is a better way for us to get to the truth than the alternative, or else we shall not have shown that open-mindedness is an *epistemic* goal.[2] This will depend, of course, on what is required of us to be open-minded. If the demand is too great, there will presumably be more efficient ways of expending our resources to achieve our goals. Thus, the resource allocation question must ultimately be addressed in order to resolve our original puzzle.

In the remainder of this chapter, I consider a succession of accounts of open-mindedness, assessing them both in terms of their ability to resolve these puzzles and in terms of their success in preserving a sense of open-mindedness that is interesting in its own right.

Accounts of Open-Mindedness

It is interesting to note that so much of the discussion of open-mindedness has taken place in the field of philosophy of education, rather than in epistemology. The purposes of philosophers of education are different from mine, but it is still instructive to look at their work. I will look particularly at William Hare's and Jonathan Adler's discussions of open-mindedness.

According to Hare, "[A] person who is open-minded is disposed to revise or reject the position he holds if sound objections are brought against it, or, in the situation in which the person presently has no opinion on some issue, he is disposed to make up his mind in the light of available evidence and argument as objectively and as impartially as possible. . . . [W]e may adopt the attitude of open-mindedness with respect to highly particularized and specific beliefs or to more general and wide-ranging hypotheses, theories, and conceptual frameworks. The *object* of one's open-mindedness varies, but the *meaning* of open-mindedness remains constant" (1979, 9). This might seem a very natural way to characterize open-mindedness, at least on a first pass. However, as Hare describes it, open-mindedness seems nothing short of rationality itself. That is, if someone is "disposed to revise or reject the position he holds if sound objections are brought against it, or . . . make up his mind in the light of available evidence as objectively and impartially as possible," what is left to say about the quality of his reasoning (1979, 9)? Hare seems to virtually equate being open-minded with being intellectually virtuous tout court. This runs afoul of the first desideratum of an interesting view of open-mindedness: that it be a distinct and specific kind of excellence.

Moreover, this seems to just get open-mindedness wrong. There are a great many ways one can fail to be disposed to respond properly to cogent objections to one's view that do not amount to a failure of open-mindedness. One might consistently make mistakes in one's reasoning, such that cogent objections do not appear to be so. One might be unable to keep all

---

[2] This assumes that truth is the only epistemic value. There may well be others, and if there are, then open-mindedness may derive additional epistemic value via its relationship to these other values.

the relevant considerations in mind at once, hence unable to formulate opinions on the basis of all the relevant evidence. It might simply be easier to remember certain kinds of considerations rather than others, and hence one might fail to be impartial in one's evaluations, but not in the kind of biased way that seems necessary to being closed-minded. None of these failings seems incompatible with being open-minded. Hare's account would implausibly count a great many quite distinct objective cognitive failings under the rubric of a failure of open-mindedness.

Let us, then, turn to an alternative view. In "Reconciling Open-Mindedness and Belief" (2004), Adler proposes a very different way of understanding open-mindedness. It focuses more on the attitude of the agent than his characteristic reactions to evidence that runs counter to his views. As we shall see, one can develop the account in ways that make it easy to explain why open-minded people are likely to act in those characteristic ways, but we also get a much deeper understanding of open-mindedness itself.

In his paper, Adler is concerned specifically about one of the puzzles mentioned at the outset of this chapter, which has been debated amongst philosophers of education. It is encapsulated by the following question posed by Adler: "*How can one be open-minded about a strongly held belief; and why should one?*" (2004, 123; emphasis in original). The question makes evident a tension between two plausible claims. On the one hand, it seems as though strong belief in a proposition implies that one regards it as "not seriously possible that it is wrong" (2004, 128). On the other hand, as Hare says, being open-minded appears to require that we are "prepared to entertain doubts about our views" (qtd. Adler 2004, 128). It would appear that either one cannot be open-minded about one's strongly held beliefs, or else one cannot hold any belief both open-mindedly and strongly.

Let us look a little more closely at why this seems to be so. Suppose we believe that p very confidently and strongly. To be open-minded about p seems to imply that we should take challenges to p seriously. In other words, we should take seriously the possibility that $\sim p$ is true. But this seems tantamount to having actual doubts that p is true, which suggests that we aren't really as confident about p as we assumed at the beginning. Thus, strongly believing p and being open-minded about p seem incompatible.

This certainly could be an accurate description of someone's reaction to being challenged regarding one of her beliefs. The challenge itself might be enough to lower the believer's confidence in her belief to the point that it is no longer correct to say that she believes it strongly. But that seems less a description of open-mindedness than a description of epistemic insecurity or even cowardice. Thus, there must be a way to reconcile strong belief and open-mindedness.

What needs to be done is to block the chain of reasoning that leads from the stipulation of being open-minded about p to having significant doubts about p, rendering the belief no longer strongly held. The beginning and end of that chain seem unassailable. Being open-minded surely requires at least that we take challenges to our beliefs seriously, at least sometimes. And having significant doubts about whether p is true does seem to undercut the possibility of believing p strongly. The weak link is the inference from one's taking a challenge seriously to one's entertaining doubts about the truth of p.

I think the reason we find it so easy to move from the one to the other is that it seems as though the only explanation for one's taking some challenge to her belief that p seriously is that she has doubts about the truth of p. Why bother worrying about the challenge otherwise? The key to breaking the above chain of inference is to provide an alternative explanation for taking such challenges seriously.

Adler's account of open-mindedness provides us with just such an explanation. The key move is to define open-mindedness as "a second-order attitude toward one's beliefs as believed, and not just toward the specific proposition believed, just as fallibilism is a second-order doubt about the perfection of one's believing, not a doubt about the truth of any specific belief" (2004, 130). The idea here is that open-mindedness is primarily an attitude toward oneself as a believer, rather than toward any particular belief. To be open-minded is to be aware of one's fallibility as a believer, and to be willing to acknowledge the possibility that anytime one believes something, *it is possible that one is wrong*.

When an open-minded person encounters a challenge to one of his beliefs, he responds by (at least sometimes) taking such a challenge seriously. This can be so even if he believes the challenged belief quite strongly. But what explains his willingness to take the challenge seriously is not any sudden or latent doubts about the truth of the belief but rather his acknowledgment that, being human, he could always have got things wrong in this case. This need not affect the strength of his belief at all. If it did, then the mere commitment to fallibilism would render strong belief impossible.

It may still sound strange to some that one can seriously consider the case for $\sim p$ when one strongly believes that p. To address such lingering doubts, Adler offers a powerful analogy. Consider the position of a quality-control officer in a factory that makes widgets. The officer knows that the factory is highly reliable, and hence that nearly every widget that comes down the assembly line is nondefective. But, to safeguard against even the occasional defective widget making it to market, it is the officer's job to inspect one of every ten widgets before it leaves the factory. Suppose the officer selects widget number 30. Before inspecting it, she confidently believes that it will be nondefective. The fact that she is willing to check to see if it really is nondefective does not indicate some doubt about widget 30. It is not insecurity about widget 30 that prompts the check but rather an awareness of the possibility, albeit low, that the factory might produce a defective widget. Consequently, her belief that widget 30 is nondefective is no weaker than her belief that widget 29 is nondefective, even though she checked one but not the other.

The Puzzles

Adler's definition, then, does what he intended it to do. It explains how open-mindedness is compatible with strongly held belief, thus solving the first puzzle posed for accounts of open-mindedness. Can it also address the motivational puzzle? For instance, why should anyone want to be open-minded in Adler's sense? How is it good for us epistemically?

We have to keep in mind the assumption that everyone has similar cognitive goals, which include having true beliefs and avoiding false ones. Given these goals, simple awareness of our fallibility (a condition of open-mindedness) should motivate us to be open-minded. We can be nearly certain that some of our beliefs are false, given our fallibility. We want to be rid of those, and paying attention to evidence that indicates we are wrong about something is a good way to do so. At the very least, it would seem that being closed-minded virtually guarantees that you are stuck with whatever false beliefs you get on your own.

Once again, we can appeal to the widget example. There is no puzzle about why the officer is motivated to check the widgets (besides the fact that it is her job, which we shall conveniently ignore for the moment). She could say to herself, "I'm sure of each widget that it's nondefective, so there's no reason to check any of them." But she knows that this is a losing strategy if her goal is to keep any defective widgets from making it out the door.

What, then, of the otherwise virtuous believer? Has he reason to be open-minded? This is a much more difficult question. The answer given above for why a normal cognitive agent should want to be open-minded is a little strained when applied to the otherwise virtuous believer. He, too, is fallible, and will have false beliefs, but the likelihood of his discovering these by engaging with other, generally less virtuous, believers seems very low indeed. Even at best, he likely wastes his time, and at worst he is misled into exchanging a truth for a falsehood.

I believe that an account of open-mindedness along the lines Adler describes can answer this question. However, Adler does little to develop the characteristics of the open-minded agent. He does not offer details about how having the appropriate second-order attitude leads consistently to the kind of unbiased, objective assessment of beliefs and views that is characteristic of the open-minded person. But these are the details we need in order to assess whether open-mindedness remains a virtue if one has mastered the other cognitive virtues. To that end, I shall offer a characterization of the open-minded agent, taking Adler's definition of open-mindedness as a starting point.

The Open-Minded Agent

Our starting point is Adler's characterization of open-mindedness as "a second-order attitude toward one's beliefs as believed, and not just toward the specific proposition believed." But this attitude alone will not constitute open-mindedness. The attitude must be efficacious in our cognitive lives. It must intrude upon our habits of thought consistently and productively to produce the cognitive and overt "behavior" typical of those we take to exemplify open-mindedness. Though I make no claims to offering a complete description of this, I shall propose two general characteristics of thought that one must have in order to translate one's second-order awareness into genuine open-mindedness.

Self-Knowledge

The first and most important of these characteristics is the disposition to seek, and when found, accept, self-knowledge about one's cognitive weaknesses and strengths. Most of us are prone to many bad habits of thought or simply have imperfect cognitive equipment. For instance, I am prone to making careless mistakes when adding more than two or three numbers in my head. If I and another person were both calculating the same sum in our heads, and our answers came out different, I should seriously consider the possibility that I made a mistake. But, of course, this is not the typical situation in which questions of open-mindedness arise.

In those situations where one's more significant beliefs are challenged, one is subject to different cognitive weaknesses that can keep one from seeing the truth of an alternative view. These weaknesses include bias, overconfidence, wishful thinking, and so on. These habits tend to be domain-specific to a certain extent. For example, I might be overconfident when defending my beliefs about the domestic economy. Or I might have a bias in favor of the United States, so that I shall be unmoved by any considerations that suggest the United States suffers by comparison with any other nation. Rarely does someone exhibit these bad habits of thought across the cognitive board (overconfidence may be an exception).

To the extent one defeats these habits of thought, one is more open-minded. But to do this requires that one be aware of when and with regard to what one is likely to fall into these habits. This is hard knowledge to come by, and harder still to accept. We all think that we have come to our beliefs in a rational, objective manner. But the open-minded person is moved by her awareness of her own fallibility to search for domains and situations in which she is prone to these habits of thought that produce closed-mindedness.

Self-Monitoring

But supposing one comes by such knowledge, what is one to do with it in order to be open-minded? Gaining the knowledge may be the hardest part, but having it is not enough. This knowledge must be efficacious in the moment that one is facing the challenge to one's beliefs. For it to be so, one must self-monitor for signs that one is in a domain or situation in which one is likely to be biased, say. The signs might be the subject matter of the discussion or reading matter or whatever prompted the challenge to one's beliefs. Or it might be the tone of your voice as you respond to someone. If you are really self-aware, you might even notice characteristic gestures or body postures that you tend to adopt when overconfident, for example.

When one "catches" oneself at engaging in one of these bad habits of thought, one should take whatever prompted the habitual response seriously, out of an awareness not just of one's general fallibility but of one's particular fallibility under these sorts of circumstances. It's important to note here that catching oneself in one of these bad habits of thought regarding one's belief that *p* does not imply that one's belief that *p* is false, or even that you don't have excellent reasons for believing it. As Adler says, one can be prompted to take a challenge seriously without lowering one's confidence in the belief itself.

So, it is through gaining self-knowledge, which one applies in the moment of challenge through self-monitoring, that the open-minded person makes her awareness of her own cognitive fallibility efficacious in her cognitive practice. One nice feature of this understanding of open-mindedness is that it makes sense of how it is possible to strive to become *more* open-minded. Self-knowledge is something that can be sought and cultivated, and self-monitoring can be practiced. Of course, there is the problem that our biases and tendencies to overconfidence and wishful thinking tend to be hidden from us. How can we become better at discovering these? The obvious answer is through exposing oneself to a variety of ideas and worldviews. Closed-mindedness can be the result of taking one's own assumptions to be obvious and universal, hence incontrovertible. To discover that those assumptions are not shared by people across time, place, and culture can help one see that one's assumptions are controvertible after all. These are, of course, truisms about open- and closed-mindedness, which makes it all the more important that an account of open-mindedness be able to explain them.

A Final Reckoning

How does this account fare with regard to our initial desiderata? Though it is still just a sketch, I think the description of open-mindedness that has emerged is very richly detailed, with both descriptive and normative elements, and gives us a great deal of guidance about how to become more open-minded. Open-mindedness is also clearly a trait of the person. That is, one is the sort of person who is aware of his fallibility and self-monitors to combat it, or one is not. Yet we can also make sense of the common usage in which people are accused of being closed-minded about something in particular. Even a generally open-minded person can be closed-minded about some specific domain or in some specific situation. In that case, while the *person* remains open-minded, he is clearly not exhibiting his open-mindedness in that circumstance.

The final test is that of the puzzles. We have already dispensed with the first two, which brings us back to the difficult problem of why an otherwise cognitively virtuous person should be open-minded. What has she to gain? I think it is fair to say that even the most excellent cognizers are still subject to the bad habits of thought alluded to above. A thinker who is sober, careful, conscientious, thorough, and the like, can still be subject to things like bias, overconfidence and wishful thinking. Indeed, we are likely to pick up some of these habits of thought from the intellectual community we grow up in. Because of the self-disguising nature of these habits, nothing short of the kinds of self-knowledge and self-monitoring that are constitutive of open-mindedness will serve to eliminate them.

And these habits of thought can affect not just how we assess the evidence we have but also what we take to be evidence in the first place. If we have a bias, say, to the effect that people under thirty don't know anything, we shall dismiss testimony from such sources as even being relevant to anything we believe or are considering. Thus, having the virtues relevant to assessing evidence well will not redress all the effects of such bias. Only coming to recognize that the bias exists and learning to recognize when it is affecting our deliberations can offset its perverse effects on our cognition.

This may sound like an awful lot of work, and this brings us back to the issue of resource management. Even given the payoffs for the virtuous agent, is it worth it? There are really two questions being asked here. One is a question about the relative benefits of developing the self-knowledge and habits of self-monitoring that have been described. The other is a question about the relative benefits of spending the time to take challenges seriously as they arise.

As to the first question, I would say the benefits gained are worth the cost. Even an otherwise virtuous agent is not immune to all the bad habits of thought that can lead to closed-mindedness, and closed-mindedness seems to lead away from the cognitive goods, such as truth. So, the otherwise virtuous agent should develop the self-knowledge and self-monitoring necessary to detect and avoid such habits.

The second question is the harder one, and the one that has been hanging over these accounts of open-mindedness from the beginning. Why should an otherwise cognitively virtuous person pay any attention to challenges to her belief, given that she is so much more likely to be right than her compatriots? A related question is whether her open-mindedness requires her to. If we understand "taking a challenge seriously" to mean "devote time and energy at the moment of the challenge to soberly and thoroughly reflect on the merits of the case being made," then an open-minded person would have to spend an inordinate amount of time on such reflections. Perhaps so much so that it would interfere with pursuing what most of us would consider a normal life.

Some small amount of comfort might be gained by recognizing that the demands of open-mindedness are not the only demands placed on us, nor are they often the most stringent. Hence, we are often in a position in which devoting resources to such a challenge would keep us from fulfilling other, more pressing, obligations. But this might simply show that the hurly-burly of most of our lives prevents us from developing our virtue to the highest degree. This still leaves the ideally open-minded agent as someone who does address every challenge as it arises, with full thoroughness and care. But, this seems not to describe the behavior of an ideal epistemic agent, so it would be better if we had an account that didn't require it of virtuous cognizers.

To make further progress on this issue, we need to distinguish carefully between what it takes to be an open-minded *person*, on the one hand, and what it is to be open-minded *about some matter*, on the other. We began our investigation talking primarily about the latter but have ended talking primarily about the former. We need to understand the relationship between *open-mindedness*, on the one hand, and *being open-minded about p*, on the other.

Following Adler, I claimed that being open-minded about *p* requires that we take challenges to *p* seriously. But what, exactly, does it mean to take challenges seriously? And does the open-minded person have to take *every* challenge seriously? In other words, can an open-minded person decline to entertain a challenge regarding her belief that *p*, while remaining open-minded regarding *p*? I think the answer has to be yes, which means either that not every challenge must be taken seriously or that taking a challenge seriously does not imply that one devotes cognitive resources to seriously *considering* the challenge.

I'm not sure that very much turns on which of these strategies one pursues. I find the first to be modestly preferable, so I shall briefly sketch how such an approach would solve the problem at hand. On this approach, an open-minded person need not take all challenges to her beliefs seriously. Moreover, such a person can decline such a challenge regarding *p while being open-minded about p*. Put another way, one can reject a challenge to one's views *open-mindedly*. Obviously, the plausibility of this move depends upon being able to explain just when such a dismissal of a challenge is open-minded and when it is not. It is not enough to say simply that a dismissal is open-minded if done by an open-minded person. Virtuous agents are not perfect. They, too, can behave viciously at times.

However, the open-minded person will at least have the self-knowledge to discriminate those situations and domains in which he is more likely to go astray due to his bad habits of thought. He has put in the time and energy to develop that knowledge and the habits of self-monitoring that render him typically judicious in his assessment of such things. Hence, it is reasonable for him to follow those judgments regarding whether he need take some given challenge seriously. If he is fairly confident that he is not in a situation in which he is likely to exhibit his bad habits of thought, then there is less pressure on him to bother with the challenge. He can fairly confidently brush it aside, assuming that his confidence in his belief is already very high.

So, when an open-minded person dismisses a challenge from a confident judgment both that she is well-justified in her belief that p and that she is not being led astray by the relevant bad habits of thought, *and she is correct about the latter*, her dismissal is open-minded. Being wrong about how well-justified her belief is would not render her closed-minded about p, it would make her merely mistaken in her estimation of the weight of the evidence regarding p. But if she is mistaken about her not being led astray by these bad habits of thought, then she is being led astray in just such a way. And that is sufficient in itself for being closed-minded.

Hence, the worry that an open-minded person must spend his whole life wrestling with his justifications and reasons for even his most confidently held beliefs is misplaced. To the extent that he has become genuinely open-minded, he has a great deal of latitude for ignoring many challenges, especially to his most confidently held beliefs. On the other hand, if one has not already invested resources in gaining the self-knowledge about one's bad habits of thought and developing the good habits of self-monitoring, then one has less latitude about this. For any given challenge, one cannot always be confident that one is not in a domain or circumstance within which one is likely to exhibit bad habits of thought. This puts more pressure on the otherwise virtuous person who lacks open-mindedness to invest resources in each challenge that comes along, just in case. As we've seen, this is not a practical or desirable way to live, nor, I would venture, a cognitively virtuous one. Hence, the otherwise virtuous person actually has good reason to develop the virtue of open-mindedness as well, and so the final and most difficult puzzle—Why should an otherwise virtuous person be open-minded?—can be given a fairly substantive and at least somewhat satisfying answer.

Conclusion

A great deal remains to be said about open-mindedness, but I hope to have made a start on developing an account of it that is interesting in the sense I articulated at the outset, and that has promise for solving the puzzles unique to the virtue. This has obvious ramifications for so-called virtue epistemology, but open-mindedness is a cognitive virtue that might well have import for other normative domains. I shall close with just one example for future elaboration.

Being open-minded might be necessary not just for cognitive excellence but for civic excellence as well. Tolerance is an important civic good in modern pluralist democracies. It depends upon the conviction that everyone has the right to pursue the good as she sees fit, so long as this does not violate certain side constraints (harming others, for example). This conviction is hard to maintain if too many citizens begin to lose sight of their fallibility. Open-mindedness is an important personal virtue for such societies. No doubt this is one reason that much of the debate about open-mindedness takes place in the philosophy of education literature. For those who agree that the personal virtue of open-mindedness is necessary for the civic virtue of tolerance, the state has a legitimate interest in promoting the personal virtue in the institutions of public education. All the more reason to get clear on what it is we want to inculcate in future generations of excellent citizens.

References

Adler, Jonathan. 2004. "Reconciling Open-Mindedness and Belief." *Theory and Research in Education* 2, no. 2:127–42.

Axtell, Guy. 1997. "Recent Work on Virtue Epistemology." *American Philosophical Quarterly* 34, no. 1:1–26.

Fricker, Miranda. 2007. *Epistemic Injustice*. Oxford: Oxford University Press.

Greco, John. 2003. "Further Thoughts on Agent Reliabilism." *Philosophy and Phenomenological Research* LXVI:466–80.

Hare, William. 1979. *Open-Mindedness and Education*. Montreal: McGill–Queen's University Press.

Montmarquet, James. 1993. *Epistemic Virtue and Doxastic Responsibility*. Lanham, Md.: Rowman and Littlefield.

Roberts, Robert C., and W. Jay Wood. 2007. *Intellectual Virtues*. Oxford: Oxford University Press.

Sosa, Ernest. 2007. *A Virtue Epistemology*. Oxford: Oxford University Press.

Zagzebski, Linda. 1996. *Virtues of the Mind*. Cambridge: Cambridge University Press.

11

EPISTEMIC MALEVOLENCE

JASON BAEHR

There is considerable structural symmetry between moral and intellectual character virtues. This is evident in the fact that many moral virtues have clear and straightforward counterparts among the intellectual virtues. We speak, for instance, of moral but also of *intellectual* courage, honesty, integrity, fairness, humility, and the like. The same holds for many moral and intellectual *vices*. A person can be a moral or intellectual coward, morally or intellectually dishonest, morally or intellectually unfair, and so on.[1] Given this symmetry, it is surprising that what is perhaps the paradigm moral vice has no obvious intellectual counterpart. The moral vice in question is *malevolence*. While there may be such a thing as intellectual or epistemic malevolence, this is hardly a familiar notion. It does not appear on any standard lists of intellectual vices; nor does it occupy anything like the central role in our thinking about intellectual vice that malevolence proper or moral malevolence occupies in our thinking about moral vice. This, then, suggests a notable structural asymmetry between moral and intellectual vice.

The aim of this chapter is to explore this asymmetry in some depth. The discussion is guided by three main questions: (1) Is there a counterpart to malevolence proper or moral malevolence among the intellectual virtues? (2) If so, what does it amount to? (3) Why does it fail to occupy the central role in our thinking about intellectual vice that malevolence proper occupies in our thinking about moral vice? To begin to answer these questions, we first must attempt to get clarity on the basic character of malevolence proper. This, it turns out, is no easy task. Accordingly, the first half of the chapter is spent addressing a range of questions concerning the specific character of this trait. I then go on, in light of this discussion, to develop and illustrate a conception of *epistemic*

---

[1] As this suggests, I am thinking of intellectual virtues as character traits, rather than as cognitive faculties or powers like memory, vision, introspection, reason, or the like. This difference corresponds to the difference between "responsibilist," or character-based, and "reliabilist," or faculty-based, approaches to virtue epistemology. For a discussion of this distinction, see Baehr 2006. For an up-to-date account of character-based virtue epistemology, see Baehr 2008.

malevolence. In the final part of the chapter, I address the aforementioned question concerning the role of epistemic malevolence in our ordinary ways of thinking about intellectual vice.[2]

1. Malevolence Proper

I begin by with a concise and general account of malevolence proper or moral malevolence. As I am thinking of it, malevolence is essentially or paradigmatically a matter of *opposition to the good as such*.[3] Its spirit is captured in the infamous manifesto of Milton's Satan: "Evil be thou my good," which, to better fit the definition just noted, may be recast as: "Good be thou my enemy."[4] While an acceptable first approximation, this conception bears considerable scrutiny and elaboration.

1.1. Opposition to the Good

First, what kind of opposition is essential to malevolence? Very briefly, malevolence involves opposition to the good that is *robustly volitional, active, and "personally deep."* To say that this opposition is "robustly volitional" is to say that it centrally and fundamentally involves the will. Malevolence it is not a mere conviction that the good should be opposed, nor a mere preference for such. Rather it involves a kind of hostility or contempt for the good. To say that the opposition characteristic of malevolence is "active" is to say that it tends to issue in actual attempts to stop, diminish, undermine, destroy, speak out, or turn others against the good. It is not primarily a passive orientation.[5] Finally, the opposition in question is "personally deep" in the sense that it reflects the malevolent person's fundamental cares and concerns. A malevolent person cannot simply or easily give up or repudiate her opposition to the good. This opposition is importantly tied to her self-conception: it is, at least to some extent, what she is *about*.

---

[2] While I do hope to identify the defining features of epistemic malevolence, I want to leave open the question of whether epistemic malevolence is *always* or *necessarily* an intellectual or epistemic *vice*. Specifically, I wish to leave open (though admittedly am not certain what to think about) the possibility of a person who is epistemically malevolent in the sense I lay out, but whose malevolence is driven by a sufficiently epistemically appropriate *ultimate* motivation, such that it is not really an intellectual vice. Thanks to Wayne Riggs for forcing me to think about this point.

[3] Some modifications to this definition will be called for; however, these should be viewed as qualifications or amendments, not as a rejection of the core idea behind the definition. It is also worth noting that malevolence may not be a fully univocal concept: that is, that there may be more than one kind of vice or character defect picked out by our ordinary thinking and speach about "malevolence." Accordingly, my aim in this section is merely to elucidate *one* such concept.

[4] See Milton's *Paradise Lost*, book IV, line 110.

[5] It might involve some passive elements (e.g., certain feelings); the point is that it is principally and necessarily active.

Clearly there is a close connection between the elements of malevolence just noted. It might be wondered, in fact, whether there is any meaningful distinction between, say, the first and third elements: that is, between a state's being "robustly volitional" and its being "personally deep." While closely connected, these notions are neither identical nor coextensive, for, at a minimum, a psychological state (e.g., certain desires, beliefs, or wishes) might be "personally deep," in the sense of playing a role in making its possessor the person that she is or of being very difficult to give up or repudiate, while nevertheless failing to be "robustly volitional" (since the state in question may largely be outside the person's control). Moreover, something can be "robustly volitional" without being "personally deep." I might, for instance, care very deeply about succeeding at X simply because X is a means to some cherished goal Y. While my efforts at X might "centrally and fundamentally" involve my will, I might have no, even partially, self-defining attachment to X. It may be that were X not a means to Y, or were I to pursue some other means to Y, I would not care in the least about succeeding at X. It is important, then, to maintain a distinction between the relevant aspects of malevolence.[6]

1.2. Opposition to the Good as Such

A second, trickier aspect of malevolence concerns the idea that it involves opposition to the good *as such*.[7] What exactly is it to be against the good—or anything, for that matter—"as such"?

While I cannot fully defend the view here, I think this notion is plausibly understood in terms of making something or someone an *enemy*. Just as we can choose to make someone a friend—to befriend another person—so too we can choose to make or "take up" another person or thing as an enemy. To coin a phrase, we can *enemize*. My suggestion is that to be opposed to X as such is to take up or regard X as an enemy; it is to enemize X. This fits well with the idea that the kind of opposition characteristic of malevolence is "personally deep," since our friends and enemies are among the things most personal to us. It also fits the gloss of Satan's manifesto noted above ("Good be thou my *enemy*").

In a recent discussion of *malice*, Robert Adams suggests an alternative conception of what it is to be opposed to something as such. He defines malice as "opposition to the good for its own sake" and maintains that a person is opposed to X "for its own sake" just in case she is opposed to X "noninstrumentally," that is, just in case she is opposed to X not merely for the sake of achieving some other end or goal (2006, 42–43). I shall assume

---

[6] Thanks to Heather Battaly for raising this issue with me.

[7] It might be wondered whether such an orientation is even possible. That is, to be opposed to something, mustn't one regard it as *bad*? I address this worry below.

that Adams's "malice" is essentially the same trait as my "malevolence" and that his "for its own sake" is interchangeable with my "as such."

Noninstrumental opposition and "enmity" do typically go hand in hand. However, the latter provides a better way of understanding the claim that malevolence is opposition to the good as such, for malevolence is apparently consistent with *instrumental* opposition to a good—a possibility that is ruled out by Adams's account. Note, first, that in the same way that "the enemy of my enemy is my friend," we can say that "the friend of my enemy is my enemy." Accordingly, suppose Jones is my enemy and Smith is the good friend and close ally of Jones. Apart from his relation to Jones, I have nothing against Smith. Nevertheless, in an effort to harm or spite Jones, I might make or declare Smith my enemy.[8] This in turn might bring about an opposition to Smith that is robustly volitional, active, and personally deep. I see no reason why this orientation might not also be malevolent, notwithstanding the fact my only reason for opposing Smith is to bring down Jones. Alternatively, imagine a soldier who, out of a love for his country, becomes deeply, actively, and personally opposed to his enemies in combat. These are people whom, if not for the war, the soldier would have nothing against. Here again it seems the soldier's orientation toward his enemies might count as malevolent while nevertheless being instrumental in nature. Thus while malevolence may typically involve noninstrumental opposition, this is not a requirement. And if so, it is a mistake to think of the relevant "as such" qualification in terms of such opposition. A better account of this qualification is one that appeals to the notion of making someone or something an enemy.

1.3. Impersonal Versus Personal Malevolence

A third important point concerns the *object* of malevolence. If we take Milton's Satan as a paradigm, it looks as though the immediate object of malevolence is rather abstract or impersonal, for Satan is apparently opposed to *the* good or to good*ness* itself. While I do think malevolence can take something like this form, surely this is not a requirement. A person can be malevolent simply on account of his orientation toward other persons, for example, by opposing another person's well-being or this person's share in the good. Such an orientation is independent of the malevolent person's orientation toward goodness in general. This, then, suggests a distinction between "impersonal" and "personal" malevolence. In the case of impersonal malevolence, the object is impersonal in the sense just noted; in the case of personal malevolence, the object is a person's or a group of people's well-being or share in the good.

---

[8] Interestingly, Adams himself seems to want to allow for something like this possibility, for he claims that Satan might show malice toward God "simply to spite God" (2006, 40). This makes it sound as though Satan's opposition to "important goods," as Adams puts it, is indeed instrumental to a certain end (viz., that of frustrating or angering God).

It might be thought, however, that the very notion of impersonal malevolence is problematic: that, for instance, there is something odd or implausible in the idea of opposition to something abstract or impersonal like goodness or the good in general. While I share this reservation to some extent, I think there remain good reasons to take seriously the idea of impersonal malevolence. First, we sometimes think or speak of, say, a person's love of justice or of beauty. Here the object in question presumably is justice or beauty *itself*, not merely, say, the set or any subset of just states of affairs or beautiful objects. But if we can be *for* an impersonal end like justice or beauty, why doubt that we can be *opposed* to the good or to goodness in general? Second, the notion of impersonal malevolence does have at least some intuitive traction. Again, Milton's Satan would not appear to be opposed merely or even primarily to the well-being of any one person or group of people. Nor does it seem quite right to think that he is opposed merely, say, to the well-being of every person besides himself. Instead, his wickedness seems to run deeper and to be more formal in character. He is, it seems, opposed to goodness *itself* or to the good *in general*.

Moreover, we need not limit our attention in this context to the Judeo-Christian character of Satan. Supervillains like the Joker, for instance, while no doubt opposed to the well-being of many individuals, also seem fundamentally opposed to goodness itself or to some such general or abstract end.[9] The latter, rather than the well-being of any individual or group of individuals, is an intuitively more plausible characterization of the object of the Joker's and similar villains' malevolence. Indeed, this would appear to be what makes such characters so unsettling and wicked.

Finally, note that the notion of impersonal malevolence is consistent with the possibility that the object of such malevolence is a kind of abstraction or idealization. It may be, for instance, that Milton's Satan shifts (over time) from being against, say, the well-being of God or of God and God's followers, to being against the good or goodness in general, where the latter is, in Satan's mind at least, an abstraction of the former.[10] It does not follow from this that Satan's malevolence is "personal" in the relevant sense; nor that his malevolence is *itself* an abstraction or idealiza-

---

[9] Thanks to Tom Hurka for this example. Another would be a Grinch- or Scrooge-like character who is—by appearances—opposed to something like human happiness *in general*, not necessarily to the happiness of any particular person or group of persons. Thanks to Damon Evans for this example.

[10] As this suggests, one needn't be a Platonist about properties to accept this conception of malevolence. It is also worth noting that the end in question may be more or less "abstract" or "impersonal." A malevolent person might, for instance, be against a certain kind of good *activity* (versus, say, the property of goodness or some conceptualization of it). As long as the object here is the activity understood *generally*, it still makes sense to think of this person's malevolence as "impersonal" in the relevant sense. Thanks to Anne Baril for raising this point.

tion. Thus while there may be something prima facie odd about impersonal malevolence, I shall continue to treat it as a coherent concept.[11]

1.4. The Scope of Malevolence

A fourth and related aspect of malevolence is its *scope*. Particularly when thinking of malevolence on the impersonal model just identified, it is difficult to escape the impression that the scope of malevolence is maximally broad. However, there is something at least prima facie problematic about this suggestion. For instance, if I am really opposed to goodness itself, then it seems I shall be opposed to all that is good, and thus to anyone's share in the good, including my *own*. But of course we do not tend to think of malevolent persons as being opposed to their own well-being. Similarly, suppose that human well-being consists partly in an ability to freely choose what to be for and what to be against. If so, then a person opposed to the good as a whole or to goodness itself apparently must be opposed to his own opposition, since this opposition represents an exercise of the relevant valuable ability. But again, this conflicts with our intuitive understanding of malevolence, for malevolent persons certainly need not—and perhaps cannot—be against their own opposition to the good. This suggests that there is, after all, something problematic about the very idea of impersonal malevolence.

There are two problems with this objection. First, it is not difficult to imagine that someone like Satan or the Joker might be opposed to the good in general in the sense that he takes it to be something worth opposing, and even enemizes the good as he conceives of it, but nonetheless fails to appreciate or take seriously the fact that this opposition "commits" him to being opposed even to his *own* well-being and opposition to the good. Impersonal malevolence might, in other words, be accompanied by a combination of logical inconsistency and self-deception. The malevolent person might be committed, in principle at least, to opposing his own good; but he might fail, through intellectual carelessness or dishonesty, to see that this is so, and thus to actually or actively "follow through" with his commitment.[12] Again, while this might involve ascribing to the person in question a certain kind or degree of irrationality, such irrationality seems entirely consistent with malevolence.

---

[11] Another potential worry about the notion of impersonal malevolence, suggested by Miranda Fricker, is that benevolence—the contrary of malevolence—would not appear to admit of an impersonal variety. I feel the force of this worry; but again, when weighed against the reasons for thinking that there is such a thing as impersonal malevolence, I think the more reasonable conclusion is that malevolence and benevolence simply are not structurally isomorphic in every respect.

[12] This would be similar to the person who declares with conviction that "there is no truth" or that "only empirically verifiable statements have any meaning." There is a definite sense in which such a person is "opposed" to truth in general or to the possibility that a nonverifiable statement might have meaning, notwithstanding the problematic self-referential implications of these convictions.

Second, the scope of impersonal malevolence need not be maximally broad. For an impersonally malevolent agent, instead of being opposed to the good as a whole, might be opposed to some limited part or dimension of the good. Such a person might, for instance, actively and vehemently oppose *generosity* or *neighborliness*; and she might oppose it universally—opposing even the show of generosity or neighborliness toward herself. Here the object of malevolence is still abstract or impersonal in the relevant sense, and yet it is not so broad as to raise any of the self-referential worries just noted. For this reason as well, the notion of personal malevolence remains worth taking seriously.

1.5. The Psychological Coherence of Malevolence

A fifth and closely related feature of malevolence also concerns an apparent tension within its psychology. We have said that to be malevolent is to be opposed to the good as such (or to some dimension of the good or to one or more person's share in the good). It is plausible to think, however, that to be *opposed* to something—at least in any sense relevant to malevolence—is to regard it "under the aspect" of the *bad* or to regard it *as* bad. If so, it can look as if to be malevolent is to regard as bad that which one regards as good: that it is ascribed contrary qualities to the object of malevolence. We have already seen that it would be a mistake to think of malevolence as an especially rational state. I take it, however, that it is not this irrational or irrational in this particular way. Intuitively, the malevolent person is not confused or of two minds about that which he opposes. In the two sections that follow, I consider how we might think about the psychology of malevolence so as to accommodate these facts. Doing so will require addressing some even "deeper" and more complicated aspects of the psychology of malevolence. The payoff, however, is that we shall finally be in a position to identify an epistemic counterpart to malevolence.

1.5.1. Subjective versus objective conceptions of the object of malevolence.

We may begin by noting that the worry just noted arises—or arises in full force, at any rate—only if malevolence is understood as opposition to that which one in some sense "regards" as good. If malevolence is better understood as, say, opposition to that which *in fact* is good, then the aforementioned point entails merely that malevolence is a matter of regarding as bad that which in fact is good; and this, on the surface at least, is considerably less objectionable than the claim that malevolence is a matter of regarding as bad that which one also regards as good.[13] We would do well, then, to distinguish between what I shall call a "subjective conception" of the object of malevolence and an "objective conception,"

---

[13] Though even here the worry might arise, since the objective conception allows for the *possibility* that a malevolent person will be opposed to something that she "regards" as good.

and to try to determine which of these conceptions is the more plausible one. Again, according to the subjective conception, malevolence is a matter of being opposed to something that one *regards* as good; and according to the objective conception, it is a matter of opposition to something which *in fact* is good.[14]

Which of these two conceptions is more plausible? There are, I think, good reasons for preferring a version of the subjective conception. My objection to the objective conception is twofold: namely, that X's being objectively or in fact good is neither necessary nor sufficient for a person's opposition to X to count as malevolent. That it is not necessary is evident from certain cases in which a person is deeply and vehemently opposed to what she *mistakenly* regards as a genuine good. Suppose, for instance, that a person S is firmly convinced that a certain end E is a good thing and that S comes to oppose E as such, to make an enemy of E. Suppose further that S has good *grounds* for thinking that E is good—that S's conviction is well supported by her evidence (perhaps S has good testimonial grounds for her belief or perhaps moral appearances are somehow misleading in this case). Finally, suppose that E is not, in fact, a genuine good (that E is, say, evaluatively neutral or even disvaluable).[15] While the object of S's opposition is not a genuine good, I take it that, from an intuitive standpoint, it might still make sense to regard S as malevolent. If so, then a thing's being objectively good is not necessary for a person's opposition to this thing to count as malevolent.

It might be wondered, however, whether an agent like S should instead be regarded as a kind of misguided bungler and therefore not really as *malevolent* at all.[16] While I would agree that opposition to what one mistakenly regards as good might be of this (relatively benign) sort, it need not be so. Recall, for instance, that S is firmly convinced and has good grounds for believing that E is a genuine good, but that she is also deeply and personally—even violently, say—opposed to E. E is the *enemy* of S. Given these features of S's psychology, it would be a mistake to regard her as confused, bumbling, quixotic, or the like. Indeed, on the contrary, S's opposition to E is rather disturbing—and sufficiently so, I take it, that S might reasonably be regarded as malevolent. Again, while she is ultimately mistaken about the worth of E, and while she may not be doing any genuine harm (since E is not a genuine good), S certainly *intends* to be undermining a genuine good and firmly *believes* (and with good reason) that she is doing so. Put another way, it is completely a matter of luck, relative to S's perspective

---

[14] Alternatively, we might distinguish between a *de re* (objective) opposition to a good and a *de dicto* (subjective) opposition. It is also worth noting that the two conceptions are not mutually exclusive, in the sense that one can be opposed to something which in fact is good and which one also regards as such.

[15] I am assuming, plausibly, that "good reasons" are not conclusive reasons, that is, that fallibilism about good reasons is correct.

[16] Thanks to Heather Battaly for raising this objection.

on the matter, that she is *not* "opposed" to a genuine good.[17] It is, then, plausible to think that opposition to a genuine good is not necessary for malevolence.[18]

There are also good reasons to think that opposition to a genuine good is not sufficient for malevolence. Imagine, for instance, that a person S has grown up in a community the identity of which is rooted in its opposition to what is in fact a genuine good G. S has long been taught of the problems, limits, even evils, associated with G. As a result, S has good testimonial grounds for thinking that G is bad; and nothing about S's own experience of G has threatened to defeat or undercut these grounds. As S matures, he develops a staunch personal opposition to G, one that manifests itself in his actively and vehemently opposing G. While S is opposed in the relevant sense to a genuine good, I take it that we might not regard S as *malevolent*. For again, S is opposing what he has good reason to think is a genuine *evil* (which typically would be a good or appropriate stance to take). This suggests that a thing's being objectively good is not sufficient for a person's opposition to this thing to count as malevolent.

One might worry, however, that the scenario just described could be that of a racist, say, or of some other vicious moral agent who in fact might be a paradigm instance of malevolence. Imagine, for example, a person who has grown up in a community in which she has been taught to believe that members of a given race are subhuman and lack any inherent dignity. Over time, this person comes to enemize the individuals in question and to actively oppose their well-being. Surely such a person could be malevolent, the objection goes, even if, given her background knowledge and experience, she has good reasons for thinking that the people in question deserve the relevant treatment.

There is, however, an important difference between the racist just described and most *actual* racists: namely, that most actual racists do not really have good reasons for thinking that the objects of their racism deserve the kind of judgment or treatment they dole out. A racist upbringing

---

[17] See Baehr 2007 for a discussion of the role of luck in moral and intellectual virtue attributions. For a related, contrasting discussion, see Hurka 2001, 171–80. Parts of Hurka's discussion suggest that he might opt for an objective conception of the object of malevolence and specifically that he might think of malevolence as involving a kind of brute, noncognitive, or, in his terms, "simple emotional" opposition to its object.

[18] A related question or worry is whether the subjective account is inconsistent with motivational internalism. My response, very briefly, is that it is consistent with any *plausible* version of motivational internalism. It is consistent, for instance, with the view that if S judges X to be valuable, then S will experience *some* (potentially very minimal) motivation to comply with this judgment; and it is consistent with even weaker versions of motivational internalism (e.g., Smith 1994) according to which the foregoing principle holds only for "good and strong-willed" agents (which, needless to say, a malevolent person is not). It is inconsistent with the view that if S judges X to be valuable, then S will experience an *overriding* motivation to comply with this judgment. But this view is much too strong.

notwithstanding, the total experience and knowledge base of most racists does not, I take it, really support their beliefs to the effect that the members of the target race are inferior, worthless, subhuman, or the like.[19] In light of this, our inclination to think of racists as malevolent should not be mistaken for evidence that opposition to a genuine good is (contra the argument above) sufficient for malevolence.

Nevertheless, it is worth considering the possibility of a person whose knowledge and experience base really does support his racist beliefs.[20] Again, we might imagine that these beliefs have been inculcated by otherwise reliable cognitive agents and thus that they enjoy reasonably good testimonial support. Further, we might imagine that this person's occasional run-ins with members of the race in question have (by chance) served only to confirm his negative view of them. Accordingly, this person has enemized a group of people who, given his background knowledge and experience, he has good reason to think merit his opposition. Here I take it that it is much less clear (if indeed it is clear at all) that the person in question should be considered malevolent. He is morally deceived, to be sure; and his disposition is morally bad in a deep and important sense.[21] But this does not amount to a charge of malevolence, for the latter at least connotes (possibly denotes) a kind of moral perniciousness or personal wickedness that is not exemplified by this agent.

We have, then, considered some forceful reasons for thinking that the objective conception of the object of malevolence is mistaken. This in turn bodes well for the subjective conception, according to which malevolence is a matter of opposing what one *regards* as good (but which may or may not be such). But neither is this conception immune from criticism.

One worry concerns what might be involved with "regarding" something as good. If to regard something as good is, say, to have a settled *conviction* or *belief* that it is good, then the subjective conception is problematic, for presumably some malevolent agents do not really believe (let alone firmly believe) that the object of their opposition is good. It is plausible to think,

[19] Presumably most racists have good reason to believe, for instance, that the targets of their racism share certain morally relevant features with other people they regard as having significant moral standing. More could be said, of course, about the operative notion of "good reasons"; but this is a very complex topic that I cannot take up here. I shall assume that the notion of good reasons as I have described it thus far is sufficiently intuitive.

[20] It may be thought that this is impossible: that no one's knowledge and experience base could ever be such that it really supports any racist beliefs. While I think such cases are extremely unlikely, surely they are not impossible, and all we need to disprove the objective conception is a single in case in which a person is opposed to a genuine good but is not actually malevolent. At any rate, if such cases were not possible, then so much the worse for the objection to which I am responding.

[21] The sense in question is (at least) a consequentialist one. Accordingly, if at least some virtues and vices can be defined in terms of the quality of their moral outputs (see, e.g., Driver 2001), then this person might even have certain moral *vices*.

for instance, that a malevolent agent's deep and unyielding opposition to some end might over time cause her to lose her grip on the value of this end and that she would not thereby cease to be malevolent.

In light of this possibility, we would do well to opt for a relatively weak or minimal understanding of what it is to regard something as good. Accordingly, I propose the following elaboration on the subjective conception: namely, that malevolence is a matter of opposing what one regards as good, where to "regard" X as good is, at some conscious or at least semiconscious level, to be *aware* of the value or apparent value of X (though not necessarily to *believe* that X has this value).[22] This formulation is capable of handling a range of cases that might otherwise be thought to pose a problem for the subjective conception. It might be thought, for instance, that many racists are malevolent, but that they do not (in a doxastic sense) regard the objects of their racism as good.[23] It is plausible to think, however, that in many (if not most) cases of this sort, the individuals in question do have at least a semiconscious awareness of the value or worth of the people they are "against," in which case they would qualify as malevolent on the present account.

But this more precise rendering of the subjective conception may not be weak enough. For it seems possible, not just that a malevolent person might fail to *believe* that the object of his opposition is good, but that he might lose his awareness of its value altogether. While such cases are, I would think, quite rare, it is not inconceivable that someone might, say, be opposed to the members of a particular racial (or other kind of) group for so long and with such vigor that he eventually lacks even a semiconscious awareness of the inherent dignity or worth of these people. And I see little reason to deny that such a person might still qualify as malevolent. Let us refer to cases of this sort as cases of "hardened malevolence." These are cases in which a malevolent agent's opposition to a given end so distorts her cognitive perspective on this end that she loses any awareness of its value (or apparent value). The phenomenon of hardened malevolence poses a significant challenge even to the relatively weak formulation of the subjective conception specified above.[24]

---

[22] I say "apparent" value to allow for cases of the sort discussed above in which a malevolent person opposes that which he mistakenly regards as good.

[23] Such cases are not equivalent to the one noted above in which a person's racists beliefs are well supported by her background knowledge and experience. For, at a minimum, a person might fail (in a doxastic sense) to "regard" the objects of her racist beliefs as good while *lacking* the relevant evidential or experiential support for this attitude.

[24] I did not consider cases of "hardened malevolence" in connection with the earlier discussion of well-supported racist beliefs, first, because it is not at all clear that a "hardened racist" might have good reasons in support of his beliefs, and second, because such cases clearly would *not* have been a compelling illustration of the claim that a person might be opposed to a genuine good *without* actually being malevolent—which, again, was the central point of the earlier discussion.

One response to this problem would be to try to locate the object of malevolence entirely outside the subjective perspective of the agent, for instance, by claiming that malevolence is opposition to an objective or actual good (regardless of the malevolent person's awareness of this value). We have seen, however, that this is not a promising strategy; for again, something's being objectively good is neither necessary nor sufficient for a person's opposition to this thing to count as malevolent. How, then, might we modify the subjective conception so as to accommodate cases of hardened malevolence?

We can begin to answer this question by contrasting such cases with the (highly improbable but possible) case above in which a person's racist beliefs happen to be well supported by his background knowledge and experience. Both sorts of cases have something in common: namely, that the person in question has a mistaken view of the value or worth of that to which he is opposed. In the former kind of case, however, it is plausible to regard the subject as malevolent, while in the latter kind of case it is not. What, then, explains the apparent normative difference between these two kinds of cases? Why might a "hardened racist" count as malevolent while a "misled racist" (as we might refer to him) does not?

The answer, it seems, concerns the *source* of the agents' mistakes about the worth or value of the people they oppose. The misled racist's mistake arises largely from the "outside," so to speak. Again, this person has been inundated with misinformation (by otherwise reliable sources) about the members of the relevant group; and her few encounters with these people have (uncharacteristically) served to confirm her view of them. Accordingly, there is a sense in which the misled racist's beliefs are "justified" or "warranted."[25] But the same cannot be said of the hardened racist. The main source of his false beliefs is his own malevolence: his own hatred, contempt, and opposition to the persons in question have completely "blinded" him to their moral standing. As a result, there is a sense in which the hardened racist's beliefs are irrational, unjustified, or unwarranted. There is a sense, that is, in which he (but not necessarily the misled racist) *ought to be aware* of the dignity or worth of the people to whom he is so virulently opposed.

In light of this assessment, I propose the following rendering of the subjective conception: namely, that malevolence is a matter of *opposing what one regards, or ought to regard, as good, where to "regard" X as good is, at some conscious or at least semiconscious level, to be aware of the value or*

---

[25] It bears repeating that this is a highly unusual case; indeed, it is not obvious that there are any *actual* cases of racism that fit this description. But, as noted above, all that matters is that such a case be *possible*. It is also worth noting that there may be other legitimate senses of "justification" or "warrant" in which the beliefs in question are unjustified or unwarranted. Finally, saying that the misled racist's beliefs are justified (in some legitimate sense) clearly does not amount to saying that they are epistemically good on the whole. The beliefs in question are, after all, *false*.

apparent value of X (but not necessarily to believe that X has this value).[26]

Not only does this account of the object of malevolence rule correctly vis-à-vis the sorts of cases just considered, it also has the advantage of being able to explain why malevolence is widely regarded as such a wicked or pernicious vice. On the present account, malevolence is a kind of "opposition to the good"; however, it is not essentially a *de re* opposition. Rather, it is a matter of opposing or enemizing what one is *aware* of (or *ought* to be aware of) as good. There is, then, no accidental connection between the psychology of the malevolent agent, on the one hand, and the fact that this person is malevolent, on the other. It involves a kind of "knowing" (or "ought-to-have-known") opposition to the good.[27] This sheds at least some light on the ostensibly pernicious character of malevolence.[28]

1.5.2. Resolving the tension. We are now in a position to return to the challenge noted earlier concerning how to make coherent sense of the psychology of malevolence. Recall that to the extent that malevolence involves an opposition to what one "regards" as good, and to the extent that "opposing" something in the relevant sense requires that one also regard this thing as bad, it turns out that malevolence involves regarding as bad that which one also regards as good.[29] But again, this suggests that malevolence involves a kind of psychological duality or incoherence that we do not tend to ascribe to it. In what coherent and intuitively plausible way, then, might malevolence involve the relevant contrasting attitudes?

It is important to note that there need not be just a single right answer to this question. There may be multiple ways in which the psychological tension can be resolved—multiple ways, that is, in which malevolence can plausibly be thought of as involving both a positive and a negative assessment of its object. In what follows, I identify four such ways.

First, in certain cases, there may exist a semantic gap between the relevant judgments, such that the malevolent person does not, strictly

[26] Again, the notion of "ought" employed in this formulation is aimed at picking out the species of epistemic normativity identified in the previous paragraph: that is, the species that the misled racist instantiates but that the hardened racist does not. And this, again, may be but one of many viable notions of "ought," not all of which are instantiated by the misled racist.

[27] Of course "knowing" should not be taken literally here, since the malevolent agent's belief about the value of the object of his opposition might be false. It also bears repeating that on a purely *de re* account of the object of malevolence, this connection can be accidental in the relevant sense. For again, it allows that a person who is opposed in the relevant way to a good that by all appearances, and as far she is concerned, is a genuine evil might still count as malevolent. Such an account faces the formidable challenge of explaining how or why such a person might embody the kind or level of personal wickedness that we intuitively associate with malevolence.

[28] I am very grateful to Heather Battaly for some excellent and very challenging comments on an earlier (and considerably briefer) version of the discussion in this section.

[29] Where malevolence involves opposition to something that one merely *ought* to regard as good, the present puzzle does not arise. However, as suggested by the discussion above, this is not the typical case.

speaking, ascribe contrary qualities to the object of her malevolence, and thus may not exhibit an obviously problematic level or kind of irrationality. For instance, someone might acknowledge the object of her opposition as a "good," on the one hand, but nevertheless regard it as "worthy of opposition" or as "meriting destruction or diminishment," on the other. Such an orientation would not involve an acceptance of two explicitly contrary propositions. Would it be consistent with malevolence? It seems to me that it might. Nonetheless, if the person were to regard the relevant object as "good" and as "worthy of opposition" at the same cognitive "level," so to speak, and to do so while invoking a univocal standard of goodness or worth, then perhaps she might be of two minds or ambivalent in a way that malevolent persons intuitively are not. For this reason, the present possibility is best considered in conjunction with some of the other possibilities identified below.

A second way in which a malevolent person might plausibly regard the object of his malevolence as both good and bad, just alluded to, is where this person employs alternate concepts of good and bad in his assessment of this object. Someone might, for instance, oppose the well-being of a particular group of people, which he regards as *morally* significant or valuable, on the grounds that doing otherwise would have *politically* adverse results. Thus he might regard as politically bad something which he nevertheless regards as morally good. Assuming that his opposition is sufficiently personal, volitional, and so forth, and that he enemizes the relevant people or their well-being, there is little reason to deny that his opposition might be malevolent.

A third way of alleviating the relevant tension, also alluded to above, requires distinguishing between two different ways of "regarding" something as good or bad. It is not difficult to imagine a malevolent person who, say, in an *immediate* or *personal* way, regards as bad that which, in a rather *distant, abstract,* or *impersonal* manner, he also acknowledges or regards as good.[30] This person might *experience* the object of his malevolence as bad, while still acknowledging, at some level or in some way, that this object is good or has positive worth or value. While actually making or holding to the relevant judgments in this case might involve a certain amount of self-deception or irrationality, it represents a genuine psychological possibility—one that falls within the boundaries of intuitive ways of thinking about malevolence. It does not make malevolence look implausibly irrational or cognitively dissonant.

Fourth, a malevolent person might regard the object of her malevolence as both bad and good by regarding it as bad *in one respect* or *under one*

---

[30] This is, of course, suggestive of Aristotle's discussion of *akrasia* in book VII of *Nicomachean Ethics*. The malevolent person here described lacks the kind of deep knowledge or awareness of the value of the object of his malevolence, which, on Aristotle's description, the akratic person lacks of the good.

description and as good in a different respect or under a different description. Suppose I acknowledge that the professional success of Jones would add to his happiness and in this respect regard it as a good thing. But suppose I am also filled with contempt for Jones and everything he stands for, such that, relative to my *own* happiness, I regard Jones's success as bad. This characterization does not employ different standards of "good" and "bad": *happiness* is the sole normative criterion. Further, the co-instantiation of the relevant judgments, while perhaps not fully rational, is not irrational or incoherent in a way that conflicts with our ordinary ways of thinking about malevolence. Again, while I regard Jones's success as both "good" and "bad" in a single sense, I regard it as good under one description (as a contributor to *his* happiness) and bad under a different description (as a potential threat to my *own* happiness).

We have examined four different ways in which a malevolent person might, in some sense, at some level, or in some respect, regard the object of his malevolence as both good and bad without manifesting a problematic kind or level of irrationality.[31] We may conclude that the dual judgments central to malevolence do not ultimately generate a problematic psychological conflict within the psychology of malevolence as we are conceiving of it.

2. An Epistemic Counterpart of Malevolence

We are now in a position to turn our attention to the idea of *epistemic* malevolence, and specifically, to the question of whether there *is* such a thing as epistemic malevolence, and if so, just what it amounts to. In fact, the groundwork for an answer to these questions has already been laid. In the previous section, we saw that malevolence proper is reasonably understood in terms of "opposition to the good as such," and that it admits of both impersonal and personal varieties. It is plausible, I submit, to think of epistemic malevolence as opposition to the *epistemic* good as such, and to maintain that it too admits of both impersonal and personal varieties. Let us for the moment identify the epistemic good with knowledge. Accordingly, we may think of "impersonal" epistemic malevolence as (roughly) opposition to knowledge as such, and of "personal" epistemic malevolence as (roughly) opposition to another person's share in knowledge or to her epistemic well-being as such. I turn now to consider

---

[31] It is worth noting that the ways in question are not mutually exclusive. On the contrary, it is plausible to think that malevolence can, and often does, involve some combination of these ways. For instance, an individual might, in an immediate and experiential way, regard the object of his malevolence as "worthy of opposition," while, at another, more distant and perhaps semiconscious level, regarding it as "good." This scenario combines the "semantic gap" and "different ways of regarding" possibilities identified above. Alternatively, a malevolent person might regard the object of his malevolence, at one level and in one respect, as bad, while at another level and in a different respect regarding it as good, thereby illustrating the "different ways of regarding" and "different respects" possibilities.

five candidate cases of epistemic malevolence, all of which involve some kind of opposition to knowledge. Doing so will add some flesh and bring some clarity to the concept of epistemic malevolence just noted. While several of the cases are rather extreme or hypothetical, it should not be difficult to recognize elements of them from ordinary experience.

(1) Consider, first, the philosophical skeptic. This person is, in some sense at least, "opposed to knowledge as such," for he denies the very *possibility* of knowledge, or at least of some significant variety of it (moral, philosophical, religious, scientific, and so on). However, given the model just sketched, he does not really qualify as epistemically malevolent. Among other things, the skeptic is not opposed to knowledge in a robustly *volitional* or *active* way; rather, his opposition consists merely in a denial of the possibility of knowledge. Similarly, he does not regard knowledge as an *enemy*. He might even wish that knowledge were possible and that skepticism were false: he might value knowledge as something that would be well worth pursuing if only it could be achieved. Finally, a commitment to skepticism seems actually to *rule out* the possibility of epistemic malevolence. For presumably malevolence of any sort requires, at a minimum, belief in the possibility of its object. But this is precisely what the skeptic lacks.

(2) Next consider a (roughly) Foucaultian "suspicionist." This person regards knowledge as a dangerous idea or concept. She thinks knowledge has an inherently corrupting effect on human beings. On her view, persons who pursue and acquire knowledge do so as a way of trying to control and dominate others. Thus she sees all (or nearly all) knowledge claims as *power plays*. Suppose, further, that the suspicionist is adamantly *for* social justice. The result is that she is personally, vehemently, and actively opposed to knowledge: she regularly speaks out against this alleged "good," discourages its pursuit among her friends and colleagues, and so on.

Is the suspicionist an example of epistemic malevolence? This depends on the precise character of her opposition. We stipulated that she is for social justice and that this goes some way toward explaining her opposition to knowledge. This underscores the possibility that she is not really opposed to knowledge *as such*: that she may just be strongly in *favor* of social justice, while not really regarding knowledge as an *enemy*. But of course it is also possible that she does regard knowledge as an enemy: that her opposition to knowledge is sufficiently or relevantly entrenched in her psychology such that she is not merely for social justice and only "incidentally" against knowledge. To the extent that the latter description is right, the suspicionist would seem to be a good illustration of epistemic malevolence (and of *impersonal* epistemic malevolence in particular).

It might be objected that the suspicionist is not really epistemically malevolent on the grounds that there is, after all, something right about her belief that knowledge corrupts and fosters social injustice in the relevant way.[32] It might be thought, that is, that her opposition to knowledge is rational or justified in a way that malevolence is not. While I am dubious about the epistemic credentials of the suspicionist's belief, I shall not stop to examine them here. Rather, in keeping with the discussion in section 1.5.1 above, I shall simply note that *were* the suspicionist's belief about the disvalue of knowledge rational or well supported, then it might indeed be a mistake to think of her as an illustration of epistemic malevolence.[33]

The case of the suspicionist also illustrates an earlier point related to the scope of epistemic malevolence. It is tempting to think of this person as being opposed to knowledge in *general* or to *all* knowledge. But this is implausible. First, the suspicionist may very well take herself to *know* that knowledge is dangerous in the relevant sense, but without regarding this knowledge as dangerous. Second, her campaign against knowledge is *itself* likely to involve knowledge. For instance, convincing her friends and acquaintances of the disvalue of knowledge is likely to involve a considerable amount of practical or circumstantial knowledge (e.g., knowledge about their concern for knowledge, their likely reaction to her diatribes against knowledge, better and worse ways of convincing them of the disvalue of knowledge, and so on). But again, there is no reason to think that the suspicionist will take a low view of *this* knowledge. Therefore, as with the impersonal variety of malevolence proper discussed in section 1.4 above, the scope of impersonal epistemic malevolence is not maximally broad.[34]

(3) A third candidate case of epistemic malevolence is found in the character of O'Brien in George Orwell's *1984*. O'Brien's aim is to acquire absolute control over the thinking and reasoning capacities of Winston Smith and his other subjects. He attempts to condition in them various submissive, shallow, and contradictory ways of thinking, and to prohibit any kind of intellectual autonomy or reflective questioning. O'Brien remarks, for instance, that his subjects must undergo "an elaborate mental training ... [which] makes [them] unwilling and unable to think

---

[32] Thanks to Aimée Koeplin for raising this worry.

[33] The case also underscores the point, mentioned in footnote 2 above, that epistemic malevolence is consistent with good motives (in this case social justice), and thus that it is not always a *vice* (or at least not always a *moral* vice). I shall not stop to elaborate on or defend this position. Rather, I shall simply note that a similar question arises in connection with many other virtues and vices. One is hard pressed, for instance, to deny that a terrorist or other villain can be courageous or careful, and yet it seems implausible to think that the courage and carefulness of such figures are genuine *virtues*.

[34] The considerations just noted should not lead us to be skeptical about the possibility of *impersonal* epistemic malevolence. First, while a completely general opposition to truth or knowledge may be problematic, such opposition to *other* epistemic ends or values (e.g., theoretical understanding) may not be. Second, the same combination of logical inconsistency and self-deception discussed in section 1.4 above may be operative in cases of impersonal epistemic malevolence. Thanks to Linda Zagzebski for forcing me to be clear about this.

too deeply on any subject whatsoever." His goal is that they develop "the power of not grasping analogies, of failing to perceive logical errors, of misunderstanding the simplest arguments," as well as "the power of holding two contradictory beliefs in one's mind simultaneously, and accepting both of them" (Orwell 1992, 174, 177).[35]

While ultimately a good illustration of epistemic malevolence, this case does not fit perfectly with the model sketched above. For it appears that the object of O'Brien's opposition is not principally or primarily his subjects' acquisition of *knowledge*, rather it is their capacity to *think* and *reason* in a free and rational way.[36] We might, then, draw the conclusion that O'Brien is not really epistemically malevolent (since again, we are thinking of epistemic malevolence as opposition to the epistemic good as such and have identified the epistemic good as knowledge). A more plausible response, however, would be to expand our conception of the epistemic good or of epistemic well-being such that it *includes* an ability to think and reason in a free and rational way. Surely a person with a great deal of knowledge, but without the ability to think and reason in the ways forbidden by O'Brien, would not be very epistemically well off. If we broaden our conception of the epistemic good along these lines, and if we assume that O'Brien regards his subjects' intellectual autonomy as an "enemy," then we may conclude that O'Brien is indeed epistemically malevolent (in the personal sense).[37]

(4) A similar, though more realistic (and hence more tragic) example of personal epistemic malevolence is found in Frederick Douglass's famous autobiography, in which he recounts some of his early attempts at self-education. Douglass's mistress, Sophia Auld, initially strikes him as "a woman of kindest heart and finest feelings" who had "been in a good degree preserved from the blighting and dehumanizing effects of slavery." As Douglass explains, she "commenced to teach me the A, B, C. After I had learned this, she assisted me in learning to spell words of three or four letters." At this point, however, Sophia's husband Tom intervenes, insisting that Sophia cease all instruction, "telling her, among other things, that it was unlawful, as well as unsafe, to teach a slave to read. To use his own words, further, he said, 'If you give a nigger an inch, he will take an ell. A nigger should know nothing but to obey his master—to do as he is told. Learning would spoil the best nigger in the world. Now,' said he, 'if you teach that

---

[35] Thanks to Daniel Ambord for turning my attention to this example and for helpful discussions of this and related examples of epistemic malevolence.

[36] Of course, one might be against the relevant kind of intellectual autonomy because one regards it as a means to knowledge (where knowledge is what one is "really" against). But this need not be the case; and it seems clearly not to be the case with O'Brien.

[37] I am assuming, further, and in keeping with the discussion in section 1.5.1 above, that O'Brien has or at least ought to have some sense of the worth or value of that which he is diminishing. If only the latter is true, then O'Brien would be a good example of hardened epistemic malevolence.

nigger (speaking of myself) how to read, there would be no keeping him. . . . He would at once become unmanageable, and of no value to his master. As to himself, it could do him no good, but a great deal of harm. It would make him discontented and unhappy'" (1999, 42). Before long, the corrupting influence of slavery lays hold of Sophia as well, divesting her of all of her "heavenly qualities": "Under its influence, the tender heart became stone, and the lamblike disposition gave way to one of tiger-like fierceness. The first step in her downward course was in her ceasing to instruct me. She now commenced to practice her husband's precepts. . . . Nothing seemed to make her more angry than to see me with a newspaper. She seemed to think that here lay the danger. I have had her rush at me with a face made up all of fury, and snatch from me a newspaper, in a manner that fully revealed her apprehension" (43). The Aulds seem clearly to enemize Douglass's epistemic well-being. They staunchly oppose and take active measures to thwart his acquisition of knowledge and attempts to think critically and autonomously. Specifically, they would appear to embody a kind of "hardened" malevolence. For it is not too difficult to imagine that Mr. and Mrs. Auld no longer have any sense of the worth or value of Douglass's education.[38]

(5) A final illustration is the notorious Cartesian demon—a *systematic deceiver*. The demon, we may imagine, delights in filling his subjects' minds with lies, in creating an ever-deepening and insurmountable chasm between appearance and reality. Unlike O'Brien and Mr. Auld, he is not principally concerned with controlling or manipulating his subjects' thought processes. Rather, his goal is that his subjects *end up* with as many false beliefs and as few true beliefs as possible, even if this involves their thinking or reasoning in a fairly autonomous and rational way.[39] On the surface, this seems to be a rather pure and straightforward case of personal epistemic malevolence (and, of course, Cartesian demons are sometimes referred to as "malevolent").

My only reservation concerns the possible motivation for the demon's deception. Our characterization—as with many other characterizations of Cartesian demons—at least leaves open the possibility that the demon's motivation is mere *amusement*: that he simply gets a kick out of systematically misleading his subjects. But if this is right, then while the deceiver may be epistemically twisted or perverse, it is not clear that he is malevolent, for his opposition to his subjects' epistemic well-being may not be sufficiently personal or negative. He may not regard their flourishing as bad or as a genuine *enemy*, and thus his orientation may not be adversarial enough to count as malevolent. That said, if we were to

---

[38] The two remain epistemically malevolent, according to the subjective conception of the object of malevolence discussed in section 1.5.1, however, for clearly they *ought* to have an awareness of the value of Douglass's epistemic well-being.

[39] Thus he might focus his efforts on systematically imparting false "basic beliefs," from which his subjects might reason impeccably, but to little epistemic avail.

stipulate that the demon is personally opposed to their epistemic well-being, that he is bent on deceiving them, and that his opposition is fueled by something like spite or anger or hatred, then indeed it would seem apt to view him as a paradigm example of personal epistemic malevolence.[40]

One central aim of this chapter is to shed some light on what an epistemic counterpart of malevolence proper or moral malevolence might look like. Between the discussion of malevolence proper in the previous section, and the analysis of several cases in the present section, the basic nature and structure of epistemic malevolence should be fairly clear. Again, epistemic malevolence is plausibly understood as opposition to the epistemic good as such, where the good in question includes, but is not limited to, knowledge. It is also plausible to think of epistemic malevolence as admitting of both "personal" and "impersonal" varieties in the senses outlined above.

3. Epistemic Malevolence and Intellectual Vice

We may now turn now to address the third of our initial three questions: Why don't we think of epistemic malevolence as epitomizing intellectual vice in the way that we think of malevolence proper as epitomizing moral vice? There are, in fact, two separate questions here, and they are best dealt with in turn. First, *does* epistemic malevolence epitomize intellectual vice? Is it a clear and informative paradigm element of it? And second, in the event that it is, why don't we think of it as such? Why doesn't epistemic malevolence top (or at least make an appearance on) any standard lists of intellectual vices? The first question concerns the place of epistemic malevolence within the normative structure of intellectual vice. The second concerns its place in our *thinking* about intellectual vice.

In response to the first question, I think that epistemic malevolence conceived in the present way does in fact epitomize intellectual vice. This is evident from certain standard ways of thinking about intellectual virtues and vices. First, several virtue epistemologists have thought of something like a desire for truth or knowledge as the underlying and unifying feature of intellectual *virtues*: that intellectual virtues, by definition, are traits that arise or flow from a "love" of knowledge (see, e.g., Zagzebski 1996 and Montmarquet 1993). Second, consider what apparently underlies the traits that do tend to appear on standard lists of intellectual vices. These include traits like intellectual carelessness, superficial thinking, laziness in inquiry, dogmatism, narrow-mindedness, ignoring of evidence, and so forth. Argu-

---

[40] Here again I am assuming that the agent in question is either aware, or ought to be aware, of the value of that which he is diminishing. A related example, suggested to me by Clifford Roth, is that of a politician who aims, for the sake of political victory, systematically to deceive voters about his opponent's policies, character, and the like. Here again, as long as the person genuinely *enemizes* the relevant epistemic end, and so on, his orientation would seem to be a clear case of epistemic malevolence. It would also appear to be a good example of the kind of *instrumental* opposition discussed in section 1.2 above.

ably, what these traits have in common, and what (at least in part) explains their status as intellectual vices, is either a straightforward lack of desire for knowledge or an insufficient concern with knowledge relative to other concerns (e.g., a concern with power or status, or a fear of being mistaken). Given, then, that intellectual virtue is fundamentally a matter of loving or being for epistemic goods, and that many intellectual vices have in common a lack of or otherwise inadequate concern for such goods, it stands to reason that an outright *opposition* to these goods would epitomize intellectual vice. Indeed, such opposition, which we identified as the very essence of epistemic malevolence, seems as much as or more than any other intellectual vice to represent a kind of epistemic *wickedness*.

Now for the second question: Why don't we tend to *think* of epistemic malevolence as epitomizing intellectual vice? I shall assume that this is because epistemic malevolence is less familiar to us than malevolence proper, and that this in turn is because epistemic malevolence is less *common*, that it occurs or is manifested less frequently than malevolence proper. But why is it less common?

There are, in fact, two problems with this question that need to be addressed before we can attempt to answer it. First, I have thus far left unclear how I am conceiving of the relation between malevolence proper and epistemic malevolence. At times I have suggested that the latter is an "application" of the former, in which case there is a sense in which epistemic malevolence is part of and can be subsumed under malevolence proper, while elsewhere I have described epistemic malevolence as a "counterpart" of malevolence proper, which at least leaves open the possibility that it is a separate or distinct trait. Fortunately, we need not settle this issue before answering the question at hand. For instead of comparing the relative incidence of epistemic malevolence and malevolence proper, we can compare that of epistemic malevolence and what I shall now refer to as "moral malevolence," which is opposition to the moral good or to a person's moral well-being, and where the latter consists in a person's share in certain recognizably moral values like life, health, the experience of higher and lower pleasures, freedom of movement, freedom from physical and mental suffering, and so forth. I take it that moral malevolence at least approximates what we have thus far been discussing under the label "malevolence proper." But whether this is so, or whether the latter is a considerably broader concept, need not worry us here, for epistemic malevolence remains much less common than moral malevolence thus defined. And again, our concern is why this should be.

The question stands in need of one additional refinement. As stated, it suggests that both personal and impersonal epistemic malevolence are less common than their moral counterparts. But I am not sure that this is right. Specifically, it is questionable whether *impersonal* epistemic malevolence is really less common than impersonal moral malevolence. Neither, it seems, is really very common at all. Impersonal moral malevolence is, perhaps, more *familiar*, but I suspect this is due more to certain memorable and compelling portrayals of characters like Satan and the Joker than it is to an actual higher incidence of impersonal moral malevolence. Assuming this is right, we would do best to limit our attention to the question of why personal epistemic malevolence is less common than personal moral malevolence.

How, then, might we go about explaining this discrepancy? Here again I think that there need not be, and in fact *is* not, just a single right answer. That is, I suspect the higher incidence of personal moral malevolence is attributable to a confluence of factors, four of which I attempt to identify below.[41]

First, the moral good or moral well-being arguably includes a greater *plurality* of goods or values than does its epistemic counterpart. For reasons already indicated, I would not insist that the epistemic good be *identified* with knowledge; nevertheless, as my earlier enumeration of the goods associated with moral well-being suggests, there does appear to more packed into the notion of moral well-being than into the notion of epistemic well-being. Consequently, it seems that, other things being equal, the greater breadth of moral well-being, or the greater number of moral goods, is likely to make for a greater number of occasions for personal moral malevolence. In short, within the moral realm, there is considerably more to be *against*. This provides at least a partial explanation of the higher incidence of personal moral malevolence compared with personal epistemic malevolence.

Second, I think the higher incidence of personal moral malevolence can be attributed in part to our tendency to place greater *value* on the goods to which this kind of malevolence is opposed by comparison with the value we place on the goods relevant to epistemic malevolence. If person A is filled with contempt, hatred, spite, vengeance, and the like, for person B, and consequently wishes significantly to harm B, A is more likely, I take it, to strike at B's share in certain fundamental moral goods—life, health, pleasure, freedom of movement, and the like—than he is to strike at B's share in knowledge. And this, it seems, is due at least in part to the perceived superiority of the relevant moral goods.[42] Thus, to the extent

---

[41] Clearly the answer to our question is largely an empirical one. However, as I hope to demonstrate in a moment, I think several helpful things can be said about it from the philosophical armchair.

[42] My use of "apparent" or "perceived" is not accidental, since I want to leave open the possibility that at least some epistemic goods are more valuable than some moral goods. A related point is that our tendency to place greater value on the relevant moral goods may partly be attributable to a certain kind of priority that at least some of these goods enjoy vis-à-vis certain epistemic goods: acquiring knowledge, for instance, typically requires that one have adequate food, water, and shelter (and certainly that one be *alive*). This is consistent, however, with the possibility that the relevant moral goods are not themselves more valuable.

that malevolence is motivated, as it typically is, by hatred, revenge, spite, and the like, we have at least some reason to expect personal moral malevolence to be more common than personal epistemic malevolence.

Third, there is a sense in which individual moral well-being is more *vulnerable* vis-à-vis other agents compared with individual epistemic well-being. For it is generally easier, in a world like ours, to undermine another person's moral well-being than it is to undermine her epistemic well-being.[43] It is, for instance, generally easier to undermine the pleasure, health, or practical autonomy of other people than it is to block their access to truth or knowledge or a good education. This underscores the more (though by no means exclusively) social and interpersonal dimension of morality and moral well-being compared with that of epistemic well-being. The acquisition of knowledge, while by no means a strictly solitary enterprise, is generally *more* solitary (or capable of being so) than the acquisition of moral goods. This difference goes some way toward explaining the higher incidence of personal moral malevolence, for our greater vulnerability vis-à-vis moral goods makes it more likely, other things being equal, that others will be opposed to, and more likely to attempt to undermine, our share in these goods.

A fourth and final explanation is somewhat more complicated. It is rooted partly in the fact that malevolence often arises in connection with *competition* for certain goods. If you and I must compete for a certain mutually desired good, this increases the probability, other things being equal, that enmity or malevolence will arise between us. My suggestion is that there is generally greater competition for moral goods than there is for epistemic goods and thus that we should expect a higher incidence of personal moral malevolence than of personal epistemic malevolence.

In what sense or why is there greater competition for moral goods? I think that here too the explanation is manifold. First, as indicated above, we generally value moral goods more than we do epistemic goods, in which case we are more likely to compete and to compete more fiercely for these goods. Second, our world and the goods in question are such that it is generally easier to come by the relevant epistemic goods than it is the relevant moral goods. Knowledge, for instance, is easily transmitted via testimony; books can be purchased at reasonable prices; the Internet and related media place a wealth of knowledge about a vast range of subjects at our fingertips. Knowledge is also relatively easy to come by in the sense that one person's acquiring knowledge about some subject matter X generally does not make it any less likely that someone else will be able to acquire knowledge about X. Knowledge is, in this respect, a nondepleting resource.[44] The relevant

---

[43] I owe this point to Wayne Riggs.

[44] There are, of course, exceptions to this and each of the considerations or suggestions I am putting forth in this section. My aim here is merely to identify the way things tend to be or how they tend to go relative to the goods in question (and, indeed, only how they tend to

moral goods, however, are often more expensive and less easily accessible. Maintaining good health, for instance, requires resources that are finite and often in short supply: this includes anything from affordable nourishment to state-of-the-art medical treatments. Here, one person's laying hold of the relevant resources and resulting goods *is* more likely to pose a threat to another person's laying hold of the same goods. The result is that, other things being equal, there is likely to be more competition associated with the relevant moral goods than there is with the relevant epistemic goods. Third, epistemic well-being is generally easier to sustain compared with moral well-being. Life, health, the experience of various pleasures, and so forth, require ongoing attention and investment. The good of knowledge, however, is relatively easy to sustain. This is due in no small part to the faculty of *memory*. If I satisfy a particular epistemic appetite—a desire to know about X—this appetite will remain satisfied as long as I retain and can recall the relevant information about X. But if I satisfy a particular bodily appetite—a desire for food or sleep, for instance—this satisfaction will quickly dissipate. There is, in other words, no counterpart to memory in connection with the relevant moral goods. Because moral well-being is more difficult to sustain than epistemic well-being, there is likely to be more competition, and thus more malevolence, associated with the former than with the latter.[45]

We began with the observation that there is no well-known counterpart to malevolence proper or moral malevolence among the intellectual character vices. This led to the question of what epistemic malevolence might amount to, or whether in fact there is such a thing. In section 2, we saw that there is indeed such a thing as epistemic malevolence and that its structure is analogous to that of malevolence proper or moral malevolence. But this left open the question of why epistemic malevolence is not nearly as central to our thinking about intellectual vice as moral malevolence is to our thinking about moral vice. In the present section, we have seen that this is likely due to a rather wide range of factors. While a good deal more could be said about epistemic malevolence and its relation to epistemic vice at large, much of the initial puzzlement surrounding this notion has, I hope, been dispelled.

Acknowledgments

I am grateful to many participants in the 2008 Fullerton International Philosophy Conference for helpful comments and feedback on this chapter (see specific acknowledgments spread throughout the notes above). I owe a special thanks to Michael Pace for several hours of helpful conversation

be or go *ceteris paribus*). This is all that is required for answering the central question of this section.

[45] Thanks to Damon Evans for helping me think through this complicated point.

about epistemic malevolence and related issues and to Heather Battaly for a set of very helpful and insightful comments on an earlier draft of the chapter.

References

Adams, Robert. 2006. *A Theory of Virtue*. Oxford: Oxford University Press.
Baehr, Jason. 2006. "Character, Reliability, and Virtue Epistemology." *Philosophical Quarterly* 56:193–212.
———. 2007. "On the Reliability of Moral and Intellectual Virtues." *Metaphilosophy* 38:457–71.
———. 2008. "Four Varieties of Character-Based Virtue Epistemology." *Southern Journal of Philosophy* 46:469–502.
Douglass, Frederick. 1999. *Narrative of the Life of Frederick Douglass, An American Slave*. Oxford: Oxford University Press.
Driver, Julia. 2001. *Uneasy Virtue*. Cambridge: Cambridge University Press.
Hurka, Thomas. 2001. *Virtue, Vice, and Value*. Oxford: Oxford University Press.
Montmarquet, James. 1993. *Epistemic Virtue and Doxastic Responsibility*. Lanham, Md.: Rowman and Littlefield.
Orwell, George. 1992. *1984*. Everyman's Library Series. New York: Knopf.
Smith, Michael. 1994. *The Moral Problem*. Oxford: Blackwell.
Zagzebski, Linda. 1996. *Virtues of the Mind*. Cambridge: Cambridge University Press.

12

EPISTEMIC SELF-INDULGENCE

HEATHER BATTALY

We are all familiar with self-indulgent acts. One might remember with regret (if *akratic*) or conviction (if vicious) stuffing oneself with chocolate cake, drinking scotch at breakfast, or having sex with one's best friend's partner. Moral self-indulgence is a well-established vice. What of epistemic self-indulgence? Is it possible to take pleasure in the wrong epistemic objects, or to excessively desire the right ones? I will argue that there is an epistemic analogue of moral self-indulgence.[1]

Section 1 analyzes Aristotle's notion of moral temperance, and its corresponding vices of self-indulgence and insensibility. Section 2 uses Aristotelian moral self-indulgence as a model for an account of epistemic self-indulgence. One is epistemically self-indulgent only if one *either*: (ESI1) desires, consumes, and enjoys appropriate and inappropriate epistemic objects; or (ESI2) desires, consumes, and enjoys epistemic objects at appropriate and inappropriate times; or (ESI3) desires and enjoys epistemic objects too frequently, or to an inappropriately high degree, or consumes too much of them. These conditions are necessary, not sufficient, for possessing epistemic self-indulgence. I argue that we need not look far to locate the epistemically self-indulgent: philosophers, especially skeptics, are likely candidates.

1: Aristotle on Moral Temperance, Self-Indulgence, and Insensibility

Aristotle devotes *Nicomachean Ethics* III.10–12 and parts of VII.1–9 (Aristotle 1998) to the analysis of moral temperance (*sophrosune*) and its corresponding vices. He makes seven key points that will help structure the present analysis. (1) He argues that temperance is a mean with respect to pleasures and desires. (2) He zeroes in on the differences between temperance and its corresponding vices of self-indulgence and insensibility (III.11). (3) He argues that though *akratic* and self-indulgent people perform the same acts, the self-indulgent person chooses such acts, while

---

[1] This is meant to be a contribution to the "responsibilist" wing of virtue epistemology. On "virtue-responsibilism," see Axtell 2000, Baehr 2006, Battaly 2008, Montmarquet 1993, and Zagzebski 1996. Relatively little has been written about epistemic vices. See Baehr's analysis of epistemic malevolence in this volume, and Fricker's analysis of epistemic injustice in her 2007.

the *akratic* person acts contrary to choice (VII.8). (4) He restricts the
purview of temperance and its vices to bodily pleasures and desires,
excluding pleasures of the soul (III.10). (5) He further restricts their
purview to desires and pleasures that are peculiar to individuals, excluding desires and pleasures that are common to all (III.11). (6) He contends
that the temperate person desires and enjoys "things that . . . make for
health or for good condition . . . and also other pleasant things if they are
not hindrances to these ends, or contrary to what is noble, or beyond his
means" (1119a15–18). Finally, (7), he remarks that the self-indulgent
person enjoys objects "more than . . . most men do" (1118b27).

(1) Aristotle famously defines virtue to be "a state of character concerned with choice, lying in a mean, the mean relative to us, this being
determined by a rational principle, and by that principle by which the
man of practical wisdom would determine it" (1006b36–1107a2). In II.6
he argues that each virtue is a *mean* in two different ways. First, each
virtue lies between a vice of excess and a vice of deficiency (1107a3).
Accordingly, Aristotle argues that the virtue of temperance, the mean
with regard to bodily pleasures (1118a2), lies between the vice of self-
indulgence (excess) and the vice of insensibility (deficiency). But he also
contends that insensible people "are not often found" (1107b5), since
human beings "tend more naturally to pleasures, and hence are more
easily carried away towards self-indulgence" (1109a15).

Second, virtues are *means* with respect to actions and passions: the
vices either "fall short of or exceed what is right in both passions and
actions," while the virtues "find and choose what is intermediate"
(1107a4–5). The passions associated with temperance and its correlative
vices are pleasure and desire, most notably pleasure and desire for food,
drink, and sex (1118a32). Aristotle remarks that pleasure "may be felt
both too much and too little, and in both cases not well; but to feel [it] at
the right times, with reference to the right objects, towards the right
people, with the right motive, and in the right way, is what is both
intermediate and best, and this is characteristic of virtue" (1106b20–23).
To explicate, one might enjoy or desire appropriate *or* inappropriate
objects (e.g., sex with one's own or one's best friend's partner), enjoy or
desire them at appropriate *or* inappropriate times (e.g., scotch at a party
or while teaching a class), enjoy or desire them too much (ecstatically or
too frequently) *or* too little (listlessly or too seldom), and so on.[2] The
virtue of temperance requires hitting the mean with respect to bodily
passions; it requires (for starters) enjoying and desiring appropriate
objects, to the appropriate degree, at appropriate times.

---

[2] Howard Curzer points out that since pleasure and desire can be independent—e.g., one
can enjoy sex too little (listlessly), but desire it too frequently (hourly)—the temperate person
must hit the mean both with respect to pleasure and with respect to desire. See Curzer 1997,
especially 12, 16.

The actions that fall under the domain of temperance and its vices are acts of consumption—for example, eating cake, drinking scotch, engaging in sex with one's partner—and corresponding acts of omission, which consist in not doing such things. Aristotle assumes that one must consume a physical object in order to take bodily pleasure in it.[3] Hence, to hit the mean with respect to bodily pleasures, one must first hit the mean with respect to acts of consumption.[4] As was the case with pleasures, one might consume appropriate *or* inappropriate objects, consume them at appropriate *or* inappropriate times, consume too much of them *or* too little, and so on. Hitting the mean with respect to acts of consumption requires consuming appropriate amounts of the appropriate objects at appropriate times. In sum, Aristotle argues that the temperate person hits the mean between insensibility and self-indulgence by hitting the mean in her passions and actions. She desires, consumes, and takes pleasure in appropriate objects, in appropriate amounts, to the appropriate degree, at appropriate times.

(2) In III.11, Aristotle further delineates the differences between temperance and its corresponding vices. He contends that the vice of self-indulgence requires three types of excess (1118b24). To be self indulgent, one must desire and enjoy both appropriate and inappropriate objects, one must desire and enjoy objects "in the wrong way," and one must do so "more than most people do" (1118b24). In his words, self-indulgent people "delight in some things that they ought not to delight in (since [the things] are hateful), and if one ought to delight in some of the things they delight in, they do so more than one ought and than most men do" (1118b25–27). In short, the self-indulgent person (i) desires and enjoys appropriate and inappropriate objects indiscriminately; and when he has per chance fastened on appropriate objects, he (ii) desires and enjoys them at inappropriate times, and (iii) desires and enjoys them too much. To illustrate, the self-indulgent person desires and enjoys, say, having sex with his best friend's partner (an inappropriate object) as well as having sex with his own partner (an appropriate object); and when he desires and enjoys the latter, he does so during funerals and job interviews (at inappropriate times), and does so too much (hourly).[5] The self-indulgent person exceeds with respect to objects, occasions, and degrees and amounts because he wants and chooses pleasure. Not only does he think that pleasure is good, he values it above all else. In this vein, Aristotle remarks that "the self-indulgent man ... craves for all pleasant things ... and is led by his appetite to choose these at the cost of everything else" (1119a1–2). Because the self-indulgent person overvalues pleasure, he fails to discriminate objects (and occasions and amounts) that are appropriate from objects (and so on) that are not—he thinks all objects

---

[3] Aristotle restricts consumption to touch and, arguably, taste (1118a26).

[4] If one is not consuming the appropriate objects at the appropriate times, then one cannot take pleasure in the appropriate objects at the appropriate times.

[5] For an excellent account of temperance with respect to sex, see Halwani 2003, chap. 3.

(and so on) are appropriate. Overvaluing pleasure also prevents him from recognizing and pursuing other things of value.

The character Aristotle identifies in the passages above is undeniably self-indulgent, since she exceeds with respect to all three of his parameters. But Aristotle's account of self-indulgence is too strong: one need not go to excess in all three ways to be self-indulgent; excess with respect to any one parameter is all that is needed. After all, the person who desires, consumes, and enjoys all sorts of appropriate and inappropriate sexual objects (best friend be damned!) is still self-indulgent, even if she only does so at appropriate times. Something similar can be said of those who desire, consume, and enjoy only appropriate sexual objects, but do so at every opportunity—for example, having sex with one's own partner during a funeral is indeed self-indulgent. Likewise, those who desire and consume appropriate objects (bread) but desire them too frequently (every quarter-hour) or consume too much of them (a whole loaf) at any one sitting are self-indulgent. Hence, one is morally self-indulgent *only if* one either: (MSI1) desires, consumes, and enjoys appropriate and inappropriate objects; or (MSI2) desires, consumes, and enjoys objects at appropriate and inappropriate times; or (MSI3) desires, consumes, and enjoys objects too much. (MSI3) may be further analyzed into frequencies, degrees, and amounts, so that it reads: "One desires and enjoys objects too often, or to an inappropriately high degree, or consumes too great an amount of an object." One can desire and enjoy objects too much by wanting or enjoying them too *frequently*; that is, wanting or enjoying them at too many times, as when one wants scotch hourly. One can also desire and enjoy objects too much by having an inappropriately high *degree* of longing for an object at a given time ("dying" for a latte), or taking an inappropriately high degree of pleasure in an object at a given time (ecstatically enjoying a sandwich).[6] Finally, one consumes objects too much by consuming them too frequently (drinking scotch hourly); and one consumes too much of an object by consuming an extreme *amount* at a single time (stuffing oneself with chocolate cake).

Aristotle contends that in contrast with the self-indulgent person, the temperate person "neither enjoys the things that the self-indulgent man enjoys most—but rather dislikes them—nor in general the things that he should not, nor anything of this sort to excess" (1119a11–14). The objects that the temperate person enjoys, and the occasions on which she does so, are subsets of the objects that the self-indulgent person enjoys, and the occasions on which he does so. The temperate person desires, consumes, and enjoys only appropriate objects, only at appropriate times, and only to the appropriate amount, degree, and frequency. In Aristotle's words, the temperate person "craves for the things he ought, as he ought, and when he

---

[6] Of course, it is appropriate to ecstatically enjoy and/or long for some objects, but sandwiches and lattes are not among them.

ought" (1119b16). Hence, the morally temperate person (MT1) desires, consumes, and enjoys only appropriate objects; and (MT2) desires, consumes, and enjoys them only at appropriate times; and (MT3) desires, consumes, and enjoys them only to the appropriate amount, degree, and frequency. It is important to note that the morally temperate person *does* enjoy appropriate objects: she ecstatically enjoys sex with her own partner at appropriate times, she is pleased by a good cup of coffee in the morning, and so on. She enjoys the right objects at the right times because she values pleasure appropriately. She thinks that physical pleasure is good, but does not overvalue it. Unlike the self-indulgent person, her pursuit of pleasure does not crowd out other worthwhile pursuits.

Accordingly, Aristotle argues that the insensible person places too little value on physical pleasure, denying its importance in his life. Aristotle spends little time examining defect with respect to bodily pleasures because he thinks that "people who fall short with regard to [such] pleasures and delight in them less than they should" are rare and, perhaps, even inhuman (1119a6–7). But we can assume that unlike the self-indulgent person, who desires, consumes and enjoys appropriate and inappropriate objects, and the temperate person who desires, consumes, and enjoys only appropriate objects, the morally insensible person (MI1) chooses not to desire, consume, or enjoy some objects that it would be appropriate to enjoy (e.g., he does not enjoy sex with his partner because he thinks that he shouldn't enjoy it). Further, unlike the self-indulgent person, who desires, consumes, and enjoys objects at appropriate and inappropriate times, and the temperate person who desires, consumes, and enjoys objects only at appropriate times, the morally insensible person (MI2) chooses not to desire, consume, or enjoy objects on some occasions when it would be appropriate to do so (e.g., he does not consume champagne at a wedding). Finally, we can assume that unlike the self-indulgent person who desires, consumes, and enjoys objects too much, and the temperate person who desires, consumes, and enjoys objects to the appropriate amount, degree, and frequency, the morally insensible person (MI3) chooses to desire, consume, and enjoy objects too little (e.g. he consumes, but does not sufficiently enjoy, a delectable meal because he thinks it is bad to do so). As was the case with self-indulgence, one need not satisfy all three conditions to be insensible; deficiency with respect to one parameter is all that is needed.

(3) Moral temperance, self-indulgence, and insensibility all require choice. For Aristotle, choice requires rational desire (*boulesis*). Roughly, one rationally desires physical pleasure when one wants it because one thinks it is good; when one desires it because it plays a role in one's conception of the good life. Though the self-indulgent person and the *akratic* person perform the same acts—both stuff themselves with chocolate cake—the self-indulgent person chooses to do so, while the *akratic* person acts "contrary to his choice" (1148a10). The self-indulgent person "pursues the excesses of things pleasant . . . and does so by choice,

and for their own sake and not at all for the sake of any result distinct from them" (1150a18–20). The self-indulgent person's conception of the good life is dominated by the value he places on pleasure. When he stuffs himself with chocolate cake, he is "led on in accordance with his own choice, thinking that he ought always to pursue the present pleasure" (1146b22–23). That is, he thinks that it is good to stuff himself with chocolate cake, and does so without regret. In contrast, the *akratic* person does not rationally desire large quantities of chocolate cake. In fact, she thinks that it is bad to stuff herself with chocolate cake, but she does so, despite her rational desires, because of appetite (a desire that is decidedly not rational). Because the *akratic* person acts contrary to her rational desire, she regrets her action. So, one who consumes too much chocolate cake at a single sitting, and regrets doing so, is *akratic*, not self-indulgent. She is *akratic* even if she enjoys eating the cake at the time (provided that she regrets it later). Since I agree that self-indulgence and *akrasia* are two different states, and that the vice of self-indulgence is more blameworthy than *akrasia* (VII.8), I endorse Aristotle's contention that self-indulgence requires choice.[7]

1.A. Which Objects Are Appropriate?

Which objects does the temperate person desire, consume, and enjoy? Aristotle provides three criteria—points (4), (5), and (6) above—that help us zero in on appropriate objects. (4) He argues that temperance and its correlative vices are only concerned with bodily pleasures, not pleasures of the soul. (5) He restricts their purview to desires and pleasures that are acquired and peculiar to individuals, excluding those that are natural and common to all. Finally, (6) he contends that the temperate person desires and enjoys both objects that "make for health or for good condition" and "other pleasant things if they are not hindrances to these ends, or contrary to what is noble, or beyond his means" (1119a15–18).

(4) III.10 restricts temperance, self-indulgence, and insensibility to bodily pleasures for food, drink, and sex, excluding pleasures of the soul such as "love of honor and love of learning" (1117b29). Aristotle remarks that the person who loves honor and learning "delights in that of which he is a lover, the body being in no way affected, but rather the mind" (1117b30–31). On his view, people who love learning and honor are "called neither temperate nor self-indulgent" (1117b32). The same is true of "those who are concerned with other pleasures that are not bodily; for those who are fond of hearing and telling stories . . . are gossips, but not self-indulgent" (1117b33–35). Here, Aristotle is distinguishing between

---

[7] Without reference to rational desire and a conception of the good life, it will prove difficult to distinguish between *akrasia* and vice. The appetites that produce the *akratic's* actions may be cognitively impenetrable. For a discussion of cognitive impenetrability, see Amy Coplan's "Feeling Without Thinking" in this collection.

physical pleasures and cognitive pleasures. Physical pleasures require direct contact (touch) with the body, whereas cognitive pleasures do not. The pleasures of story-telling are cognitive. In section 2, I argue that epistemic pleasures are a subset of cognitive pleasures.

Arguably, Aristotle restricts temperance and its vices to physical pleasures, because he thinks that "temperance and self-indulgence . . . are concerned with the kind of pleasures that the other animals share in" (1118a23). III.10 even goes so far as to exclude the pleasures of vision, hearing, and smell from the purview of temperance and its vices on the grounds that other animals do not share them. In short, Aristotle thinks that we share desires for food, drink, and sex with nonhuman animals. What sets us apart from nonhuman animals is our capacity to regulate those desires via reason. The temperate person succeeds in regulating those desires: his appetites "harmonize with reason" (1119b15). He neither overestimates nor underestimates the value of the pleasures of food, drink, and sex.[8] In section 2, I contend that this line of argument does not preclude an account of epistemic self-indulgence.

Aristotle has a second motivation for excluding love of learning from the purview of self-indulgence. In III.10, he takes love of learning and love of honor to be of a piece because he thinks learning and honor are both objects that are worthy of choice. In VII.4, he contends that we are not blamed for "desiring and loving" objects that are worthy of choice, but only for "doing so in a certain way; i.e. for going to excess" (1148a28–29). In his words, "there is no wickedness" with regard to learning and honor, because each is "by nature a thing worthy of choice for its own sake; yet excesses in respect of them are bad and to be avoided" (1148b2–5). In other words, one cannot be vicious with respect to desiring, consuming, and enjoying objects that are worthy of choice for their own sakes. Since learning and honor are appropriate objects, one cannot satisfy (MSI1). Recall that for Aristotle one must satisfy all three conditions, including (MSI1), to be self-indulgent. For this reason, he refuses to extend the category of self-indulgence to those who take excessive pleasure in learning and honor. He implies that if such people are to be called "self-indulgent" at all, they can only be self-indulgent in a qualified sense: "self-indulgent with respect to honor."[9] In these passages, Aristotle assumes that all truths (that are learned) are worthy. In section 2, I suggest that some true beliefs may be less worthy than others.

(5) In III.11, Aristotle further restricts the purview of temperance and its vices to bodily desires that are acquired and "peculiar to individuals," rather than those that are "common" or "natural" (1118b8). In Aristotle's words, "The appetite for food is natural, since everyone who is without it craves for

---

[8] Unlike self-indulgent and insensible people, the temperate person appropriately values her animal appetites. See Young 1988.

[9] Aristotle does imply that we can satisfy (MSI3) with respect to learning and honor.

food or drink ... and for love also ...; but not everyone craves for this or that kind of nourishment or love, nor for the same things. Hence, such cravings appear to be our very own" (1118b9–13). In analyzing this passage, Charles Young astutely argues that "common" desires are for food, drink, and sex *simpliciter*—basic hunger, thirst, and lust. To illustrate, if I am "starving," I may want to eat something, anything, without caring what. We all have these "common" appetites because we all need nourishment. In contrast, desires peculiar to individuals are for specific kinds of food, drink, or sex—gin, Tanqueray gin—and differ from one person to the next. Each of us has the peculiar desires she does, not because of biological needs, but because of what she enjoys: she wants chocolate cake because she likes it, and may want it even when she isn't hungry (see Young 1988, 528–31).

Aristotle insightfully argues that those who go wrong with respect to natural desires are "brutish": they are sick rather than vicious (see also VII.5). In his words, with respect to the natural appetites, "few go wrong, and only in one direction, that of excess; for to eat or drink whatever offers itself till one is surfeited is to exceed the natural amount, since natural appetite is the replenishment of one's deficiency" (1118b15–18). Aristotle thinks that people who indiscriminately consume food, filling "their bell[ies] beyond what is right," are "belly-gods" (1118b19). They are "slavish" and sick, rather than self-indulgent. This is as it should be. One can be blamed for possessing the vice of self-indulgence, but compulsive eating, compulsive drinking, and sex addiction are pathological rather than blameworthy. In fact, alcoholism and sex addiction are now widely thought to be diseases, not vices.

But Aristotle wrongly overlooks deficits with respect to natural desires. Those who are anorexic, and those who suffer from deficiencies with respect to sex drive, are sick rather than insensible. Since we can be blamed for possessing vices like self-indulgence and insensibility, but cannot be blamed for excesses or deficiencies with respect to natural desires, Aristotle is right to restrict the purview of temperance and its vices to peculiar desires.

(6) III.11 ends with Aristotle's claim that the temperate person desires, consumes, and enjoys both objects that "being pleasant, make for health or for good condition" and also "other pleasant things if they are not hindrances to these ends, or contrary to what is noble, or beyond his means" (1119a15–18). To borrow further analysis from Charles Young, the temperate person desires and enjoys objects that actively contribute to health, and objects that are "merely consistent" with health provided that they are not ignoble or too expensive (1988, 534). Young brilliantly dubs the latter "treats." To illustrate, broccoli actively contributes to health, whereas reasonably priced chocolate cake is a treat—it does not make one healthier, but neither does it undermine health. According to Young, Aristotle thinks that "a temperate person will on occasion eat or drink something solely for the sake of the pleasure it brings" and not because it

contributes to health (1988, 535). This is good news: temperate people sometimes eat chocolate cake! They recognize that it is sometimes appropriate to desire, consume, and enjoy foods that do not directly contribute to health. Temperance just became easier to attain. Given (6), (MT1), (MSI1), and (MI1) will read: (MT1) the temperate person desires, consumes, and enjoys both objects that contribute to health and treats; (MSI1) the self-indulgent person desires, consumes, and enjoys objects that contribute to health and treats, *and* objects that either undermine health, are ignoble, or are beyond her means; (MI1) the insensible person chooses not to desire, consume, or enjoy some objects that either contribute to health or are treats.

One might worry that the inclusion of treats in (MT1) is too liberal, blurring the line between temperance and self-indulgence. In reply, first, recall that the temperate person must not only consume and enjoy appropriate objects, he must do so at appropriate times, in appropriate amounts and degrees, and with appropriate frequencies. Occasionally, the temperate person will desire, consume, and enjoy chocolate cake, but he will not desire, consume, or enjoy more chocolate cake than he should. Consuming chocolate cake too often, or in large quantities, does undermine health.[10] Those who exceed with respect to the amount, degree, or frequency of treats are self-indulgent, not temperate. Second, the category of treats is not as wide as it may first appear. The temperate person will not consume any objects that he cannot afford, or any objects that are ignoble. Though one "Golden Opulence Sundae" would not undermine his health, it is excluded from the category of treats because it is (presumably) beyond his means.[11] Nor will sex with his best friend's partner count as a treat, since it is ignoble. Third, arguably, those who do not occasionally desire, consume, and enjoy treats are insensible. People who only consume foods that contribute to health, and *never* consume or enjoy treats like chocolate cake, have placed too much value on health (they may be obsessed) and too little value on pleasure.

1.B. How Much Is too Much?

Aristotle offers no guidance with respect to *when* it is appropriate to enjoy the objects in question; and the little guidance he does offer with respect to appropriate amounts, degrees, and frequencies cannot be correct by his own lights. (7) Aristotle argues that the self-indulgent person desires, consumes, and enjoys objects "more than most people do" (1118b27). Here, he keys appropriate amounts of consumption and appropriate degrees and frequencies of desire and enjoyment to "most people." This is

---

[10] In the film *Supersize Me*, Morgan Spurlock argues that a thirty-day diet of fast food undermined his health.

[11] This ice cream sundae is served at Serendipity 3 in Manhattan at a price of $1,000.

a radical departure from his standard way of answering such questions, which defines appropriateness in terms of the practically wise person (see also Curzer 1997, 16). Presumably, it does not matter how much desire and enjoyment most people have, or how much they consume, since most people are not temperate.

Aristotle should have claimed that the appropriate amounts, degrees, and frequencies are those of the practically wise person. Can we offer any guidance that is more specific? We can at least claim that desire, enjoyment, and consumption are excessive when they prevent one from pursuing or attaining other things of value. Too much desire, enjoyment, or consumption can stall us out, derailing other worthwhile projects. To borrow an illustration from Raja Halwani, the self-indulgent person spends "yet another afternoon watching yet another pornography movie rather than writing the philosophy paper they had been planning on writing" (2003, 184). She loses sight of other values (e.g., writing philosophy papers) as a result of overvaluing bodily pleasures.

2. Epistemic Temperance, Self-Indulgence, and Insensibility

Using the analysis in section 1 as a model, I will argue that there are epistemic analogues of moral temperance, self-indulgence, and insensibility. I will endorse epistemic versions of points (1) to (3) and (5) to (7), and argue that (4) does not preclude an account of epistemic self-indulgence. For starters, (1′) like its moral counterpart, epistemic temperance lies in a mean between a vice of excess—epistemic self-indulgence—and a vice of deficiency—epistemic insensibility. It, too, is a mean with respect to passions and actions. The passions associated with epistemic temperance and its vices are the desire for and enjoyment of epistemic objects (e.g., beliefs, knowledge). One might enjoy or desire appropriate *or* inappropriate epistemic objects (e.g., true beliefs about the current global economy or false beliefs about the current global economy), enjoy or desire them at appropriate *or* inappropriate times (while teaching a class or while having sex with one's partner), and enjoy or desire them too much (ecstatically or too frequently) or too little (listlessly or too seldom). Hitting the mean with respect to epistemic passions requires enjoying and desiring appropriate epistemic objects, to the appropriate degrees and frequencies, at appropriate times. The actions associated with epistemic temperance and its vices are acts of "consuming" epistemic objects, in much the same way that one can be said to "consume" information or misinformation. The epistemic objects consumed are often (but not exclusively) claims or propositions; that is, propositions count as *epistemic* objects when, in consuming them, we form *beliefs* about their contents.[12] The acts of researching and reading

---

[12] Nonpropositional objects like works of art can also count as epistemic objects.

are paradigmatic acts of epistemic consumption. Such acts are voluntary—we choose which topics to research, which sources to read and consult, and when. Hitting the mean with respect to acts of epistemic consumption requires consuming appropriate amounts of appropriate epistemic objects at appropriate times.

Accordingly, (2') a person will be epistemically temperate only if he: (ET1) desires, consumes, and enjoys only appropriate epistemic objects; and (ET2) desires, consumes, and enjoys them only at appropriate times; and (ET3) desires, consumes, and enjoys them only to the appropriate amount and degree and with the appropriate frequency. A person will be epistemically self-indulgent only if he *either*: (ESI1) desires, consumes, and enjoys appropriate and inappropriate epistemic objects; or (ESI2) desires, consumes, and enjoys epistemic objects at appropriate and inappropriate times; or (ESI3) desires and enjoys epistemic objects too frequently, or to an inappropriately high degree, or consumes too much of them. (As above, satisfying any one of these conditions is all that is needed.) Finally, a person will be epistemically insensible only if he *either*: (EI1) chooses not to desire, consume, or enjoy some epistemic objects that it would be appropriate to enjoy; or (EI2) chooses not to desire, consume, or enjoy epistemic objects on some occasions when it would be appropriate to do so; or (EI3) chooses to desire and enjoy epistemic objects too seldom, or to an inappropriately low degree, or to consume too little of them. Moral insensibility may well be rare, but I will argue that epistemic insensibility is not rare, and may even be more prevalent than epistemic self-indulgence.

Briefly, (3') epistemic *akrasia* and epistemic self-indulgence are distinct states. The epistemically self-indulgent person and the epistemically *akratic* person perform the same acts—both consume inappropriate epistemic objects, like engaging in wishful thinking. But unlike the epistemically *akratic* person, the self-indulgent person chooses to do so, and does so without regret. She pursues epistemic pleasure for its own sake; she thinks that she ought to pursue epistemic objects that produce pleasure. In short, she believes that it is good to employ wishful thinking because it is pleasurable. In contrast, the *akratic* engages in wishful thinking, but regrets doing so.[13]

Section 2.A contends that Aristotle's argument for (4) does not preclude an account of epistemic self-indulgence. Section 2.B takes steps toward identifying appropriate epistemic objects. I endorse (5'), which restricts the purview of epistemic temperance and its vices to epistemic desires that are peculiar and acquired rather than natural. I also argue for (6'): the epistemically temperate person desires, consumes, and enjoys both objects that contribute to valuable epistemic ends and epistemic treats. Section 2.C provides illustrations of epistemically self-indulgent

---

[13] For an excellent analysis of epistemic *akrasia*, see Hookway 2001.

people and epistemically insensible people, whose epistemic desires are excessive and deficient, respectively (7').

2.A. Why Do We Need an Account of Epistemic Self-Indulgence?

Despite Aristotle's restriction of temperance and its vices to physical pleasures, I will argue that his view invites, perhaps even requires, an account of epistemic self-indulgence. Aristotle argues that pleasures of the soul—cognitive pleasures—fall outside the purview of temperance and its vices. Cognitive pleasures, like the pleasures of story-telling, reading novels, and playing video games, do not require direct physical contact with the body. Epistemic pleasures are a subset of cognitive pleasures: they are the pleasures one takes in learning, beliefs, knowledge, and belief-forming activities. Not all cognitive pleasures are epistemic: we often enjoy films and novels solely because they are entertaining, not because we form beliefs about their contents.

Aristotle excludes all cognitive pleasures from the purview of temperance and its vices on the grounds that we do not share these pleasures with animals. But Aristotle also famously argues that rationality sets us apart from other animals. Young reminds us that for Aristotle "our animality is not the distinguishing aspect of our humanity" (1988, 539). Physical pleasures are not "distinctively human." Rather, distinctively human pleasures are found "in activities [Aristotle] associated with rationality . . . and it is these activities, according to him, that should fill our lives, so far as possible" (1988, 540). Not only do the above remarks fail to preclude an account of epistemic temperance, they positively cry out for one. Since Aristotle thinks that the distinctively human pleasures are epistemic ones, providing an account of epistemic temperance should be even more important for him than providing an account of temperance that addresses physical pleasures.[14]

Aristotle also excludes love of learning from the purview of self-indulgence on the grounds that (roughly) all truths are equally worthy. In the next subsection, I suggest that this may not be the case. But even if those arguments fail, Aristotle should still admit the need for an account of epistemic self-indulgence. After all, the restrictions that he places on self-indulgence are too strong. We need not meet (MSI1), (MSI2), and (MSI3) to be self-indulgent; meeting any one condition is all that is needed. And Aristotle implies that we *can* meet (MSI3)—we can desire, consume, and enjoy learning too much. The same is true of epistemic self-indulgence.

Finally, accounts of epistemic temperance, self-indulgence, and insensibility are needed in education. Few high school students are taught to

---

[14] Aristotle is also wrong to exclude nonepistemic cognitive pleasures, e.g., the pleasures of story-telling and playing video games, from the purview of moral self-indulgence. Surely, we can be self-indulgent with respect to such pleasures.

desire and enjoy epistemic objects, perhaps because we are still influenced by a hard-line distinction between reason and emotion, or because epistemic pleasures are difficult to attain. And even if students were encouraged to desire, consume, and enjoy epistemic objects, they would no doubt find it difficult to muster up and sustain desire for appropriate epistemic objects (e.g., the activity of weighing evidence), when inappropriate objects (e.g., the activity of wishful thinking) are tempting and easy. Aristotle himself recognizes that "the pleasures arising from thinking and learning will make us think and learn all the more" (1153a22–23). If we follow his lead, and train students to desire and enjoy appropriate epistemic objects, we can produce an educational system that recognizes the importance of acquiring virtuous epistemic habits.[15]

2.B. Which Epistemic Objects Are Appropriate?

For starters, what counts as an "epistemic object"? What sorts of things in the epistemic realm are candidates for being desired and enjoyed? There are at least two types of candidates: end-states, and activities. Epistemic end-states include beliefs, knowledge, and understanding. For simplicity's sake, I will focus on beliefs. Beliefs can be true or false, theoretical or practical, and potentially harmful or helpful to other human beings. They can be about anything, from the whereabouts of Paris Hilton, to Derek Jeter's batting average, to the latest views about consciousness, global warming, or the world economy.[16] Sometimes we desire and enjoy epistemic end-states: we want true beliefs, or want to avoid false beliefs, about the side-effects of medication X, or about whether quantum particles are wave functions. Sometimes we desire and enjoy engaging in epistemic activities. Epistemic activities include belief-forming and -sustaining processes and practices, epistemic actions, methods of inquiry, and the epistemic virtues and vices themselves. Epistemic activities can be reliable or unreliable, acquired or natural, and voluntary or involuntary. Those that are acquired and voluntary can be employed or avoided by epistemically virtuous people.[17] Hence, epistemic activities are a motley group, including, for example, vision, induction, deduction, hasty generalization, wishful thinking, open-mindedness, dogmatism, entertaining alternative views, and ignoring objections.

Let's begin to narrow this field. Do any of the above candidates for being desired and enjoyed fall *outside* the purview of epistemic temperance and its

---

[15] See also Homiak 1981; and Roberts and Wood 2007, 172.

[16] I assume throughout that celebrity and sports trivia are not acquired via violations of privacy.

[17] The category "epistemic activities" is much broader than the category "epistemic acts (of consumption)." Epistemic acts (of consumption) are voluntary; epistemic activities need not be.

vices? Recall Aristotle's restriction of the purview of moral temperance and its vices to acquired desires that are "peculiar" to individuals. Is there a useful epistemic analogue here? I argue that there is: (5′) the purview of epistemic temperance and its vices is restricted to epistemic desires that are peculiar and acquired, excluding those that are common and natural.

Which epistemic desires are common and natural? Arguably, the desire for perceptual information about one's immediate surroundings is natural. Aristotle agrees: "All men by nature desire to know. An indication of this is the delight we take in our senses ... and above all others the sense of sight" (Aristotle 1984, 980a22). Like the desire for food, the desire for perceptual knowledge is hard-wired in humans. Just as we all need nourishment, we all need to know whether there is a tiger in the bushes. Likewise, the desires associated with other hard-wired belief-forming processes, like memory and basic induction and deduction, are also natural. By way of contrast, epistemic desires peculiar to individuals are acquired, and directed at specific types of knowledge that are not desired by all: knowledge of baseball statistics, of bird migration, of metaphysics. Each of us has the peculiar epistemic desires she does, not because of biological needs, but because of what she likes and values.

We should restrict the purview of epistemic temperance and its vices to epistemic desires that are "peculiar" and acquired because we can be praised and blamed for peculiar desires, but not for natural ones. One can be praised for wanting to understand the conflict in the Middle East, or wanting knowledge about the global economy, and blamed for wanting to read tea leaves. But one cannot be praised for possessing natural (hard-wired) epistemic desires or be blamed for lacking them. People who "err" with respect to such natural desires are "epistemic brutes": they are disabled, not vicious. People who lack the natural desire for perceptual information about their surroundings likely suffer from neurological or developmental disorders or disabilities, for which they are clearly not blameworthy. Nor would we blame people who possess excessive or compulsive natural desires for perceptual information, should such people exist. Since we can be blamed for epistemically self-indulgent and insensible desires, but cannot be blamed for excesses or deficiencies with respect to natural epistemic desires, such natural desires fall outside the purview of epistemic temperance and its vices.

Let's narrow the field further. Which of the remaining candidates do epistemically temperate people desire, consume, and enjoy? Section 1 argued that the morally temperate person desires, consumes, and enjoys *both*: particular sorts of food, drink, and sex that actively contribute to health; *and* treats. Analogously, I submit that (6′) the epistemically temperate person desires, consumes, and enjoys *both*: particular sorts of beliefs, knowledge, and methods that actively contribute to valuable epistemic ends; *and* epistemic treats. What is an epistemic treat? Moral treats neither undermine health nor are ignoble or beyond the agent's means. Analogously, at the very least, epistemic treats do not undermine valuable epistemic ends. We can add analogues of the remaining two conditions—nor are they epistemically ignoble or beyond the agent's epistemic means—should the need arise. But, here, I focus on the first condition: epistemic treats do not undermine epistemically valuable ends.

Which ends are epistemically valuable? Roughly, if any ends are epistemically valuable, avoiding falsehoods and attaining truths are. False beliefs and unreliable practices and methods of inquiry do not, as such, actively contribute to epistemically valuable ends. Nor are they epistemic treats, since they undermine the end of avoiding false-hoods. True beliefs and reliable practices and methods of inquiry do appear to actively contribute to epistemically valuable ends. But true beliefs peculiar to individuals can be about anything: celebrities, sports, philosophy, or medicine. They can be theoretical or practical, and harmful or helpful to other human beings. Are all true beliefs equally epistemically valuable?

I will mark some of the key questions in this tricky terrain, and suggest that some true beliefs, like celebrity and sports trivia, may be less epistemically valuable than others. But even if these truths do prove to be of lesser value, they are still epistemic treats. Hence, epistemically temperate people will sometimes desire, consume, and enjoy celebrity or sports trivia.

(A) Trivial versus important truths. Are people who desire, consume, and enjoy true beliefs about the details of celebrities' lives or about sports statistics epistemically temperate? One might argue that such beliefs are trivial; that is, that they are not, or not very, epistemically valuable, and that those who desire, consume, and enjoy them are epistemically self-indulgent. After all, at universities we are discouraged from pursing such truths. We are redirected toward important truths, like those of physics, history, biology, and philosophy.

(B) Theoretical versus practical truths. Are people who desire, consume, and enjoy true beliefs that have little (or no) practical import epistemically temperate? One might argue that the truths of, say, philosophy are largely irrelevant to the practical world, and as such are not very epistemically valuable.[18] Are we, as philosophers, epistemically self-indulgent? Should we abandon our current projects and direct our energy toward projects that are more practical?

(C) Harmful versus helpful truths. Are people who desire, consume, and enjoy true beliefs that are harmful epistemically temperate? One might argue that true beliefs about the workings of biological weapons are not valuable because they are harmful, whereas true beliefs about the practice of medicine are valuable because they are helpful. Is it

---

[18] Mr. Casuabon, of George Eliot's *Middlemarch* (Eliot 1984), is a case in point. Arguably, he desires truths that are theoretical, impractical, and trivial.

epistemically self-indulgent to want true beliefs about the workings of biological weapons?

I begin with some brief remarks about (C) and (B). It may well be *morally* vicious to desire and pursue true beliefs about biological weapons. But this does not entail that it is *epistemically* vicious to desire and pursue such beliefs. After all, the demands of the epistemic and moral virtues can conflict. In this vein, Michael Lynch argues that "while being true always makes a proposition prima facie good to believe, it may be better, all things considered, not to believe it" (2004, 47). Though true beliefs about biological weapons *are* epistemically valuable, this does not entail that we should, in the end, pursue them. Arguably, in such cases, the value of truth is outweighed by the value of preventing mass destruction; the practically wise person would not desire such truths. As Lynch asserts, "truth is a value," but "it is not the only value" (2004, 50). The value of truth can, and sometimes should, be outweighed by competing moral values.

We can say something similar about (B). It may well be *pragmatically* inappropriate to desire and pursue purely theoretical truths. But this does not entail that it is *epistemically* inappropriate to desire and pursue such beliefs. If we can prise apart epistemic and pragmatic value, then we can allot epistemic value to purely theoretical truths. Since the role of pragmatism in epistemology is hotly debated, we can hardly settle this issue here. Suffice it to say that *if* we can prise the two apart, there will be some situations in which epistemic value is and should be outweighed by pragmatic value.

The arguments for (A) are stronger. In their analysis of a virtue they call "love of knowledge," Robert Roberts and Jay Wood argue that those who possess this virtue desire knowledge that is worthy. They explicitly address which sorts of truths are worthy. In their words, "People differ as to the kinds of truths they take an interest in, and the differences can be differences of intellectual virtue, according to the quality of the goods the people care about. Individuals who are concerned about the truths they read in *Science* . . . the *Atlantic Monthly* . . . *National Geographic*, the *New York Review of Books*, or *Books and Culture* are in this respect more virtuous than people who are most interested in the truths they read in *People* magazine . . . because the truths that are found there are mostly trivial" (Roberts and Wood 2007, 159). Those who possess the virtue of love of knowledge desire and pursue important truths about the sciences and literature; not trivial truths about which dress Angelina Jolie wore to the Oscars or the whereabouts of Paris Hilton. Roberts and Wood go on to argue that this conclusion cannot be avoided. They think that the aim of universities is both to transmit important knowledge to students, and to "produce people with a taste" for important knowledge (2007, 160). There are some worries about this line of thought: (i) it risks restricting epistemic virtues like love of knowledge and epistemic temperance to academics; and (ii) it demands clear criteria for what makes one sort of knowledge more epistemically valuable than another. Still, Roberts and

Wood's view has intuitive appeal. It seems that truths about Jolie's clothing and Jeter's batting average are not as epistemically valuable as truths about evolution or about what makes life meaningful. It also seems that any decent analysis of epistemic value must account for this phenomenon.

We cannot say exactly which truths the epistemically temperate person will desire, consume, and enjoy. But, if Roberts and Wood are correct—if trivial truths about celebrities are less valuable than truths about science—then the epistemically temperate person will value some truths more than others. Presumably, truths about science will actively contribute to valuable epistemic ends, and will be desired, consumed, and enjoyed by the epistemically temperate. But trivial truths about celebrities will also be desired, consumed, and enjoyed by the epistemically temperate, since such truths are epistemic treats. Epistemic treats cannot be falsehoods, since falsehoods undermine that which is epistemically valuable. But, they can be truths of "lesser" value. Of course, consuming trivial truths too often, or in large quantities, may well undermine epistemically valuable ends. Hence, the epistemically temperate person will sometimes desire, consume, and enjoy trivial truths, but will not do so more than she should. She will occasionally consume trivial truths solely for the sake of pleasure. So, just as morally temperate people do not always desire and consume broccoli, epistemically temperate people do not always desire and consume knowledge of physics. Just as the morally temperate sometimes enjoy chocolate cake, the epistemically temperate sometimes enjoy celebrity trivia.

Accordingly, (ET1), (ESI1), and (EI1) will read: (ET1) the epistemically temperate person desires, consumes, and enjoys both objects that contribute to valuable epistemic ends and epistemic treats; (ESI1) the epistemically self-indulgent person desires, consumes, and enjoys objects that contribute to valuable epistemic ends and epistemic treats, *and* objects that undermine valuable epistemic ends; and (EI1) the epistemically insensible person chooses not to desire, consume, or enjoy some objects that either contribute to valuable epistemic ends or are epistemic treats. The epistemically self-indulgent person desires, consumes, and enjoys appropriate and inappropriate objects indiscriminately. Those who predominantly desire and consume celebrity trivia (treats)—only occasionally consuming important truths—and who love astrology, the horoscopes, hasty generalization, and wishful thinking are epistemically self-indulgent. The epistemically insensible person chooses not to desire, consume, or enjoy scientific truths, because he thinks they are not valuable; or consumes scientific truths, but does so without pleasure, perhaps solely because they are required readings for a course.

2.C. How Much Is too Much or too Little?

Finally, how much does the epistemically temperate person desire, consume, and enjoy appropriate epistemic objects? Here, too, the appro-

priate amount of consumption and the appropriate degrees and frequencies of desire and enjoyment are those of the practically wise person,
rather than those of "most people." As before, desire, enjoyment, and
consumption are excessive when they prevent one from pursuing or
attaining other things of value. They are deficient when they prevent
one from pursuing, attaining, or enjoying valuable objects. Here, I
provide a brief illustration of epistemic insensibility, and several examples
of epistemic self-indulgence.

Moral insensibility *is* less common than moral self-indulgence. But
epistemically, the reverse seems to be true. Generally speaking, human
beings are far more likely to desire and enjoy appropriate epistemic objects
too seldom and too little than to desire and enjoy them too much. In fact,
there seems to be plenty of epistemic insensibility to go around—(EI1) and
(EI3) are readily satisfied. Those who are epistemically complacent consistently choose not to desire, consume, or enjoy some epistemic objects that
it would be appropriate to enjoy, satisfying (EI1). For instance, they may
choose not to consume truths about politics or history, even basic practical
ones. Surely, some undecided voters are insensible in this way. As Roberts
and Wood note, the complacent might also choose not to pursue appropriate activities like "test[ing] . . . cherished beliefs" (2007, 170). When the
going gets tough, they stop searching for evidence, considering alternatives,
and following up on leads. Moreover, even when one consumes appropriate
objects, one might still choose to desire and enjoy them too seldom, or to an
inappropriately low degree, or consume too little of them, satisfying (EI3).
For instance, some students consistently consume appropriate truths and
activities, but fail to desire or enjoy them, as when they do the required
reading for a course but take no pleasure in it.

Though epistemic self-indulgence is less common than epistemic insensibility, there are good reasons to think that it, too, is actual.[19] I will
provide examples of individuals who desire and consume appropriate
epistemic objects too much and too frequently, satisfying (ESI3). First, I
turn to the character of Dr. Gregory House, the protagonist of the
television drama *House*.[20] Dr. House is head of the department of
diagnostic medicine at Princeton-Plainsboro Hospital. He reliably solves
his cases and saves patients, correctly diagnosing patients whom no one
else can diagnose. House is obsessed with solving his cases. Truths about
patients' illnesses are appropriate epistemic objects (they are important,
practical, and helpful to others), so House does not satisfy (ESI1). But, he
does satisfy (ESI3). In nearly every episode, the strength of his desire for

---

[19] The Basque language, Euskara, even contains a word, "egizalekeria," that means
"excessive love of truth." Thanks to Nomy Arpaly for pointing this out. See also Zagzebski
1996, 194–97. Zagzebski suggests that Uncle Toby's desire for knowledge is excessive. Uncle
Toby is a character in Laurence Sterne's *Life and Opinions of Tristram Shandy*.
[20] See Battaly and Coplan 2009a and 2009b.

such truths causes him to inappropriately choose them over the pursuit of objects that are morally valuable. For instance, in "Human Error," House treats a patient who was rescued from a shipwreck while emigrating from Cuba. She dies, but he keeps her on bypass for hours, without informing her husband that she has died, because he wants to figure out why she died. Dr. Cuddy, the hospital's administrator, asks House: "Other than your curiosity, do you have any reason to keep her on bypass? Do you want a storybook ending . . . ? I know you care." House replies: "I don't care. My motives are pure." That is, House only cares about the truth, not about the husband's right to know about his wife's death. In "Last Resort," a sick and dangerous gunman takes hostages in the hospital, demanding a diagnosis from House. House eventually convinces the gunman to give him the gun, so that they can get clear images on a CAT scan. House, in possession of the gun, reads the images, determines that his diagnosis was incorrect, and *returns the gun* to the gunman so that he is forced to continue to diagnose him. House's degree of desire for truth clearly exceeds that of the practically wise person's, blinding him to objects that are morally valuable.

Of course, Dr. House is a fictional character. But arguably, some philosophers are self-indulgent in the same ways. Even if we assume that the truths philosophers desire, consume, and enjoy *are* appropriate, some of us still satisfy (ESI3). Some of us consistently chose not to attend to things that are of great moral value (friends, students, teaching, ill parents) in order to work on a paper, or to read a new article in the field. This is not to say that it is never inappropriate to choose the pursuit of philosophical truths over the pursuit of other valuable objects. It is only to say that for some of us the strength of our desires for such truths prevents us from seeing just how valuable friends, teaching, and so forth, are, and causes us to choose the pursuit of philosophical truths over these other things even when the practically wise person would do the reverse. Some of us also consistently choose to pursue philosophical truths at inappropriate times—satisfying (ESI2)—when we should instead be enjoying a party, or our partner's accomplishments.

Within the field of epistemology, skeptics about knowledge and justification are arguably epistemically self-indulgent.[21] In contrast with Dr. House, skeptics are not epistemically self-indulgent because of the strength of their desire for *truth*, or because their desires blind them to *moral* value (though that may also be the case). Skeptics are epistemically self-indulgent because the strength of their desire to *avoid falsehoods* blinds them to the *epistemic* value of attaining truths. This is not to say that skepticism is never appropriate; sometimes the stakes are indeed high. But the stakes are not always high. Because of his obsession with

---

[21] Thanks to Michael Pace for this example. Thanks also to Amy Coplan.

avoiding falsehood, the skeptic will sometimes deny knowledge when the practically wise person would not. In sum, I have argued that there is an epistemic analogue of moral self-indulgence. Those who are epistemically self-indulgent desire, consume, and enjoy truths, treats, and falsehoods indiscriminately, or at inappropriate times, or too much. I have suggested that philosophers and skeptics are epistemically self-indulgent. If this is correct, then we need not look far to find epistemic vice.

Acknowledgments

Thanks to Nomy Arpaly, Amy Coplan, Roger Crisp, Thomas Hurka, Ryan Nichols, Michael Pace, Clifford Roth, Jay Wood, and Linda Zagzebski for thoughts on an earlier draft. Special thanks to Jason Baehr for written comments. Thanks also to my students, Kyle Bova, Hoa Liu, and Maura Priest.

References

Aristotle. 1984. *Metaphysics*. In *The Complete Works of Aristotle*, edited by Jonathan Barnes. Princeton: Princeton University Press.

———. 1998. *The Nicomachean Ethics*. Translated by David Ross. Oxford: Oxford University Press.

Axtell, Guy, ed. 2000. *Knowledge, Belief and Character*. Lanham, Md.: Rowman and Littlefield.

Baehr, Jason S. 2006. "Character in Epistemology." *Philosophical Studies* 128:479–514.

Battaly, Heather. 2008. "Virtue Epistemology." *Philosophy Compass: Epistemology* 3, no. 4:639–63.

Battaly, Heather, and Amy Coplan. 2009a. "Is Dr. House Virtuous? Using *House* to Teach the Moral and Intellectual Virtues." *Film and Philosophy* 13:1–18.

———. 2009b. "Diagnosing Character: A House Divided?" In *House and Philosophy*, edited by Henry Jacoby, 222–38. Hoboken, N.J.: John Wiley and Sons.

Curzer, Howard J. 1997. "Aristotle's Account of the Virtue of Temperance in *Nicomachean Ethics* III.10–11." *Journal of the History of Philosophy* 35, no. 1:5–25.

Eliot, George. 1984. *Middlemarch*. New York: Modern Library.

Fricker, Miranda. 2007. *Epistemic Injustice: Power and the Ethics of Knowing*. Oxford: Oxford University Press.

Halwani, Raja. 2003. *Virtuous Liaisons: Care, Love, Sex, and Virtue Ethics*. Chicago: Open Court.

Homiak, Marcia L. 1981. "Virtue and Self-Love in Aristotle's Ethics." *Canadian Journal of Philosophy* 11, no. 4:633–51.

Hookway, Christopher. 2001. "Epistemic *Akrasia* and Epistemic Virtue." In *Virtue Epistemology: Essays on Epistemic Virtue and Responsibility*, edited by Abrol Fairweather and Linda Zagzebski, 178–99. New York: Oxford University Press.

Lynch, Michael P. 2004. *True to Life: Why Truth Matters.* Cambridge, Mass.: MIT Press.

Montmarquet, James A. 1993. *Epistemic Virtue and Doxastic Responsibility.* Lanham, Md.: Rowman and Littlefield.

Roberts, Robert C., and W. Jay Wood. 2007. *Intellectual Virtues: An Essay in Regulative Epistemology.* Oxford: Oxford University Press.

Young, Charles M. 1988. "Aristotle on Temperance." *Philosophical Review* 97, no. 4:521–42.

Zagzebski, Linda T. 1996. *Virtues of the Mind: An Inquiry into the Nature of Virtue and the Ethical Foundations of Knowledge.* Cambridge: Cambridge University Press.

INDEX

Printed and bound by CPI Group (UK) Ltd, Croydon, CR0 4YY

13/04/2025